MICRO MIRACLES

DISCOVER *the*

HEALING POWER

of ENZYMES

ELLEN W. CUTLER, DC
WITH JEREMY E. KASLOW, MD

RODALE

© 2005 by Ellen W. Cutler, DC

Cover photograph © 2005 by Jeanette Vonier/Elegant Images

Printed in the United States of America

Rodale Inc. makes every effort to use acid-free ♾, recycled paper ♻.

Book design by Judith Abbate/Abbate Design

Library of Congress Cataloging-in-Publication Data

Cutler, Ellen W.
    Micromiracles : discover the healing power of enzymes / Ellen W. Cutler with Jeremy E. Kaslow.
        p.   cm.
    Includes bibliographical references and index.
    ISBN-13 978–1–59486–076–9 hardcover
    ISBN-10 1–59486–076–9 hardcover
    ISBN-13 978–1–59486–221–2 paperback
    ISBN-10 1–59486–221–4 paperback
    1. Enzymes—Therapeutic use.   I. Kaslow, Jeremy E.   II. Title.
RM666.E55C88   2005
615'.35—dc22   2004030175

Distributed to the trade by Holtzbrinck Publishers

2   4   6   8   10   9   7   5   3   1   hardcover
2   4   6   8   10   9   7   5   3   1   paperback

RODALE
LIVE YOUR WHOLE LIFE™

We inspire and enable people to improve their lives and the world around them

For more of our products visit **rodalestore.com** or call 800-848-4735

Healing is about

our connection to

Absolute Consciousness and Love.

I dedicate the book to this Truth.

Contents

Acknowledgments vii

Introduction xi

PART I

WHY ENZYMES MATTER

CHAPTER 1: Enzymes: The Basic Catalysts of Life 3

CHAPTER 2: Your Personalized Enzyme Program 21

CHAPTER 3: Getting the Most from Enzyme Supplements . .29

PART II

THE ENZYME-DIGESTION CONNECTION

CHAPTER 4: A Digestion Primer 39

CHAPTER 5: Intolerances, Enzymes, and Your Health 49

PART III

ENZYME THERAPY FOR COMMON HEALTH CONCERNS

CHAPTER 6: Ensure Optimal Digestion 59

CHAPTER 7: Reduce Cravings and Lose Weight 79

CHAPTER 8: Revitalize Your Skin and Hair 101

CHAPTER 9: Recharge Your Energy and Vitality 127

CHAPTER 10: Enhance Emotional Balance 147

CHAPTER 11: Maintain a Healthy Immune System 169

CHAPTER 12: Lower Your Risk of Heart Disease 187

CHAPTER 13: Treat and Prevent Diabetes 205

CHAPTER 14: Fight Inflammation 225

CHAPTER 15: Defend against Cancer 249

CHAPTER 16: Slow the Aging Process 267

RESOURCES

Carbohydrate-Intolerance Diet 295

Protein/Fat-Intolerance Diet 307

Choosing an Antioxidant Formula 321

What to Look For in a Multivitamin 325

Acupressure Balancing Technique 329

Notes 333

References 345

Index 359

Acknowledgments

I feel blessed for the opportunity to write this book, which offers vital information for optimizing the health, wellness, and longevity of every being. We all deserve to be healthy and to live long lives, and we all deserve to know the simple truth of authentic natural medicine and healing.

This book exists because of the help, encouragement, and grace of many people. My most treasured supporters and my most precious gifts in this lifetime are my children, Aaron and Gabrielle. My son, who was a key researcher for this book and now is studying medicine, is not only my best friend but also a compassionate, understanding, and brilliant human being. I adore him beyond comprehension. I am so proud of him, and so proud to call him my son. My daughter is the sweet, precious light in my life. As I wrote this book, she sat with me day and night, doing her homework, reading, or serenading me with her exquisite violin. She was there throughout, serving me tea, smiling, hugging me, and imparting her wonderful sweetness. Her sublime energy, her encouragement, and merely her presence helped make this book complete.

I also want to acknowledge my favorite uncle and aunt, Seymour and Miriam Wagner, for their compassion, love, and support; my twin brother, Dr. Ira Wagner, for his selfless service to others, which I find most inspiring; and Dr. Deborah Cutler, my former husband's sister and still part of my family, whose heartfelt friendship I will always value.

Other essential people in my life, without whom this book never would have been published, are my literary agent, Bonnie Solow, and my business manager, Gina Del Vecchio. I don't know what I would do without them. Bonnie is always there for me, always focused, supportive, positive, and strong—one of the most admired and inspirational women I know. She has made it all come true. Gina, in her indisputable authenticity, always reflects my purest dreams with a strength of conviction and truth that astonishes me each day we work together. She is the thread that holds together BioSET, overseeing so much of my work that is disseminated to health professionals and the general public.

I thank my best friend, Deborah Santana, the purest angel in my life. She is not only beautiful, kind, compassionate, and selfless, she also emanates the highest level of integrity.

My publisher, Rodale, has blessed me with the opportunity to communicate my passion in this manuscript. Tami Booth Corwin was the most essential element. She understood my vision and my dedication. I remember talking with Tami for the first time at Los Angeles Airport; I think I was beaming with enthusiasm and excitement while we spoke. She is the spirit of this book. I thank her for her trust and her understanding of the importance of enzymes in healing.

The other person at Rodale who was there since the beginning of this project was Susan Berg. She was simply a joy to work with, and I feel as though she has been an angel watching over me.

I am so fortunate to have found Ken Howard to help shape the content of the book. I am in awe of his talent and his ability to edit my words while imparting my voice and my enthusiasm. His genius is too wonderful for words. I am also grateful for the contributions of Nancy Faas and Joy Parker, who helped with editing early on.

This book would not have been complete without the work of Lisa Maloof and Dr. Marc Girod. They, along with my son, Aaron, were steadfast in researching their assigned chapters and subjects. Thanks also to Lynn Greaves and Karen Samson, who have helped in so many ways.

Dr. Elson Haas generously shared his expertise in the area of natural healing and answered many of my questions as I wrote this book. I will always value his knowledge and support. Peter Miller, a wonderful and most brilliant friend, inspired me with his encouraging words and warmth. Dr. Wayne Dyer and Dr. David Hawkins bestowed invaluable wisdom and truth through their books and audiotapes. They taught me over and over again what true healing is really about.

I am honored to have Dr. Jeremy Kaslow as my coauthor for this book. His understanding of enzymes, and his use of them in his practice, complements my own. He also shares my commitment to the importance of optimal digestion. Thank you, Dr. Kaslow.

Finally, I thank Dr. Roy Martina for his loving support, unconditional love, and radiant healing energy. He opened my heart again to the Truth. His light and love healed my soul and guided me back to finding my service as a healer in this life. I will forever cherish his friendship and will never forget his kind spirit.

—Dr. Ellen Cutler

Introduction

FOR ME as a doctor, healer, teacher, and parent, the opportunity to write a book on enzyme nutrition and health is a dream come true. Literally not a day goes by that I don't mention enzyme nutrition or share my personal enzyme supply, which I always carry in my purse.

My study of enzyme nutrition and therapy began about 20 years ago, and enzymes have been part of my daily nutritional protocol ever since. My colleagues, students, family, and friends jokingly call me the Empress of Enzymes. Probably no one else has as much passion for the subject as I do or is more qualified to write a book about it than I am. For years, I've been telling people that enzymes would become well known in the near future; in fact, they would be regarded as the revolutionary medicine of the 21st century. Now that the 21st century is here, it's the perfect time to share the secret of these miracle supplements.

I teach doctors all over the world about a system that I developed called BioSET, which stands for Bioenergetic Sensitivity and Enzyme

Therapy. BioSET has four components, which together successfully treat and prevent many chronic conditions that suppress the immune system. One of the four components is enzyme therapy. In my workshops, I begin and end each lecture on enzymes with the following five points, which I call the Miracles of Enzymes in Your Life.

- Enzymes strengthen your immune system so that you are no longer as vulnerable to illness, especially to common cold and flu viruses.

- Enzymes restore levels of vitality and energy that you haven't experienced since you were a child.

- Enzymes rejuvenate your beauty and refresh you from within, allowing your hair, nails, and skin to become more healthy, radiant, and youthful.

- Enzymes enable you to utilize all of the nutrients from your food, which not only creates well-being but also supports weight loss and ultimately weight management.

- Enzymes restore an efficient and effective digestive system.

MY INTRODUCTION TO ENZYME THERAPY

Through my 25 years as a physician, thousands of people have entrusted me with the most private details about their health. Before you read the rest of this book, I want to share my personal story with you, so you can understand and appreciate my passion and drive to make enzymes part of your everyday life.

From age 5, I suffered from digestive problems, including constipation, cramps, bloating, and massive food sensitivities. I dreaded eating, because no food made me feel good. I would get so bloated after meals that I looked 3 months pregnant, and I could wear only loose-fitting pants with big waists.

As I grew older, I became more and more unhappy with my situation. I would look at other girls in awe, wondering how they were able to eat anything and everything and still wear tight-waisted jeans and skirts. Now that I am raising my own teenage daughter and observing how appearance is so important at that age, I look back and remember how really devastating that time was for me. For years, I believed that nothing could ever help me.

When I started chiropractic school, things took a turn for the worse. I grew up in a typical Jewish household. My parents, like many other Jewish parents of that generation, believed that my twin brother should attend medical school and become a doctor, while I should become a teacher. That is what I had heard for as long as I could remember. I was not at all interested in being a teacher. I wanted to go to medical school, but that was out of the question because my parents couldn't afford to send both of us. I realized that I was on my own.

Chiropractic training offered a way for me to enter health care and satisfied my interest in a holistic approach to medicine. In 1972, I enrolled at Western States Chiropractic College in Portland, Oregon. In order to support myself, I worked in an emergency room at night and attended school during the day. I took classes from 8:00 A.M. until 3:00 or 5:00 P.M., then went to my job from 6:00 to 11:30 P.M. When I got home, I studied for a few hours. I survived most days on only a few hours of sleep.

My schedule took a toll on my body, and my digestive problems worsened with each month. I was miserable. When I sought conventional allopathic medical care, the doctors invariably diagnosed inflammatory bowel disease or ulcerative colitis and recommended a regimen of drugs and/or surgery later in life. Drugs were not an option for me because I knew that they would treat only the symptoms and never get to the root of my condition.

I tried all kinds of supplements, colonics, therapies, and fasts. Every supplement seemed to aggravate my symptoms. Fasting, on the other hand, offered some relief, although only temporarily. I remember reading a book on grape fasts and then trying one for 3 months. I couldn't believe how much better I felt. I even considered buying a grape vineyard in California's Napa Valley so I could have as many grapes as possible. Unfortunately, sticking with the grape fast was almost impossible, not to mention quite costly. I became very tired and listless, lost a great deal of weight, and frequently came down with sore throats and flu. I also remember having chronic mouth sores at the time. I know now that I was completely under-nourished.

I managed to survive chiropractic school and start a practice in northern California. I continued to follow a very limited diet, even though my painful symptoms had become a daily occurrence. After a few years in practice, I enrolled in a postgraduate program in orthopedics to expand my knowledge about new research directions in nutrition, spinal mechanics, understanding of the extremities, and other areas relevant to treating my patients. Little did I know that this 3-year course, given one weekend each month, would change my life forever.

During this period, I became very close to one of the instructors. When I confided in him about my condition, he suggested that I read about enzymes and then try a plant digestive enzyme, which would assist my body in processing sugars and starches. No one had ever suggested this to me before; in fact, this was my first exposure to the phrase "enzyme supplement."

Because I trusted this excellent doctor, researcher, and friend, I believed that his advice was worth following, and I took the enzyme religiously before meals. Two weeks after I started supplementation, my colitis symptoms were gone. So, too, were my food sensitivities, fatigue, sore throats, colds, flu, and mouth sores. I was a different person, no longer vulnerable to life's stressful circumstances. My body had the power and spark to remain strong and balanced. I was cured, truly and permanently.

That was 22 years ago. I'm convinced that I would not be here today if I hadn't found digestive plant enzymes. I promised myself then and there that I would learn everything in the medical field about enzymes and then teach others about the power of enzyme therapy. Now I have the opportunity to share this information with an audience that I believe is ready to listen. Nothing could be more exciting.

ENZYMES FOR YOUR LIFE

When I set out to write this book, I promised myself that it would be the most comprehensive, extensively researched, accurate, and truthful account of enzyme nutrition available. I hope you will agree that I've succeeded.

It begins with an introduction to enzymes—what they are and how they work—and proceeds with chapters on the role of enzymes in digestion and the intricacies of enzyme therapy in enhancing health and appearance, strengthening immune function, and promoting longevity. I will teach you how to use enzyme supplements to restore energy and vitality as well as to sharpen mental focus and balance mood. You'll learn how enzymes can reduce your risk of heart disease and cancer and protect against inflammation and arthritis pain.

With the information in this book, you'll be able to build your own enzyme regimen—and a new, healthier lifestyle for yourself. In my opinion, enzymes are the medicine of the future. They are revolutionary and holistic. They are essential to true healing in its most basic sense: the restoration of optimal health and balance, or homeostasis.

The following story, along with many others throughout the book, illustrates the power of enzymes in healing. They are from my clinical practice, although I have changed the names to protect the privacy of my patients.

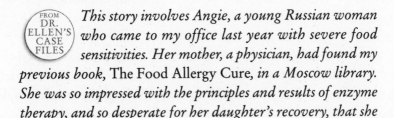 *This story involves Angie, a young Russian woman who came to my office last year with severe food sensitivities. Her mother, a physician, had found my previous book,* The Food Allergy Cure, *in a Moscow library. She was so impressed with the principles and results of enzyme therapy, and so desperate for her daughter's recovery, that she*

called me for a consultation. She explained that her daughter was wasting away because she could eat and tolerate only a limited number of foods. After speaking with me for an hour, she decided to send Angie to the United States to see if I could help her overcome her food sensitivities.

When I tested Angie, I soon realized that she was sensitive to almost everything I tried. I then performed a thorough evaluation to determine whether she was protein/fat or carbohydrate intolerant. As it turned out, Angie was unable to break down proteins and carbohydrates. (Incidentally, I gathered much of this information with an in-depth questionnaire, which appears on page 24 for your own use.) I recommended an enzyme that would enable Angie to adequately digest these foods.

If enzymes don't completely clear a person's food sensitivities, my BioSET system offers some desensitization therapies that have proven effective. Fortunately for Angie, they weren't necessary. (We were under time constraints, as she couldn't leave her job in Russia for more than a week.) Once she started enzyme supplementation, she noticed improvement in just 1 day. Eventually, she was able to eat almost anything—even foods that she hadn't touched in years.

Five days after Angie returned to Russia, her mother called me. She was crying and thanking me over and over again. I told her that I had done almost nothing; I had just helped her daughter predigest her food.

Angie's mother still calls and writes regularly, continuing to thank me. She is planning a seminar in Russia to educate her fellow doctors about enzyme therapy—and she can't wait to read this book!

—*Dr. Ellen Cutler*

PART I

Why Enzymes Matter

CHAPTER 1

Enzymes: The Basic Catalysts of Life

HUMAN EXISTENCE is a marvel—so complex, yet so efficient, orderly, and dynamic. Driving all of it is a collection of proteins collectively known as enzymes. Sometimes they go by the name *organic catalysts* because they accelerate chemical reactions in the body. In fact, many of these reactions would never take place without enzymes as catalysts. Enzymes are essential to life.

The study of enzymes is fairly new, although they've been in use for a very long time. The word *enzyme* comes from the Greek for "leaven," alluding to the fact that enzymes are closely associated with the activity of yeast in making bread. For centuries, they have also played a role in making cheese.

Even though the catalytic activity of the enzymes in yeast had been known for centuries, it wasn't until 1926 that American biochemist James Batcheller Sumner, PhD, isolated the first enzyme in pure (crystalline) form. Dr. Sumner received the 1946 Nobel Prize in chemistry for his work with the enzyme urease.

Since then, researchers have identified more than 3,000 types of enzymes in the human body, with each one performing a unique function. Literally millions of enzymes help to renew, sustain, and protect us, and they themselves renew and change at an incredible rate.

The reactions that are driven by enzymes transform one set of molecules into another, using up or releasing energy in the process, which is necessary for the construction of new substances. The original molecules are known as substrates and the new molecules as products. The products are vital to functions such as tissue repair and disease defenses, along with general body maintenance.

In order for enzymes to do their jobs, they depend on smaller molecules, such as vitamins and minerals. These so-called cofactors enable or enhance the chemical reactions in which enzymes take part. Life is a profound and vast complex of thousands of these self-regulated chemical reactions occurring constantly. Every single living cell has a huge number of reactions going on all the time.

Enzymes are essential to every bodily function, including breathing, circulation, digestion, and immune response. On a larger scale, they slow the aging process and support wellness and homeostasis (the body's ability to achieve balance among its many functions). As we get older, the quality and effectiveness of enzymes diminish; our bodies don't produce as many, and those that remain lose their spark. This leaves us vulnerable to illness. But aging isn't the only factor that depletes our enzyme levels and function. Poor diet, digestive stress, metabolic imbalance, illness, trauma, medications, and cancer treatment also have a negative impact. (We'll discuss each of these in more detail throughout the book.)

WHAT ENZYME THERAPY CAN DO FOR YOU

The use of enzymes in health care began very early. The Bible (2 Kings 20:7) describes how a cake of pressed figs was used to help

How Enzymes Get Their Names

When scientists first identified enzymes, they had no uniformly accepted method for naming the substances. The International Commission on Enzymes, established in 1956, developed the first nomenclature system. Today, enzymes take their names from the molecules, or substrates, they interact with, with the suffix -*ase* added. For example, the enzyme that breaks down protein is known as protease; lactase is responsible for digesting lactose, or milk sugar; and lipase takes care of lipids, or fats.

---

treat Hezekiah's boil. Now we know that figs contain the proteolytic enzyme ficin, which digests dead skin.

Modern enzyme therapy dates back to the turn of the 20th century. In 1906, John Beard, MD, an embryologist at the University of Edinburgh in Scotland, described the use of the enzyme trypsin in the treatment of cancer.[1] During the mid-20th century, Max Wolf, MD, rediscovered the therapeutic value of enzyme therapy, developing a method for treating various conditions with enzymes. Dr. Wolf is considered the father of systemic enzyme therapy.

As mentioned above, our bodies need enzymes in order to carry out their most basic functions. Enzymes provide the metabolic energy that fuels efficient physiological and biochemical processes. They also digest food, transport nutrients, carry away toxic wastes, purify the blood, deliver hormones, balance cholesterol and triglycerides, nourish the brain, build protein into muscle, and feed and fortify the endocrine system.

Enzymes are necessary for healthy immune function, too. White blood cells are especially rich in enzymes, which help them digest and destroy any foreign substances—such as viruses, bacteria, and food allergens—that enter the body.

While the body uses its enzymes over and over again, they can perform only a certain amount of work before they become exhausted and must be replaced. This is why we must constantly replenish our enzyme supplies. If we don't, our bodies' ability to maintain optimal health suffers. A shortfall takes a toll on virtually every system that depends on enzyme support, including digestion, immunity, and tissue repair after injury or inflammation.

Through our collective years of working with enzyme therapy, we have seen how enzymes not only prevent disease but also heal chronic health problems for which many doctors believe there are no medical solutions. Our experience has convinced us that no other class of supplements can offer such dramatic improvements.

Once our patients begin enzyme therapy, the most immediate change is in their energy levels. They routinely report that they feel rejuvenated and are back to being their "old selves." Many ask Dr. Ellen to list on the blackboard in her office all the enzymes that she takes on a daily basis. They want to experience the same vitality that she emanates each day.

TYPES OF ENZYMES

Enzymes consist of amino acids, which are the structural units of protein, as well as co-factors such as vitamins and minerals. If you imagine amino acids as the links in a chain, then the protein molecule is the entire chain. Within a cell, approximately 20 amino acids can be configured into various combinations, orders, and numbers to produce specific enzymes.

There are three main categories of enzymes: systemic, or metabolic; digestive; and food. Our bodies produce systemic and digestive enzymes, while food enzymes—as their name implies—come from what we eat.

Systemic Enzymes: For Cellular Health and More

The vast majority of enzymes manufactured by the body are systemic enzymes, which are responsible for maintaining your blood, tissues, and organs. They ensure that your heart beats regularly, your muscles contract and relax properly, and your senses (including vision and hearing) stay sharp. They remove potentially unhealthy LDL cholesterol from your blood, produce and balance your hormones, and supply the neurotransmitters that support memory and mood.

What's more, systemic enzymes are active in every cell in your body. They not only support cellular growth and repair, they also transform carbohydrates, proteins, and fats into cellular fuel. They even do some housecleaning, removing worn-out material so that the cells stay clean and healthy.

In the best of circumstances, your body can make all of the systemic enzymes it needs. But if it uses up its reserves (usually in the manufacture of digestive enzymes, which we'll discuss later), it can no longer heal or rebuild itself effectively. This is when supplementation with proper systemic enzymes can make a big difference. Otherwise, chronic illness—the result of insufficient tissue healing and repair—may set in.

Systemic enzyme supplements should be clearly differentiated from digestive enzyme supplements, which support the digestive process. Systemic enzymes target specific tissues to stimulate the body's innate therapeutic potential.

Numerous studies have documented the safety and effectiveness of systemic enzymes. They are not only natural alternatives to nonsteroidal anti-inflammatory drugs (NSAIDs) like ibuprofen and naproxen, they also compensate for diminished enzyme production as a result of the aging process. For this reason, systemic enzymes often are an important component of an anti-aging supplement regimen.

In systemic enzyme therapy, as initially developed by Dr. Wolf, enough of the enzymes enter the bloodstream intact. Once there, they can travel to tissues and then on to available cells. This quality makes systemic enzymes quite versatile as therapeutic agents. They can boost immune response, combat toxicity, fight inflammation and infection, reduce swelling and pain, improve circulation, and stimulate the body's own enzymatic processes. Since nearly every disease and disorder involves one or more of these processes, systemic enzyme therapy can be effective against a wide range of health concerns.

It can also help medications work better. It's a holistic approach to healing.

Among the systemic enzymes, the most commonly prescribed supplements are those in the protease family.[2] As the term *protease* suggests, the target of these enzymes is proteins. Specifically, proteases are able to trim and prune proteins such as those that contribute to and result from arthritic conditions.

For example, when protective cartilage in a joint deteriorates—often because of excessive irritation from repetitive motion or past injury—local inflammation increases. This leads to swelling and pain that impede joint mobility and possibly cause severe disability. In contrast to NSAIDs, which essentially mask symptoms and may aggravate joint degeneration, systemic enzymes promote healing by countering the inflammatory response. Enzymes also help in cases where proteins trigger an immune reaction, in turn promoting inflammation. They are a safe, smart, inexpensive approach to relieving arthritic pain.

FROM DR. ELLEN'S CASE FILES *At age 27, Linda had just finished her medical training and was looking forward to opening her own office in Pennsylvania. At last she'd be able to practice what she had spent so many years studying—but it would wait until after her wedding and honeymoon in Bermuda. She felt giddy with joy, excitement, and relief.*

Unfortunately, Linda's life took another turn, one that she hadn't expected so soon and so suddenly. It had been lingering in the back of her mind for a while, but she certainly wasn't prepared for it to happen just when she was ready to begin her new roles as a wife and a physician.

Linda had been diagnosed with rheumatoid arthritis (RA) in her first year of medical school, but the symptoms were mild, and she managed them well. Even when the disease went into remission and she remained symptom-free for the rest of her schooling, her years of medical training didn't allow her to forget the possibility that her symptoms would return. If they did, to what extent might they hobble her?

One week before her wedding, Linda couldn't get out of bed. Her hands, knees, and feet were severely swollen, red, and painful. She had become disabled literally overnight. She postponed not only her wedding but her career as a physician. Her dreams were shattered and her life reduced to surviving from one moment to the next. She could not get out of bed, much less walk. She struggled just to feed herself.

Linda's cousin, who happened to be a patient of mine, called her and suggested that she come to see me. Of course, Linda was in no condition to even attempt getting on a plane and flying to California. But she did call for a phone consultation, which we had within a week.

I learned that Linda was not having a good experience with the medications that she had been prescribed. They not only failed to relieve her pain, they also caused strong side effects, including severe depression and anxiety. She was determined to find something else.

I admired Linda's tenacity and optimism. Since she couldn't travel, I decided to try a long-distance evaluation and treatment. We spoke for 3 hours, during which I assessed her for toxicity, poor digestion, and food sensitivities. I determined that she had been sensitive to sugars and starches for most of her life, at times experiencing severe bloating within a couple of hours of eating—a common occurrence with carbohydrate intolerance. While in school, she had lived on breads, pastas, crackers, and cereals, with few vegetables and fruits. Not surprisingly, she always felt tired and had frequent bouts of depression and mood swings. She was also about 20 pounds overweight.

We talked extensively about Linda's family history, her first RA flare-up, and the toxic exposure she had experienced throughout her lifetime. All pointed to poor digestion, which unfortunately can set the stage for an inflammatory response and eventually, autoimmune diseases such as RA.

I immediately prescribed a carbohydrate digestive enzyme to help digest sugars and starches, a systemic protease enzyme for inflammation and pain, and a detoxification program.[3] I also advised Linda to give up sugars and starches, including simple sugars and grains, and switch to a carbohydrate-intolerance diet like the one on page 295. We agreed to talk again in 3 weeks to see how things were going. Perhaps by then, she'd be well enough to come see me in person.

Three weeks later, Linda called me. Even her voice sounded different—strong and full of life. Her pain was much better, and the swelling was nearly gone. Best of all, she was walking again. Her optimism had blossomed into a certainty that she would regain her health. I recommended that she continue following her diet and supplement regimen and said we'd talk in about 2 months.

One week before our scheduled phone conversation, I received a letter from Linda describing her complete recovery. Her plans to open a medical practice and to marry were back on track. She couldn't wait for her honeymoon. She was amazed that something as simple as enzyme therapy could make such a dramatic difference and that it had yet to be embraced by the mainstream medical establishment. She became a strong proponent of enzyme therapy and holistic health care.

Linda and I still stay in touch, and she continues to do fabulously. While we can't say that she's cured, we know that she's healthy. Just as important, she knows how to maintain her well-being. That is the gift of enzyme therapy, which truly is the medicine of the future.

Incidentally, systemic enzymes have an established role in conventional medicine. Doctors routinely use clot-dissolving enzymes to treat certain types of stroke. One example is streptokinase, which belongs to a class of medications known as fibrinolytics. They break down fibrin, the major constituent of blood clots, helping to dissolve clots and improve circulation. The Japanese have been using a similar therapy for almost 1,000 years—only theirs involves natto-kinase, an enzyme that's extracted from a traditional Japanese food, called natto, and then purified. Much like streptokinase, nattokinase helps dissolve existing blood clots and enhances the body's output of clot-dissolving agents.

Digestive Enzymes: A Nutritional Necessity

The saying "You are what you eat" is only partly correct. The truth is, you are what you digest. We cannot expect to be healthy if our digestive system isn't functioning properly. Enzymes are essential to a healthy digestive system and a healthy body because they help transform undigested food into nutrients.

—Edward Howell, MD, author of *Enzyme Nutrition*

Digestive enzymes assist with the digestion of food, the absorption of nutrients, and the delivery of those nutrients throughout the body. The most commonly known digestive enzymes are secreted from the pancreas into the small intestine, where each is responsible for breaking down a specific compound. The most prevalent of these enzymes are amylase, which processes carbohydrates; protease, which processes proteins; and lipase, which processes fats.

When foods contain sufficient amounts of enzymes, digestion begins with your very first bite. Chewing and mixing with saliva activates some enzymes so they can do their job. Unfortunately, cooking destroys most of them. Consider milk, which is subjected to high temperatures in order to kill any microbes. This process—known as pasteurization—also destroys phytase, an enzyme that enables the body to absorb and use the calcium from milk. In other words, the bioavailability of the calcium declines dramatically.

With foods depleted of their enzyme supplies, your body must manufacture its own to support the digestive process. This is an expensive proposition, as enzyme production consumes a lot of energy, among other invaluable resources. If your body is responsible for supplying the enzymes in saliva and in gastric, pancreatic, and intestinal fluids, it must curtail production for other purposes. Thus, other tissues and organs—including the brain, heart, lungs, kidneys, liver, and muscles—don't get all the enzymes they need. This enzyme "relocation" and the resulting deficiency may set the stage for heart disease, cancer, diabetes, and many other chronic health problems.

Likewise, the incomplete digestion of food can set the stage for a multitude of symptoms and conditions. One reason is that the body isn't getting nutrients in a form that it can use. Even though it may be well fed, it can suffer from poor nutrition. What's more, undigested food can trigger an immune reaction, as the body's natural defenses attempt to seek out and destroy the foreign food particles.

When a patient shows signs of an autoimmune disease, the first thing to consider is whether the person may be running low on digestive enzymes. If so, food particles may be finding their way into the bloodstream, eventually lodging in various tissues and organs. As the immune system attacks the particles, it turns the body against itself, setting the stage for autoimmune disease.

Left unchecked, the cycle of incomplete digestion and immune reaction can lead to metabolic rejectivity syndrome. It's responsible for a host of symptoms, including fatigue, headache, muscle and joint pain, depression, and poor concentration.

While both carbohydrates and proteins can cause trouble if they aren't properly digested, significant clinical evidence suggests that carbohydrates are more likely to contribute to disease. One particularly troublesome group is the lectins, which occur in about 30 percent of fresh and processed foods. Several types of lectins resist digestion. For some of these, taking digestive enzyme supplements to support their breakdown can be an effective preventive.

Many patients ask whether they can eat more enzyme-rich foods instead of taking supplements. While we're all for switching to a healthier diet, we don't recommend relying on dietary sources alone. First, as we mentioned above, cooking depletes the enzymes in foods, which means your body must manufacture more digestive enzymes to help process what you eat. Second, foods are not concentrated sources of enzymes. For example, enzymes are responsible for ripening a fruit or vegetable. Once the process is complete, the life of most enzymes is over. Some retreat to the seeds, where they wait for the life cycle to begin again, in the form of a new plant. Unfortunately, we usually discard the seeds.

In our opinion, almost everyone can benefit from digestive enzyme supplements, even if they have no apparent digestive problems or eat mainly raw foods to preserve the enzyme content. The supplements never go to waste; whatever enzymes the body can't use, it breaks down into their component proteins and co-factors.

Our bodies depend on proper digestion for adequate nutrition. Sadly, poor digestion—and consequently poor absorption—has reached epidemic proportions in the United States. Even though we seem to be eating more than ever, our bodies are starving because they aren't getting the nutrients they need. Enzymes are the solution.

Food Enzymes: Digestive Helpers

Food enzymes come solely from raw fruits and vegetables. Like digestive enzymes, they enable our bodies to digest the foods we eat by breaking down the various nutrients—sugars, starches, proteins, fats, and fibers—into smaller compounds that can be absorbed. Food enzymes are vital to maintaining optimal health.

The conventional wisdom among physicians and nutritionists is that food enzymes are destroyed once food hits the stomach, because it sits in acid for at least 30 minutes. In fact, there's a time lag between this phase of digestion and the one preceding it. As food leaves the esophagus, it drops into the top portion of the stomach, which has very little acid, and remains there for 30 to 45 minutes before moving on. All the while, the enzymes continue doing their job. Even once the food moves to the bottom portion of the stomach, the enzymes remain active until the acid level becomes prohibitive.

The real problem is that the average American diet is seriously lacking in food enzymes. As we've mentioned, any form of processing or cooking—including pasteurization, irradiation, microwaving, and steaming—destroys the enzymes that naturally occur in food. And large-scale agribusiness, with its dependence on pesticides, fungicides, and inorganic fertilizers, has dramatically reduced the enzyme content of our soil. Healthy soil is rich not only in earthworms but also in enzymes, vitamins, minerals, and essential microorganisms. Pesticides, fungicides, and inorganic fertilizers effectively kill the soil, so any foods that grow in it are nutritionally depleted.

Multiple USDA studies offer proof that organically grown foods are much richer in nutrients than their commercial counterparts. It's reasonable to assume that they'd be richer in enzymes as well. But eating organic isn't all we can do to ensure adequate enzyme intake. Thoroughly chewing food is important, too. The enzymes in food can't do their jobs unless we chew well enough to break down the cell walls and fiber that protect the enzymes. Chewing is an essential part of the digestive process.

Further hindering enzyme activity is our penchant for hormone-laden meats, pastries made with refined flour and sugar, artificial sweeteners, and artificial fats, including trans fats such as margarine and partially hydrogenated oils. All tax the body's systems without providing their fair share of enzymes and nutrients.

When we don't eat an enzyme-rich diet, we deplete our enzyme supplies without replenishing them. What's more, our bodies aren't able to store any leftover food enzymes for later use. This is why it's so important to choose organic foods whenever possible and take enzyme supplements consistently. It also explains the abundance of new enzyme products on the market and the expert recommendations to fortify our diets accordingly.

SIGNS OF DEFICIENCY

The length of life is in direct proportion to the rate of exhaustion of the enzyme potential of an organism. The increased use of food enzymes promotes a decreased rate of exhaustion of the enzyme potential. Think of it this way: Enzymes are the "labor force" that builds your body, just like construction workers are the labor force that builds your house. You may have all the necessary building materials and lumber, but to build a house, you need workers, which represent the vital life element. Similarly, you may have all the nutrients for your body, but you still need the enzymes—the life element—to keep the body alive and well.

—Edward Howell, MD, author of *Enzyme Nutrition*

As Dr. Howell notes, each of us inherits a certain enzyme potential. When we get to the point where we're not making enough of certain enzymes, and we're not making up the shortfall through diet and supplements, our bodies may not have enough to carry out vital functions. These functions slowly degenerate because the enzyme-driven chemical reactions on which they depend don't occur.

Typically, the first sign of enzyme deficiency is digestive distress, which can manifest itself as indigestion, gas, irregular bowel movements, nausea, heartburn, bloating, food cravings, and food sensitivities or reactions ranging from headaches to eczema. As you will learn in this book, though, there are many more symptoms—including ones you might never consider—that can kick in because of enzyme deficiency. These include sinusitis, weight problems, and autoimmune disorders, among others.

FROM DR. ELLEN'S CASE FILES

Susan, a 27-year-old actress, came to the BioSET Clinic/Institute seeking relief from the severe digestive symptoms—abdominal cramping, irregular bowel movements, and bloating within 1 to 2 hours of meals— that had plagued her for almost her entire life. She had been diagnosed with irritable bowel syndrome, for which she had been told to take fiber supplements and "avoid stress." She chuckled when she repeated this to me, but a split second later, she began sobbing. She felt frustrated, helpless, and hopeless. I understood completely, because I had been in the same situation.

Upon hearing about my work with enzyme therapy, Susan had called to schedule a consultation. She just wanted direction and ultimately, relief. When she arrived at my office, she was accompanied by her husband, Paul. He seemed very supportive of her efforts to get well.

As I read Susan's patient questionnaire, I noticed that she had been struggling with infertility for 1½ years. While she hadn't come to see me for this reason, she mentioned that she had tried all kinds of interventions, including nutritional supplements and herbal formulas. None of them worked, nor could her doctors determine why she couldn't conceive. At one point during our conversation, she wondered aloud whether her digestive problems were contributing to her infertility. Paul, too, wondered whether he might have some underlying imbalance that was preventing them from conceiving. He asked if I could test him as well.

In-depth nutritional and enzyme evaluations revealed that both Susan and Paul were deficient in certain enzymes. Susan was unable to digest carbohydrates, while Paul had trouble with fats. Based on this information, I prescribed a carbohydrate digestive enzyme for Susan and a protein/fat digestive enzyme for Paul.

At their first follow-up visit, Susan was remarkably better. Her cramping and bloating had subsided, as had her food cravings. While Paul hadn't been bothered by digestive symptoms, he, too, noticed a decline in cravings. As a bonus, he had lost 5 pounds within a week. They were so pleased with the results that Susan told all of her friends about enzyme therapy, and soon my clinic was swamped with celebrities!

Nothing compared with Paul's excitement 3 months later, however, when he called to say that Susan had just found out she was pregnant. They even invited me to dinner to celebrate the occasion. They were so grateful.

The proper digestion of foods and absorption of nutrients is necessary for optimal healing in all of the body's systems, including the reproductive system. Susan and Paul are just one of many couples whom enzymes have helped when other therapies failed. Dr. Ellen has a collection of baby photos from patients who are certain that they were able to conceive and give birth because of enzyme therapy.

WHAT THE SCIENCE SHOWS

As patients discover the benefits of enzyme therapy, they routinely want to know why it isn't more widely recognized and prescribed. "It has changed my life," they say. "Why didn't I hear about it sooner? Why didn't my doctor tell me about enzymes?"

One major reason is that too many patients and their doctors rely on prescription and over-the-counter drugs to relieve symptoms, especially digestive ones. Walk past the shelves of medications in your local drugstore or supermarket, and you'll see dozens of products that promise to neutralize stomach acid or prevent acid production—and that's just what's available over the counter. The prescription business for digestive upset is huge. In 2000, Americans spent nearly $7 billion on omeprazole (Prilosec) and lansoprazole (Prevacid), just two of many prescription antacids.[4]

Another challenge is that while compelling research has confirmed the effectiveness of enzymes, scientists have not always been able to replicate the study findings, a step that is necessary for scien-

Vitamins and Minerals Need Enzymes, Too

So many first-time patients arrive for their appointments with veritable suitcases of nutritional supplements that they began taking because they read an article in a magazine or newspaper or spotted a new product in a health food store. Often, they have no idea what they're taking or why—or whether it's accomplishing anything. They don't realize that if they're not properly digesting foods and absorbing those nutrients, they won't be able to process the supplements, either.

Vitamins and minerals don't activate until they unite with enzymes. If that doesn't happen, they just get flushed from the body unused. As Dr. Ellen tells her patients, they may be taking supplements, but all they're getting is expensive urine.

tific validation. Occasionally, poor study design is to blame. For example, exposing enzymes to heat in the laboratory may impair their ability to do their jobs, which would skew the results. Also, while enzymes are essential to optimal health, they seldom are the only component of a therapeutic regimen.

Despite this, research has isolated and verified certain actions of enzymes within the body. It's only a matter of time before a dramatic discovery awakens both the general public and the medical community to the life-altering benefits of enzyme supplements.

Even then, however, experts will probably continue to debate the biochemical and nutritional value of enzyme therapy. After all, they've been doing so for more than 60 years! Two issues are at the heart of the controversy: first, whether enzymes can survive in the harsh environment of the digestive tract, and second, whether they can pass from the intestines into the bloodstream.

Earlier, we discussed how food enzymes can remain active in the stomach for a rather long time, even in the presence of acid. They can tolerate surprisingly harsh acidic environments. It's known, too, that vegetarian enzyme supplements (meaning those that come from plant rather than animal sources) remain intact in the stomach, so they are able to reactivate as they travel through the remainder of the digestive tract.

The absorption of enzymes is a more controversial issue. Enzymes are large molecules, with a molecular weight of 20,000 or more. Compare that with the molecular weight of alcohol (46) or water (18), and you can see that enzymes are huge. For this reason, the general consensus has been that intact enzymes cannot pass from the intestines into the bloodstream. Yet evidence suggests that under normal conditions, macromolecules like enzymes can permeate the intestinal wall. This phenomenon is integral to the effectiveness of enzyme therapy in treating a number of chronic conditions, including food sensitivities, inflammatory bowel disorders, vascular disease, and immune dysfunction. For example, protease—a type of digestive enzyme—is able to break down dietary proteins that have leaked into the bloodstream, where they can trigger food sensitivities and corresponding symptoms, such as bloating, headache, rash, fatigue, and irritability.

More than 20 years ago, two Harvard researchers reported that "the normal adult intestine is in fact permeable to macromolecules . . . in quantities that may be antigenic or biologically active. . . ." Since then, the documentation to support the absorption of enzymes has increased exponentially. We know that some whole proteins do reach the intestines intact and then cross the intestinal wall into the bloodstream; these are enzymes. Because they can reactivate repeatedly, it takes only a few to reach a nutritionally significant level.[5]

MEDICINE FOR THE 21ST CENTURY

As we see it, much of the controversy about enzyme therapy is driven by old beliefs and theories that are no longer valid. Indeed, enzyme therapy challenges the very principles of conventional medicine because it targets the root cause of a condition rather than the symptoms.

When treating patients, mainstream physicians tend to go for the quick fix—the drug or procedure that provides fast relief. They seldom dig deeper to find the real cause of the symptoms, which, in our experience, is often poor digestion and poor absorption of nutrients. It's so simple and straightforward yet so foreign to many in the medical community. This book will reveal why this needs to change.

The good news is that a growing number of physicians are adopting a more holistic approach to care, looking at the whole person rather than just the symptoms. If this becomes standard practice, enzyme therapy will move to the forefront of disease prevention and treatment. The therapy is all about correcting underlying deficiencies so the body's systems can function as they should. This is the foundation of optimal health.

FROM DR. ELLEN'S CASE FILES *Three-year-old Richard is one of my favorite patients. He has touched my heart in so many ways that I can't help hugging and kissing him when I see him. Richard's mother brought him to see me after reading* The Food Allergy Cure. *Ever since the boy began eating solid foods, he'd been experiencing gas and abdominal cramping so severe that he'd scream in pain. This happened regularly, not only after meals but also before bowel movements. He often awakened at night as well, which kept his mother from getting much sleep.*

Richard's parents had taken him to every well-known gastroenterologist in northern California, including physicians at Stanford University School of Medicine and the University of California, San Francisco, School of Medicine. He'd been given every test imaginable, but none revealed the source of his discomfort. Some doctors thought he might have gastritis or a preulcerous condition, for which they prescribed both prescription and over-the-counter medications. Some provided temporary relief, but inevitably, the honeymoon would end. Once again, Richard would wail in pain.

When I saw Richard, I evaluated him for enzyme deficiencies and food sensitivities. The tests showed that he wasn't digesting a variety of foods and that he couldn't tolerate grains, fruits, dairy products, or simple sugars. He was okay with vegetables, eggs, and some poultry, such as chicken, but turkey, ham, and pork triggered symptoms.

I recommended digestive enzymes to help his body process sugars, starches, and fats, as well as an enzyme-herb formula to coat and heal the mucous lining of the intestines. Just 48 hours after Richard began treatment, his mother called to say that his symptoms had subsided. She was overjoyed. By the time Richard came in for his follow-up appointment, his food sensitivities had cleared almost completely.

Today, Richard is a healthy, happy, energetic little boy. He hasn't needed any other medications since he began taking enzymes. For him, and for all of my patients, I recommend continuing enzyme supplements for life.

Richard is one of thousands of success stories in Dr. Ellen's practice. Throughout this book, you'll read many more. You'll be able to see how enzyme therapy has dramatically transformed the health of so many people with a broad spectrum of symptoms and conditions.

CHAPTER 2

Your Personalized
Enzyme Program

S INCE YOUR BODY uses literally thousands of enzymes just to keep functioning efficiently, how do you go about designing an enzyme program tailored to you? This chapter will help you decide precisely which enzyme supplements you need.

As you'll see, we've organized our recommendations into two stages. Stage 1 is a basic three-part plan that everyone should incorporate into their self-care regimens. For some people, this alone will be sufficient to restore radiant health, high energy, optimal immunity, balanced emotions, and a general sense of vigor and vitality. Stage 2, which directs you to detailed supplement guidelines for particular health concerns, is outlined in the condition-specific chapters in part 3. Here you'll be able to evaluate which areas you need to focus on.

STAGE 1: THE BASICS

Don't be fooled by the simplicity of this stage, since it can have a dramatic impact on all aspects of your health and well-being. Our patients confirm it!

Choose a digestive formula. Complete and proper food digestion should be the primary objective of any self-care regimen. Beyond serving as the primary entry route for nutrients, the gastrointestinal tract is:

• The largest immune organ in your body

• The source of many of the most powerful brain chemicals

• A major exit route for toxins

• A mechanism for maintaining the body's fluid and pH balance

• A home to trillions of beneficial bacteria

It makes sense to take good care of your digestive system by eating healthfully and taking a high-quality digestive enzyme supplement, even if you have no gastrointestinal complaints. Look for a formula that contains a broad spectrum of enzymes, rather like a multivitamin. The best products supply a blend of 13 different enzymes, which assist in digesting the various components of your food. Each is responsible for the breakdown and absorption of a particular type of nutrient. (We'll elaborate on the ingredients in the next chapter.)

If you are in basically good health, take one capsule three times a day, preferably immediately before but no more than 10 minutes prior to each meal. If you have an acid-related condition, such as heartburn or acid reflux, gastritis, or ulcers, take one capsule with your first bite of food. Also take one capsule after a particularly large meal. Eating too much at once can overwhelm your body's ability to digest the food, so adjust your dose accordingly.

Before deciding whether to add individual digestive enzymes to your program, monitor how you respond to the general formula for 1 month. That alone may be enough to reduce the bloating, indigestion, belching, and gas that often follow meals. Over time, you'll notice an increase in your energy level as well because the extra enzymes mean that your body no longer needs to put so much effort into digesting food.

Because you'll be getting more nutrients—the result of improved digestion and absorption—you may notice declines in your appetite and food cravings. Your body will have the necessary nutritional reinforcements to combat illness, slow the aging process, and remain strong and resilient for life. The changes in your health and vitality could be astonishing.

Add protease to your program. Protease, the enzyme responsible for digesting protein, contributes to general good health in many ways. It breaks up molecules called circulating immune complexes, which can disrupt immune function; reduces edema (swelling) and inflammation; and prevents the accumulation of excess fibrin, which can cause dangerous blood clots. It purifies the blood and clears it of old, dead tissue and is highly beneficial for preventing and treating all manner of infections, whether caused by viruses, bacteria, fungi, or parasites.

We suggest taking one protease capsule two or three times a day, 1 hour before or 2 hours after a meal for general health maintenance. Timing is important; when using protease as a systemic therapy rather than for digestive support, you don't want the enzyme to start acting on food in the intestines. Rather, it should travel intact from the intestines into the bloodstream, where it can act on the blood and lymph systems. Washing down your protease supplement with a generous glass of water should help.

As you'll see in part 3, many of the condition-specific prescriptions include this enzyme as well.

Take a probiotic supplement every day. True, they're not enzymes, but probiotics—the friendly bacteria, such as acidophilus, that inhabit your digestive tract—are tremendously important to healthy digestion. They support the breakdown of food, the synthesis of nutrients such as B vitamins and fatty acids, and the function of the immune system.

By taking a probiotic supplement, you help maintain the natural balance among these friendly bacteria. Read product labels to find the supplement that contains the highest number of bacteria—at least hundreds of millions, but preferably more than a billion. Be sure to check the expiration date, too, so you get the freshest product available. Take one capsule a day, at least 40 minutes before or after a meal and not with food.

STAGE 2: THE SPECIFICS

Here's where you get the chance to use an evaluation similar to one that Dr. Ellen uses in her practice. It can help determine whether an enzyme deficiency is behind any particular health issues that you may be experiencing. From the information you gather here, you can add to the basic plan to develop a comprehensive enzyme program that targets your unique needs.

As you complete the evaluation, keep in mind that if you answer yes to even one question in a section, it may indicate a need for enzyme supplements. In that case, simply turn to the appropriate chapter in part 3, where we address a range of health concerns that can result from enzyme deficiency or benefit from enzyme therapy. Each condition has its own prescription, which may include dietary recommendations, lifestyle strategies, and other helpful advice in addition to enzyme guidelines. With this information, you can craft a rejuvenating self-care regimen that will optimize your disease resistance and resilience.

Ensure Optimal Digestion (page 59)

_____ 1. Do you experience bloating, gas, indigestion, or stomach pain up to 2 hours after a meal?

_____ 2. Do you have abdominal discomfort, nausea, heartburn, or acid reflux after meals?

_____ 3. Do you need to take an antacid after meals?

_____ 4. Do you have irritable bowel syndrome, diverticulitis, chronic constipation, or diarrhea?

_____ 5. Do you ever feel dizzy or emotionally out of sorts after eating certain foods?

Reduce Cravings and Lose Weight (page 79)

_____ 1. Are you carbohydrate or protein/fat intolerant? (To find out, complete the self-assessments on page 53.)

_____ 2. Have you been unsuccessful at losing weight and/or maintaining once you've reached your ideal weight?

_____ 3. Do you crave any specific foods?

_____ 4. Do you feel deprived when following a weight-loss plan or reducing your portion size?

_____ 5. Do you experience persistent hunger or low energy at specific times of day?

Revitalize Your Skin and Hair (page 101)

_____ 1. Are you prone to itchy, dry, or cracking skin, scaly patches, rashes, or eczema?

_____ 2. Do you have acne or psoriasis?

_____ 3. Do you have wrinkles or poor skin tone, or is your skin losing its elasticity?

_____ 4. Is your hair dry or brittle?

_____ 5. Is your hair thinning or falling out?

Recharge Your Energy and Vitality (page 127)

_____ 1. Do you lack stamina, strength, or endurance?

_____ 2. Do you experience fatigue, dizziness, depression, "spaciness," or poor memory?

_____ 3. Do you have low blood sugar, low blood pressure, low body temperature, or feelings of total exhaustion?

_____ 4. Before your menstrual period, are you prone to headaches, depression, tension, or an inability to concentrate?

_____ 5. Do you have trouble falling asleep or staying asleep?

Enhance Emotional Balance (page 147)

_____ 1. Are you more likely to get sick when confronted by stressful situations, whether at home or at work?

_____ 2. Do you lack motivation, drive, or perseverance?

_____ 3. Do you often feel melancholy, depressed, or withdrawn?

_____ 4. Do you experience mood swings, irritability, nervousness, anxiety, or memory problems?

_____ 5. Have you noticed degrees of inattention, poor concentration, or hyperactivity/impulsivity?

Maintain a Healthy Immune System (page 169)

_____ 1. Do you have chronic fatigue or fibromyalgia?

_____ 2. Have you been diagnosed with multiple sclerosis, rheumatoid arthritis, thyroiditis, lupus, Sjögren's syndrome, or another autoimmune disease?

_____ 3. Do you seem to always come down with colds, flu, sore throats, or similar ailments?

_____ 4. Do you have chronic or recurrent infections, such as bronchitis or sinusitis?

_____ 5. Are you susceptible to airborne allergens or sensitive to environmental pollutants and/or chemicals?

Lower Your Risk of Heart Disease (page 187)

_____ 1. Do you have poor circulation (cold hands and feet)?

_____ 2. Are you prone to heart palpitations or arrhythmia, or do you have weak valves or other cardiac symptoms from a prior infection, such as rheumatic fever?

_____ 3. Have you been diagnosed with angina?

_____ 4. Do you have high blood pressure, varicose veins, atherosclerosis (hardening of the arteries), or a personal or family history of blood clots?

_____ 5. Has anyone in your family age 55 or younger been diagnosed with any type of heart problem?

Treat and Prevent Diabetes (page 205)

_____ 1. Have you been diagnosed with diabetes, hypoglycemia (low blood sugar), or hyperglycemia (high blood sugar)?

_____ 2. Do you become irritable or shaky if you skip or delay a meal?

_____ 3. Do you experience chronic fatigue, headaches, heart palpitations, depression, dizziness, nervousness, anxiety, leg cramps, or numbness or tingling in your hands or feet?

_____ 4. Do you have hyperinsulinemia (high blood levels of insulin) or metabolic syndrome, associated with the development of type 2 (non-insulin-dependent) diabetes?

_____ 5. Do you weigh more than you should, is your waistline larger than your hips, or do you crave carbohydrates?

Fight Inflammation (page 225)

_____ 1. Do you have chronic pain or stiffness?

_____ 2. Do you have osteoarthritis, rheumatoid arthritis, back pain, fibromyalgia, or carpal tunnel syndrome?

_____ 3. Do recover slowly from exercise or experience discomfort when moving?

_____ 4. Have you been diagnosed with ulcerative colitis, Crohn's disease, bladder infection (cystitis), chronic bronchitis, or chronic sinusitis?

_____ 5. Have you experienced injury or physical trauma (as in a car accident), or have you had any type of surgery?

Defend against Cancer (page 249)

_____ 1. Have you ever had cancer?

_____ 2. Do you have a family history of cancer?

_____ 3. Have you been diagnosed with a lipoma (a fatty tissue tumor), a breast tumor, or a degenerative liver disorder?

_____ 4. Have you noticed swelling or discomfort in the prostate area, an increase in frequency of urination, or a reduction in the force of the urine stream?

_____ 5. Have you undergone chemotherapy or radiation therapy for cancer?

Slow the Aging Process (page 267)

_____ 1. Have you noticed any of the following?

- Premature aging
- Age-related illness or declines in health
- Poor balance
- Poor muscle tone and reduced muscle mass
- Slowed reaction time
- Joint pain, swelling, or stiffness
- Thinning skin, and reduced skin elasticity, and/or easy bruising
- Loss of interest in activities

_____ 2. Have you been exposed to air pollutants, pesticides, or tobacco smoke on a regular basis?

_____ 3. Do you drink alcohol or more than two cups of coffee a day?

_____ 4. Do you eat large amounts of charred meats, processed foods, or sugary foods?

_____ 5. Are you experiencing sexual dysfunction or loss of sex drive?

CHAPTER 3

Getting the Most
from Enzyme Supplements

Almost every day in my practice, at least one patient says to me: "Dr. Ellen, which enzymes do you take every day? I want to have your energy, stamina, and vitality."

When something changes your life, as enzymes did mine, you're only too happy to spread the word to everyone you meet. That's how I came to specialize in enzyme therapy. Of course, the regimen that works for me may be quite different from the one that works for someone else. That's why I developed an evaluation like the one in chapter 2, to assess my patients' enzyme status and design personalized supplement programs to address their individual needs.

Beyond identifying the right combinations of enzymes for each patient, my mission has been to educate people about selecting the best enzyme products. I must admit that as I began studying the various products available to physicians and consumers, I was deeply disappointed by the poor quality of most of them. Also troubling was the lack of knowledge among professionals and laypeople alike about the properties that constitute a superior digestive or systemic enzyme formula.

This is why I have committed myself to sharing this information with my patients and peers and with you—so that everyone can get the maximum benefit from enzyme therapy. It starts with choosing the right supplements and taking them the right way. Here's what you should keep in mind.

VEGETARIAN ENZYMES ARE BEST

When reading the labels on enzyme products, the first thing to check is whether the enzymes come from animal or nonanimal sources. For example, some enzymes—including amylase, lipase, and protease—are derived from the pancreases of pigs or sheep. Although much of the research to date has involved these pancreatic enzyme supplements, they have limitations. For one, they are vulnerable to destruction by stomach acid.[1] To prevent this, manufacturers usually apply a coating to the supplements, but in clinical studies, coated enzymes were less effective than those without coatings. [2]

Another concern about animal enzyme supplements is that they work only a specific, limited pH range usually found only in the small intestine. Unfortunately, people whose digestion is compromised may not have the necessary pH levels to activate the enzymes. In comparison, vegetarian enzymes—that is, those from nonanimal sources—remain active over a broad pH range, which means they should work throughout the entire digestive tract.

The broad spectrum of these enzymes can break down all the primary components of food—proteins, fats, carbohydrates, and fiber. Animal enzymes are most effective at digesting proteins; while they help a little with carbohydrates and fats, they do nothing at all for fiber.

Vegetarian enzymes begin digesting food almost immediately after they enter the stomach. As they pass by feedback receptors farther along in the digestive tract, the receptors signal the rest of the body that it doesn't need to produce as many digestive enzymes because some of the food is already broken down. This way, the body doesn't expend as much energy on the digestive process. On the other hand, animal enzymes don't get to work until food reaches the proper pH level, usually in the small intestine. By then, the body has already churned out extra digestive enzymes.

Manufacturers cultivate vegetarian enzymes in a carefully controlled environment that's free of pesticides and other contaminants, while animal enzymes come from pigs that have been raised on genetically and chemically altered feed and treated with steroids and antibiotics. Also, because vegetarian enzymes can be more concentrated than animal enzymes, a single capsule can have more enzymatic activity. Generally speaking, you can get the same amount of activity—or more—from fewer vegetarian supplements. In the case of the systemic enzyme protease, for example, a single capsule of a high-quality vegetarian enzyme is equal in potency to as many as five capsules of an animal enzyme.

Incidentally, when you're shopping for enzyme supplements, check to be sure that not only the enzymes but also the capsules are vegetarian. Some products that claim to be vegetarian use capsules made from an-

A Word about Bromelain and Papain

When patients hear the word *enzyme* for the first time, they often think of bromelain from pineapple or papain from papaya. Both are enzymes, and both have their place in enzyme therapy, but we tend to recommend them on a rather limited basis. The reason: They target only protein digestion and don't support carbohydrate, fat, or fiber digestion. What's more, pineapple and papaya are often exposed to environmental contaminants, such as pesticides, preservatives, and growth enhancers. Even without these toxins, the fruits are common allergens. Over the years, several patients have not been able to use products containing bromelain or papain because they were at risk for allergic reactions.

imal gelatin, even though the enzymes themselves are from nonanimal sources. Read the labels carefully. Ideally, the capsules should be made from cellulose and water and contain only the active ingredients—no fillers or encapsulating aids like magnesium stearate. Such supplements are less likely to trigger allergic reactions.

What about enzymes in tablet form? We don't recommend them, since they're likely to contain potential allergens, such as talc, lactose, starch, polyethylene glycol, and triethyl citrate. If the tablets are red, they may contain sucrose and sunset yellow food coloring as well.

SUPPLEMENTS FOR THE BASIC PLAN

Comparing the ingredients and potencies of various brands of enzymes can be something of a challenge because of discrepancies in labeling. Currently, the only recognized units of activity for vegetarian enzymes are those listed in the Food Chemical Codex, which sets forth standards to ensure the quality and safety of food chemicals. The units and their respective enzymes are as follows.

- ALU for lactase, which digests lactose (milk sugar)

- CU for cellulase, which digests fiber

- DP for malt diastase, which digests carbohydrates

- DU or SKB for amylase, which digests carbohydrates

- HUT for protease, which digests proteins

- LU or FIP for lipase, which digests fats

As you may remember from chapter 2, we recommend a basic plan that consists of a general digestive enzyme formula, a protease supplement, and a probiotic supplement. This trio alone can do wonders for your health and well-being, but for optimal results, you must start with the right products. Here's what you should look for. (For specific product recommendations, you're welcome to visit the Web site www.bioset.net.

Full-spectrum blend digestive enzyme. As mentioned in chapter 2, the ideal digestive formula contains a broad spectrum of enzymes so it can help digest every nutrient component of your food. Check the label for these ingredients, at a minimum. Avoid products that list enzyme potencies in units of measure other than those specified here.

- Alpha-galactosidase: 10 to 150 GalU (25 to 376 AGSU)

- Amylase: 6,000 to 20,000 DU

- Cellulase: 200 to 900 CU

- Glucoamylase: 4 to 8 AGU

- Invertase: 125 to 750 SU (0.25 to 1.5 LAU)

- Lactase: 200 to 1,000 ALU/LACU

- Lipase: 150 to 600 LU

- Malt diastase: 150 to 800 DP

- Protease blend (alkaline, neutral, and acid proteases, plus peptidase): 18,000 to 50,000 HUT

- One or more of the following: xylanese, pectinase, hemicellulase, phytase, or beta-glucanase

Taking one capsule of this formula before each meal will not only help release all the nutrients from your food but will also ensure their proper absorption.

Protease supplement. Of the thousands of systemic enzymes, protease is among the most versatile, facilitating a host of reactions and processes within the body. This is why we recommend it as a separate supplement in addition to the protease blend in the digestive formula. Choose a product in the range of 400,000 to 800,000 HUT, with an additional 40 to 80 milligrams of calcium citrate. Protease works best when taken on an empty stomach, either 1 hour before or 2 hours after a meal.

Probiotic supplement. A top-quality supplement contains the following beneficial bacteria in the specified amounts.

- *Bifidobacterium bifidum*: 500 million to 700 million viable organisms

- *Bifidobacterium longum:* 250 to 375 million viable organisms

- *Lactobacillus acidophilus*: 1 to 1.5 billion viable organisms

- *Lactobacillus casei*: 250 to 750 million viable organisms

- *Lactobacillus plantarum*: 1 to 2.5 billion viable organisms

- *Lactobacillus salivarius*: 250 to 375 million viable organisms

As with protease, you'll get the best results from probiotics by taking them on an empty stomach.

FORMULAS FOR HEALING

When you get to the condition-specific chapters in part 3, you'll see that a number of the recommended formulas combine enzymes with herbs, vitamins, minerals, and other nutrients. The beauty of these products is that the ingredients have an inherent synergy. Specifically, the enzymes optimize the absorption of the herbs and nutrients so you get maximum therapeutic benefit from them. Otherwise, they could pass through your digestive tract without being absorbed into your bloodstream, which means they may never reach the tissues and organs where they're needed.

We worry when we see people taking excessive amounts of supplements that aren't being absorbed properly. Rather than supporting good health, they could become a source of toxicity and stress for the body, not to mention a drain on the wallet. As we remind patients, the body needs enzymes to absorb and utilize nutrients, whether those nutrients come from foods or supplements.

If you're not able to locate one of the enzyme formulas that we recommend in part 3, you have the option of buying and taking the individual ingredients—enzymes, herbs, and nutrients—as separate supplements. This will be about the same as taking them in a single formula.

For example, since many of Dr. Ellen's patients take the herb hawthorn for healthy heart function, she advises them to add a digestive enzyme. The two supplements together are as effective as a formula containing both ingredients. What's more, the hawthorn works better because the digestive enzyme ensures optimal absorption of the herb.

For ease of use, we've listed the primary ingredients in each formula in bold. They're the ones that are most important. Look for them in a single product or as individual supplements. You can add the secondary ingredients (in italic) as you wish.

Keep in mind, too, that the dosages for individual herbs and nutrients are approximate. If you can find products of roughly the same potency, they should work fine as long as you're taking enzymes. In fact, our recommended dosages tend to be somewhat lower than other experts' because, with enzymes to enhance absorption, you don't need as much of the other substances.

DIETARY CHANGES
ARE IMPORTANT, TOO

In part 2, you'll complete another self-assessment to determine whether you're carbohydrate or protein/fat intolerant. In our experience, the vast majority of people fall into one of these two categories. Some have characteristics of both—that is, they have trouble digesting carbs, proteins, and fats.

Depending on the results of your self-assessment, we recommend one of two diets that Dr. Ellen developed and has been recommending to her patients for more than 25 years. By helping to correct the underlying intolerances, both diets enhance immune function, boost energy, and support weight loss and maintenance.

By following the appropriate diet and taking the necessary supplements (including either a carbohydrate digestive enzyme or a protein/fat digestive enzyme), you should experience marked improvement in most chronic conditions as well as your overall health within as few as 14 days. Some patients—including many of those whose stories appear in the following pages—have reported dramatic differences literally overnight, from improved digestion and diminished food cravings to stable blood sugar and relief from pain. They say they feel more vital and alive than ever. With enzymes, you can, too!

A Word about Safety

The safe use of enzymes in the human food supply, as well as in dietary supplements, is documented as far back as the early 1900s. In the 1920s, when Edward Howell, MD, began his extensive research into the health benefits of enzyme supplementation, he reported no adverse effects. Nor have the many thousands of health care professionals who have been prescribing vegetarian enzymes as a treatment for digestive and inflammatory disorders since the 1950s.

Vegetarian enzymes appear on the FDA's GRAS (Generally Regarded as Safe) list, meaning they are acceptable for use in foods and dietary supplements. Both animal and human studies have shown vegetarian enzymes to be highly safe with no toxic limit, no matter the size of the dose or the duration of treatment. What's more, there is no evidence that vegetarian enzymes interact with other ingredients in the same supplement or with other nutritional supplements or medications.

Recently, studies have compared supplemental enzymes with various nonsteroidal anti-inflammatory drugs (NSAIDs) as treatments for inflammatory conditions. Enzymes demonstrated a much more favorable safety profile than most common NSAIDs, making them a safe but effective alternative to such drugs.

PART II

The Enzyme-
Digestion
Connection

CHAPTER 4

A Digestion Primer

FROM DR. ELLEN'S CASE FILES *Many years ago, a 66-year-old woman named Betty came to the BioSET Clinic/Institute with persistent digestive symptoms that included heartburn, severe bloating, and abdominal swelling. Over the previous 2 years, she had been bothered by a chronic cough and occasional shortness of breath. Otherwise, she seemed healthy. She took great care of herself by eating a well-balanced diet with modest amounts of fat and sugar, walking a mile every day, and practicing yoga two or three times a week. She also wasn't taking any medication, which is unusual for a woman her age.*

I gave Betty a complete physical examination and enzyme evaluation, which revealed that she had trouble digesting protein. Acid reflux (heartburn) is a common problem among people who are protein intolerant. I recommended a protein digestive enzyme along with another enzyme to neutralize the acid, and her symptoms cleared up almost as soon as she started taking the supplements.

Betty was so elated with the results that she told all the women she worked out with. Pretty soon, they were calling the clinic to schedule appointments for enzyme evaluations. They became big fans of enzyme therapy.

Betty is one of an estimated 72 million Americans who aren't able to properly digest food and absorb its nutrients. The vast majority of our patients show at least some symptoms of poor digestion. In fact, these symptoms are so common that people tend to view chronic digestive problems—especially heartburn and gas—as "normal." They aren't.

Nor are they only by-products of the aging process, as many seem to believe. During Dr. Ellen's medical rotation, she spent time in a cardiologist's office. Many young people came in complaining of chest pain, only to be diagnosed with digestive ailments. Typically, they were sent home with prescriptions for antacids.

As a nation, we spend billions on prescription and over-the-counter medications that we hope will cure our heartburn, bloating, gas, diarrhea, and constipation once and for all. While these remedies may provide some relief, they do so only by masking the symptoms. They don't fix what's causing the symptoms in the first place.

In a landmark 1986 study, a team of Swedish researchers concluded that for the most part, antacids are ineffective for treating digestive complaints. Sometimes they even cause the stomach to produce *more* acid, a condition known as acid rebound, which only aggravates any existing distress.

Another drawback of antacids is that they change the pH in the gut, creating an imbalance among the beneficial bacteria that could in turn allow the overgrowth of unfriendly types. Some evidence suggests that using antacids may increase the risk of infection with *Helicobacter pylori*, the bacterium that causes ulcers.

The only real solution to digestive symptoms is to stop them at their source. In our experience, virtually every case of poor digestion is a by-product of depleted enzymes, not just in the digestive tract but also in foods themselves. Enzyme therapy can help compensate for any deficiency and, in the process, provide real relief from symptoms—sometimes overnight.

Just as important, enzyme therapy can head off the long-term health consequences of poor digestion. When your body isn't able to properly absorb and utilize nutrients, it becomes vulnerable to a whole host of chronic illnesses, including heart disease, cancer, and diabetes. As you'll learn in part 3, enzyme therapy can play an important role in managing and sometimes reversing these and other conditions. Of course, you'll be better off if you can avoid them altogether.

In this chapter, we'll explore how digestion influences your overall health and how enzymes can correct and prevent digestive problems. Let's begin with a brief tour of the digestive system.

HOW DIGESTION WORKS

The primary function of the digestive system is to break food into its component nutrients. These nutrients need to arrive at the cell walls in the appropriate form; otherwise, they can't get inside.

A healthy digestive system processes food both physically and chemically, with controlled muscle contractions (called peristalsis) and enzyme secretions. Unfortunately, most of what we eat isn't digested properly, and often, enzyme deficiencies are to blame.

Stage 1: It's All about Chewing

Digestion begins when you put food into your mouth and chew it. Chewing mixes the food with the enzymes ptyalin and amylase in saliva, plus others produced in the mouth. Research has shown that salivary amylase can digest as much as 30 to 40 percent of starches before food even reaches the stomach, so you can see why thorough chewing is absolutely crucial. To allow enzymes to do their job, you should chew each mouthful of food 30 to 40 times, which is a lot more than the average 3 to 5 times. Basically, most people inhale their food.

Insufficient chewing is the first and most significant impediment to proper digestion. When food is swallowed practically whole, digestive symptoms such as heartburn, bloating, and gas are almost inevitable. Many people probably wouldn't need antacids if they just took the time to chew their food.

If rushing through meals is a bad habit for grownups, it's even worse for children because it sets the stage for poor nutrient absorption—and therefore nutrient deficiencies—at an early age. Sadly, even our schools give short shrift to mealtimes. Most allow only a half hour for lunch, and the kids finish eating in about 10 minutes so that they can go outside to play. They can't possibly chew their food thoroughly in that amount of time. Between the brief lunch breaks and the nutritionally unbalanced lunch options, it's no wonder that our children are prone to illness.

Stage 2: Traversing the Digestive Tract

Once it has left the mouth, food travels through the esophagus before entering the upper section of the stomach. It may stay in this section (called the fundus) for up to 1 hour, allowing food enzymes and stomach acid secretions to continue the digestive process.

As food leaves the fundus and moves into the rest of the stomach, it's churned into a creamy substance known as chyme. Eventually, the chyme reaches the duodenum, the uppermost section of the small intestine, where it triggers the pancreas to produce extra enzymes to further break down carbohydrates, proteins, and fats.

The enzyme secretions continue as the chyme makes its way through the rest of the small intestine. This is where the actual absorption of nutrients takes place as the carbs, proteins, and fats cross over the intestinal mucosa, which serves as a protective barrier against bacteria and toxins. From there, the nutrients travel via the bloodstream and lymphatic system to their destinations throughout the body.

In theory, the human body shouldn't need enzyme supplements to support the digestive process, as it's quite capable of producing enough of the necessary enzymes to break down food and absorb nutrients. In reality, though, as many as 20 million Americans have some sort of digestive ailment, which suggests that their digestive systems are not operating optimally. Taking extra digestive enzymes in supplement form can improve the process by leaps and bounds.

The key to creating a state of optimal health and disease resistance is to make sure that the body receives all the necessary nutrients in adequate amounts. Even the most well-balanced diet won't do much good if the body can't break down the foods and utilize their nutrients. In this scenario, what we eat can actually be toxic to our bodies instead of rejuvenating, and we become more susceptible to degenerative illness and chronic poor health.

To build strong, resilient bodies, we need the potent nutrients from foods so every cell is amply nourished and fully functional. We don't need to rely on nutritional supplements when we're digesting food properly and thoroughly.

WHAT GOES WRONG?

In chapter 1, we discussed how each of us has a predetermined enzyme potential. This means that our bodies can make only a certain number of enzymes over the course of a lifetime, so they depend on the enzymes in food to provide a head start on the digestive process. The trouble is, most of what we eat isn't as enzyme rich as we might think.

All raw foods contain the proper enzymes in the appropriate proportions to completely break down on their own, whether through human consumption or natural decomposition. Chewing these foods ruptures the cell membranes, which releases the indigenous enzymes to launch the digestive process. Amylase reduces carbohydrates to their component simple sugars. Protease separates long protein chains into their amino acid "links," and lipase splits fats into free fatty acids.

Cellulase—the one enzyme that must come from food, as the body doesn't manufacture it—breaks the bonds of fiber that encase most of the nutrients in plants, thus enhancing the nutritional value of plant foods.

Overwhelming evidence confirms that food enzymes play a vital role in the digestive process, breaking down food even before it drops into the lower section of the stomach, where it soaks in the powerful digestive chemical hydrochloric acid. But as we've said elsewhere, the high temperatures involved in cooking and processing leave food virtually devoid of enzymatic activity. The full burden of digestion shifts to the body, overtaxing the digestive system and preventing the complete assimilation of vital nutrients.

Of course, if the body has trouble absorbing nutrients from food, it won't fare any better with nutrients from supplements. In fact, without proper enzyme support, these supplements can harm the body instead of helping it. They can also complicate medical diagnoses by interfering with the accurate assessment of symptoms.

FROM DR. ELLEN'S CASE FILES *On her first visit to the BioSET Clinic/Institute, a 56-year-old woman with breast cancer brought a full-size suitcase filled with medications and nutritional supplements. She was experiencing chronic loose bowel movements, frequent heartburn, and acid reflux at night. She wondered whether her symptoms were being caused by something she was taking.*

I knew her physician and his impressive work with cancer patients, so I was not about to ask her to discontinue any supplements without first consulting him. When I tested her, though, I found that she was sensitive to some of the supplements. I recommended that she either receive treatment for her sensitivities with my BioSET system or refrain from using the problem supplements, with her doctor's approval.

When I performed a complete enzyme evaluation, I found her to be carbohydrate intolerant, which meant that she was not fully digesting sugars and starches. As we age, our bodies' ability to produce enzymes diminishes, and one of the most common symptoms of this is chronic, sometimes explosive, diarrhea. In my experience, this symptom can almost always be traced to difficulty digesting sugars.

I suggested that she take a carbohydrate digestive enzyme and reduce her intake of dietary sugar from all sources, including cereals, breads, dairy products (which contain lactose, a milk sugar), and fruits. Her digestive symptoms quickly subsided, and her strength and vitality improved. Now, her doctor regularly refers patients to me for food sensitivity testing and enzyme evaluation.

THE STRESS OF POOR DIGESTION

These days, everyone seems to be climbing on the nutrition bandwagon. Books and articles offering dietary advice abound, and health food stores are thriving. The trouble is, much of the available information is contradictory at best and inaccurate—and potentially harmful—at worst. Too often, it overlooks one very important fact: What we digest is just as important as what we eat.

Proper digestion can't occur without the necessary enzymes. If they aren't present in foods, they must be synthesized by the body, a process that requires tremendous metabolic energy and machinery. When we evaluate the healthfulness of any diet, we must consider the magnitude of the burden that it will place on the body through the digestive process. This burden is what's known as digestive stress.

The issue of stress figures prominently in our current understanding of health and disease. Stress involves the gradual depletion of the reserve capacity to respond and adapt to challenges to the body's systems. The more reserve capacity the body has, the better able it is to cope with stressors that it encounters. By the same token, depleted reserve capacity means that the body is highly vulnerable to the damage that stress can cause.

To better understand the interplay among stress, reserve capacity, and damage, think of the tires on an automobile. Driving causes stress on the tire treads, gradually removing rubber and depleting the reserve capacity of the tires—that is, the thickness of the treads. The resulting loss of traction increases the risk of structural damage, especially in the presence of extreme challenges such as uneven road surfaces or sudden maneuvers. Reducing the wear and tear on tires through regular maintenance and driving safely on paved roads minimizes the stress on the treads and extends their longevity.

To reduce digestive stress, your best bet is to build your meals and snacks around foods that are rich in enzymes and don't overtax your digestive system. Then your body can extract and utilize the necessary nutrients with minimal energy and effort.

The Low-Stress Diet

Simply stated, a low-stress diet is one that minimizes digestive and systemic stress. The ideal diet would consist of organically grown, pesticide-free foods, with substantial amounts of raw foods in at least two meals per day, since only raw foods contain active enzymes.

Consider what happens when a freshly picked apple remains uneaten for several days. The "meat" of the apple becomes soft and liquefies due to the action of enzymes—the same ones that help your body digest the apple when you eat it. The work of the enzymes reduces the burden of enzyme secretion on the pancreas, and thus digestive stress.

While eating nothing but raw foods would be a challenge, incorporating them into your meals and snacks whenever possible can minimize the workload for your digestive system. When you add enzyme supplements to help digest cooked and processed foods, you'll improve digestive function and nutrient absorption.

The High-Stress Diet

Unfortunately, the typical American diet is almost entirely cooked or processed fare, with very few raw foods and therefore very few food enzymes. Responsibility for picking up any slack in the digestive process falls to the digestive system and, on a larger scale, the entire body, increasing the likelihood of digestive and systemic stress.

In general, a high-stress diet has one or more of the following characteristics.

- It contains foods that cannot be adequately broken down because they are loaded with preservatives or are highly processed.

- It triggers an immune response in a susceptible person.

- It contains too much or too little carbohydrate, protein, or fat, so the nutrients are substantially out of balance with the body's metabolic requirements.

- The nutrients are not available to the body because the necessary enzymes are in short supply.

All of these factors cause the digestive system to work even harder to squeeze whatever nutrients it can from the foods that are eaten. Over time, the combination of poor nutrient absorption and digestive system overload can trigger a host of symptoms, including:

- Lack of energy

- Bloating, indigestion, and gas

- Poor elimination (constipation or frequent loose stools)

- Poor weight control (underweight or overweight)

- Hormone imbalances

- Dry or oily skin

- Thin and/or brittle bones, as in osteoporosis

- Frequent illness resulting from a poorly functioning immune system

In our opinion, persistent digestive stress is a leading contributor to many of the chronic health problems that are on the rise in this country. The body does its best to keep up with nutritional demands without adequate enzyme support, but it can tolerate these conditions for only so long. Eventually, your health begins to falter, and illness sets in—the long-term consequence of enzyme and nutrient deficiencies.

WHAT'S BEST FOR YOU

When considering the ideal diet for optimal digestion and nutrient absorption, please keep in mind that what's "ideal" can vary from one person to the next. It depends on a number of factors, including metabolism, current health status, and any existing food sensitivities.

The vast majority of our patients are either carbohydrate intolerant or protein/fat intolerant. Often, these intolerances are behind the symptoms that bring people to the office in the first place. Steering clear of the offending foods—including some that they may consider healthy—can go a long way toward minimizing digestive stress.

In chapter 5, we'll take a closer look at how intolerances can challenge all of your body's systems—including digestion—and set the stage for illness. Then you'll complete a self-assessment to determine whether an intolerance may be undermining your health, even if you seem symptom-free. With this information, you'll be able to incorporate the appropriate eating plan and digestive enzyme supplements into your self-care regimen. Remember, optimal digestion plays a major role in optimal health.

CHAPTER 5

Intolerances, Enzymes, and Your Health

F OOD INTOLERANCES and enzyme deficiencies seem to go hand in hand. If you can't tolerate a particular food, you can't digest it properly. Your pancreas churns out extra enzymes to kick-start the process, but usually to no avail. All that work not only chips away at your body's enzyme potential but also siphons resources from its other systems.

Why may certain foods cause trouble for you but not for someone else? Food intolerances are highly individual, driven by a complex of factors that include genetic background, activity level, and metabolic rate. In general, though, people who have intolerances—and that's nearly everyone—fall into one of two broad categories: Either they can't digest carbohydrates (sugars and starches) or they can't digest proteins and fats. An unlucky few may have problems with all three.

After many years of studying these intolerances and tracking their symptoms in my patients, Dr. Ellen developed a simple questionnaire to help pinpoint a person's trigger foods. Drawing on this information as well as the results of allergy testing and an enzyme evaluation, Dr. Ellen recommends one of two eating plans designed especially for carbohydrate intolerance and protein/fat intolerance. In most cases, the combination of proper diet and enzyme supplements is enough to clear up any toxicity, alleviate symptoms, and foster optimal digestion and nutrient absorption.

As you'll see in part 3, these intolerances can contribute to all manner of health problems, some of which you might never connect to food sensitivities or poor digestion. This is why identifying any underlying intolerances and correcting them with diet and enzymes are so important. You'll be able to complete the questionnaire for yourself a bit later in the chapter, but first let's take a closer look at how each of the three food types—carbohydrates, proteins, and fats—can influence your health for better or for worse.

KNOW THE OFFENDERS

Make no mistake: Your body needs carbohydrates, proteins, and fats to support various functions. When it can't properly utilize these nutrients, however, they can do more harm than good. The good news is that enzyme therapy helps correct intolerances by facilitating the digestive process so you can benefit from balanced nutrition without worrying about unpleasant and even debilitating symptoms.

Carbohydrates

Among our patients, carbohydrate intolerance—that is, the inability to digest sugars and starches—is quite common. It occurs when the small intestine isn't able to secrete sufficient amounts of the appropriate enzymes, such as amylase, the enzyme responsible for breaking down starches. This can lead to digestive symptoms such as bloating and gas, which typically occur within 2 hours of a meal.

In our experience, people who don't properly digest carbohydrates tend to crave sugary foods. But eating too many of them can complicate matters by overburdening an already challenged digestive system. Besides causing digestive stress, overindulging can contribute to weight gain.

Perhaps the best-known form of carbohydrate intolerance involves a deficiency of the enzyme lactase, which is necessary to digest lactose, or milk sugar. Most mammals, including humans, have high levels of intestinal lactase activity at birth, but it can drop off during childhood and remain low through adulthood. This sets the stage for poor digestion of foods that contain lactose, such as milk, yogurt, certain cheeses, and butter.

By some estimates, up to 70 percent of the world's population is deficient in intestinal lactase. In the United States alone, more than one-third of the population is unable to adequately break down dairy products. Researchers have found that taking supplemental lactase helps alleviate symptoms of this intolerance by improving lactose digestion.

In another form of carbohydrate intolerance, problems arise from a shortage of invertase, the enzyme that breaks down sucrose (refined sugar) into glucose and fructose. The prevalence of highly refined, processed foods in the typical American diet means that we consume an abundance of sugar. The combination of too much sugar and too little invertase is a recipe for digestive stress.

According to a theory that has been gaining acceptance in medical circles, undiagnosed sugar intolerance plays a role in many kinds of allergies. In our respective practices, we routinely see sugar intolerance in patients with hay fever, environmental allergies, and even mold allergies. Supplemental invertase can help by improving the assimilation and utilization of sugar.

Proteins

If you imagine protein as a chain, amino acids are the individual links. The body employs a complex mechanism for exchanging and balancing amino acids to maintain the structure of protein in tissues and organs. If you aren't getting enough complete protein from your diet, or you aren't properly digesting it because of an enzyme deficiency, you may not have all the amino acids your body needs.

Protease is the enzyme that breaks down dietary protein into its component peptides, which are small fragments made from individual amino acids. So if you run low on protease, you probably run low on amino acids as well. To compensate for the deficit, your body begins breaking down the protein it already has, much of it from blood, muscle, and organ tissues.

People who have trouble digesting dietary protein tend to crave protein-rich foods and are prone to digestive upset immediately after meals.

Fats

In the 1990s, as all of America got swept up in the low-fat/fat-free craze, we lost sight of one very important fact: The body needs fat to function properly. Fat is a key component of cell membranes. It supports the transport and utilization of vitamins A, D, E, and K. It's necessary for the production of certain hormones, as well as for immune function, nerve conduction, and various other bodily processes. In short, we can't live without it.

While too much of the wrong kind of dietary fat can promote weight gain and inflammation, too little dietary fat can lead to other health problems. In fact, even if you're getting enough fat from foods, you can experience a deficiency if you're low on lipase, the enzyme that facilitates fat digestion. A shortage of lipase can inhibit the breakdown of essential fatty acids for absorption into the bloodstream and lymphatic system, and from there into tissues and cells.

Many people who are overweight are deficient in essential fatty acids. To compensate, they tend to develop cravings for unhealthful fatty and/or salty foods. Their bodies don't discriminate between healthful and unhealthful fats. They just want fat—even if it's fried, hydrogenated, or otherwise processed.

You might think that your body can tap its own fat stores to get what it needs. Not so. That said, your fat stores are an important source of metabolic energy. Without them, your body would need to break down the structural protein in tissues and organs for use as an energy source.

Many patients who are fat intolerant report having bloating and gas immediately after meals. The incomplete digestion of dietary fats can cause other digestive symptoms, such as cramping and diarrhea, as well.

DO YOU HAVE AN INTOLERANCE?

When Dr. Ellen first evaluates patients for underlying intolerances, she often asks them to envision a large buffet offering every food imaginable. Try it yourself: Which food would you make a beeline for? The one you are most likely to crave and overindulge in is the one to which you are most likely intolerant. This rule of thumb has two exceptions, though. If your food of choice is potato chips or corn chips, you probably crave salt—indicating a fat intolerance—rather than potatoes or corn. If it's cheese, you may crave fat rather than lactose.

To more precisely pinpoint whether you are carbohydrate intolerant or protein/fat intolerant, complete the following questionnaire by placing checkmarks next to the items that apply to you. Keep in mind that even one checkmark could indicate a possible underlying intolerance.

Carbohydrate Intolerance

_____ Cravings for sugars, breads, and pastries

_____ Excessive consumption of refined sugars

_____ Bloating within 2 hours of a meal

_____ Excessive gas after eating raw or high-fiber foods

_____ Diarrhea, especially after consuming foods that contain lactose

_____ Constipation, especially after consuming foods that contain maltose or sucrose

_____ A tendency toward outbreaks of canker sores or shingles

_____ Skin problems, such as acne, eczema, or psoriasis

_____ High levels of blood fats (total cholesterol and triglycerides)

_____ Respiratory problems, especially asthma

_____ Spaciness or dizziness

_____ Colitis or Crohn's disease

_____ Candidiasis (yeast infections)

_____ Attention deficit hyperactivity disorder

_____ Emotional distress, such as mood swings, depression, anxiety attacks, anger, or aggressive or violent behavior

Protein/Fat Intolerance

_____ Cravings for fat, protein, and/or salt

_____ Excessive consumption of fat, protein, and/or salt

_____ Bloating immediately after meals

_____ Chronic digestive symptoms, including constipation

_____ Difficulty losing weight

_____ Frequent or chronic infections (bacterial, viral, or yeast)

_____ Diabetes or excess sugar in the urine

_____ Hypoglycemia (low blood sugar)

_____ Osteoarthritis

_____ Degenerative disk problems and bone spurs

_____ Osteoporosis

_____ Gallbladder disease

_____ Hypothyroidism

_____ Menopausal discomforts, premenstrual syndrome, and/or fibrocystic breasts

_____ Anxiety

_____ Deficiencies of vitamins A, D, and/or E

If, based on your responses, you suspect that you have a carbohydrate or protein/fat intolerance, you should see a doctor for follow-up testing. For self-care, you can try the same protocol that Dr. Ellen routinely recommends to her patients. First, choose the appropriate eating plan from page 295 or page 307. Each plan offers dietary recommendations along with a 7-day menu and some recipes. Second, begin taking either a carbohydrate digestive enzyme or a protein/fat digestive enzyme. With these two strategies, you should notice dramatic improvement in any persistent or chronic symptoms—and in your overall health—in as few as 14 days.

The best carbohydrate digestive enzyme formulas are pH-balanced and contain, at minimum, the following mix of enzymes:

- Alpha-galactosidase: 10 to 150 GalU
- Amylase: 6,000 to 20,000 DU
- Cellulase: 200 to 900 CU
- Glucoamylase: 6 to 32 AGU
- Invertase: 125 to 750 SU
- Lipase: 150 to 600 LU
- Malt diastase: 150 to 800 DP
- Protease blend: 18,000 to 50,000 HUT
- Xylanase: 85 to 125 XU

For protein/fat intolerance, look for a pH-balanced, full-spectrum digestive enzyme formula with at least these ingredients:

- Amylase: 4,000 to 6,000 DU
- Cellulase: 150 to 300 CU
- Lipase: 150 to 600 LU
- Glucoamylase: 3 to 6 AGU
- Lactase: 300 to 500 ALU
- Malt diastase: 125 to 150 DP
- Protease blend plus peptidase: 18,000 to 50,000 HUT

In part 3, we'll explore how depleted enzymes and poor digestion can lay the groundwork for a host of health concerns. For each one, Dr. Ellen will share the prescription that she usually offers to the patients in her practice. Most build on a foundation of enzymes and herbal and nutritional supplements, with dietary guidelines and lifestyle advice occasionally thrown into the mix. By combining these strategies with the basic supplement plan (see page 32) and the appropriate diet and digestive enzyme, you'll have a comprehensive self-care regimen that restores and maintains your good health for a lifetime.

PART III

Enzyme Therapy
for Common
Health Concerns

CHAPTER 6

Ensure Optimal Digestion

THE MORE RESEARCH WE DO and the more patients we see, the more we're convinced that digestive stress is a factor in many if not all of the chronic illnesses prevalent in the United States today. Eating foods that not only tax the digestive system but also fail to satisfy our nutritional needs can cause damage within the body over time. As this damage accumulates, the body can't keep up with repairs, creating even more stress. It's a vicious cycle, and correcting it becomes harder and harder.

All of the digestive disorders that are discussed in this chapter are direct outcomes of persistent digestive stress. People who develop these types of disorders must contend with uncomfortable, sometimes painful digestive symptoms—as well as the increased risk of other health problems—because of enzyme and nutrient deficiencies. But just as chronic illness begins in the gut, so does vibrant health. Enzyme therapy provides essential support to the healing process.

CONSTIPATION

Constipation—difficulty passing stools or passing hard, dry stools—affects more people than any other digestive ailment. It's especially common in those over age 65. The typical American diet and lifestyle bear much of the blame. We eat too many refined foods, which are devoid of fiber and nutrients yet loaded with additives and other artificial ingredients. What's more, we practically inhale our meals, rarely if ever taking the time to chew food thoroughly.

Constipation often affects people who have difficulty digesting carbohydrates, especially high-maltose grains such as wheat, barley, oats, and rye. Sensitivity to maltose, a form of sugar, can cause constipation. Consuming a large amount of protein without a proportional amount of fiber can also disrupt normal bowel function since it overburdens the liver and inhibits detoxification.

Other contributing factors to constipation include a deficiency of essential fatty acids; poor hydration; lack of exercise; and medications that slow bowel transit time, such as cholesterol-lowering drugs, beta-blockers, diuretics, antidepressants, muscle relaxants, and iron supplements, that slow bowel transit time. Sometimes constipation occurs in conjunction with other medical conditions, including ulcerative colitis, diverticular disease, nerve disorders of the bowel, tumors, neurological disorders, thyroid disease, and diabetes.

Incidentally, medical opinion varies as to what constitutes constipation. Conventionally trained physicians tend to believe that one bowel movement a day is sufficient, while many alternative practitioners argue that two or three a day is better. Everyone has his or her own pattern, but at least one bowel movement a day seems necessary for elimination of toxins.

DR. ELLEN'S PRESCRIPTION

To prevent hard-to-pass stools and restore healthy bowel function, I recommend the following.

The Facts about Fiber

Dietary fiber, which plays a vital role in maintaining a healthy digestive tract, takes two forms: soluble and insoluble.

When mixed with liquid, soluble fiber dissolves and turns gummy. This is why manufacturers use it to add texture and consistency to low-fat and fat-free foods. Pectin, a particular type of soluble fiber, binds with fatty substances in the digestive tract, which helps lower cholesterol. Foods that contain soluble fiber include oat bran, rice bran, barley, dried beans and peas, citrus fruits, strawberries, and apples.

Insoluble fiber, or roughage, gives structure to plant cell walls. Although it doesn't dissolve, it does hold on to water. It's responsible for moving waste through the digestive tract, which is important for maintaining healthy bowels and preventing constipation, diverticular disease, and colon cancer. Food sources of insoluble fiber include cabbage, cauliflower, brussels sprouts, beets, turnips, carrots, and apple skins.

To break down cellulose, the main component of fiber, your body depends on an enzyme known as cellulase. But it can't make this enzyme on its own. It can get it only from fiber-rich foods. People who are unable to digest fiber are prone to bloating within about 2 hours of eating. They may also crave fatty foods.

Thoroughly chewing fiber-rich foods can help release the cellulase they contain, as can taking a digestive enzyme supplement with cellulase. Try adding one capsule right after eating a fiber-rich meal—that is, one that includes salad, fruits, beans, nuts, and/or soy products. Patients who've suffered with bloating, abdominal distention, and gas their whole lives immediately improve once they begin enzyme therapy.

- Take one capsule of a carbohydrate digestive enzyme before each meal. Look for a supplement that contains maltase and disaccharidase, which break down sugars. Be sure to take the enzyme regularly, or you won't get complete relief.

- If you're having a meal that's high in protein or fat, also take one capsule of a protein/fat digestive enzyme.

- Include fiber-rich foods in every meal.

- Make sure you're getting enough essential fatty acids from flaxseed, avocados, olives, and fish, among other food sources.

- Avoid processed foods as well as caffeine, alcohol, and excessive amounts of red meat.

- Drink at least half you body weight in ounces of water every day. The water should be chlorine- and flouride-free.

- Aim for 20 to 30 minutes of physical activity every day. Brisk walking, jogging, and yoga can be very beneficial for preventing and relieving constipation.

- Establish good bowel habits and even plan your "toilet time"— preferably right after breakfast or a workout. Over time, the body actually acclimates to this schedule.

CROHN'S DISEASE AND ULCERATIVE COLITIS

Both ulcerative colitis and Crohn's disease are forms of inflammatory bowel disease (IBD) and are among the most severe digestive ailments. Telling the two apart can be a challenge, since each results in an irritated, inflamed bowel. The main difference lies in where they occur. Ulcerative colitis affects the lining of the colon and rectum, while Crohn's most commonly affects the ileum—the section of the small intestine that attaches to the large intestine—and the entire intestinal wall.

Much of the mainstream medical community views ulcerative colitis and Crohn's disease as chronic, lifelong conditions with no known cure. Both may go dormant for long periods of time. Withou proper care, they invariably return. When they do, the symptoms may be more severe than in previous flare-ups.

Dr. Ellen has been treating IBD for more than 25 years with remarkable success. Most patients with IBD have severe carbohydrate intolerances. They need help digesting sugars and starches, with dietary monitoring until their conditions stabilize.

At the beginning of treatment, the usual recommendation is to take larger doses of enzymes to restore proper digestion. It's also a good idea to avoid refined sugars; grains such as rice, wheat, oats, and barley; certain starchy vegetables, including potatoes; most fruits; and all dairy products, especially ice cream. All of these foods can be highly inflammatory to people who are carbohydrate intolerant. Other potential offenders include chocolate, nuts, spicy foods, alcohol, artificial sweeteners, food coloring and other additives, and over-the-counter anti-inflammatory drugs, such as ibuprofen and aspirin.

In most cases, the combination of dietary changes and enzyme supplements brings about rapid, long-term relief from the digestive symptoms of IBD. Related symptoms—fatigue, joint pain, and depression, among others—improve quickly as well.

As you may recall, Dr. Ellen was diagnosed with ulcerative colitis at an early age. The symptoms would wax and wane, but under stress—especially in her early college years—they sometimes became unbearable. After just 2 weeks of taking a carbohydrate digestive enzyme, they disappeared forever. Dr. Ellen is living proof of the healing power of enzyme therapy, especially for digestive ailments such as ulcerative colitis and Crohn's disease.

DR. ELLEN'S PRESCRIPTION

Since both ulcerative colitis and Crohn's disease are such serious conditions, be sure to tell your doctor before incorporating these recommendations into your current self-care regimen.

- Take one or two capsules of a carbohydrate digestive enzyme with each meal. Generally, it's best to take two capsules with larger meals.

- Take one capsule of a gastric enzyme formula three to five times a day between meals. As you'll see, I recommend this supplement for virtually all of the digestive ailments in this chapter because it offers superior support and healing for the digestive system. If you can't find all of the primary ingredients (in bold) in a single product, using individual supplements will work just as well. Just be sure to pair the herbs with a full-spectrum digestive enzyme blend for optimal absorption.

Marshmallow root extract (50 to 100 milligrams). This herb helps soothe an inflamed intestinal lining, which is great for IBD.

Aloe vera juice extract (10 to 30 milligrams). Patients with IBD have used this extract with satisfying results. It may have antiviral, antibacterial, and antifungal properties and enhance immune function. Start with the smallest dose, as too much can cause cramping or diarrhea.

Deglycyrrhizinated licorice root extract (100 to 200 milligrams). Licorice not only reduces inflammation, it also stimulates mucus production to soothe the intestinal lining.

Digestive enzymes. Look for a product that contains a full spectrum of enzymes, in the following dosages: amylase (3,000 to 9,000 DU), lipase (150 to 450 LU), cellulase (200 to 600 CU), lactase (75 to 225 ALU), invertase (75 to 300 SU), peptidase (1,000 to 3,000 HUT), alpha galactosidase (10 to 30 GalU or 25 to 75 AGSU), glucoamylase (2 to 12 AGU), and malt diastase (75 to 300 DP). Make sure the product also contains pectinase, xylanase, hemicellulase, phytase, and/or beta-glucanase; these enzymes help process the nutrients from foods.

- Take 200 to 400 milligrams of quercetin before each meal. A flavonoid, quercetin inhibits the release of histamine, an allergic mediator that can trigger inflammation.

- Follow the diet for carbohydrate intolerance (see page 295). If you prefer more flexibility in your menus, concentrate on building your meals around lean meats, poultry, fish, eggs, beans, and steamed vegetables. Choose organic whenever possible.

- Avoid the inflammatory foods listed above. Many patients ask if they'll be able to reintroduce these foods to their diets as long as they're taking their carbohydrate digestive enzymes. Generally, I recommend steering clear of grains, dairy products, and chocolate for good. But you can try gradually reintroducing the other foods after 4 to 6 months or once you're completely free of symptoms.

Roy was in his early forties when he first came to the BioSET Clinic/Institute. His symptoms included severe abdominal pain, bloody stools, and diarrhea. He had also lost weight. Roy's doctor had diagnosed ulcerative colitis and prescribed steroids. In his case, though, they weren't helpful at all, and he desperately wanted to stop taking them because he knew that their long-term use posed enormous health risks. This is why he was referred to me.

I performed a complete physical and enzyme evaluation, which revealed that Roy was carbohydrate intolerant, which is typical of people with ulcerative colitis. I advised him to take a carbohydrate digestive enzyme before each meal and to follow my diet for carbohydrate intolerance.

The results were immediate and positive. Roy's bloody stools and diarrhea stopped completely, and his abdominal pain subsided by about 75 percent—and this was after conventional treatment had failed. It was remarkable.

For Roy, restoring proper digestion made all the difference in his symptoms. He saw further improvement after I treated him with BioSET, which combines enzyme therapy with nutritional interventions and detoxification to clear up food sensitivities.

DIARRHEA

Diarrhea involves passing unformed, loose or watery stools. If your bowel movements are frequent but solid, it isn't diarrhea; in fact, you may have a form of constipation.

Diarrhea can be acute or chronic, mild or severe. Since it can be a sign that the body is trying to rid itself of toxins, trying to stop it may not be the best idea, at least until you know what's behind it.

A number of underlying conditions—including viral or bacterial infections, inflammatory bowel disease, irritable bowel syndrome, bowel tumors, and diabetes—can trigger a bout of acute diarrhea. So can eating too much fiber or fruit, taking large doses of vitamin C or magnesium, using laxatives or antibiotics, menstruating, and coping with chronic stress. Sometimes diarrhea can be a sign that you've picked up a parasitic infection or ingested unfriendly intestinal bacteria, especially while traveling in a foreign country.

As for chronic diarrhea, the most common cause is difficulty digesting simple sugars, especially sucrose and lactose. In this case, it often accompanies other digestive symptoms, such as abdominal pain, bloating, and gas. Some people react to very small amounts of these sugars, while others notice symptoms only after consuming an abundance of them.

Lactose intolerance—the inability to digest the milk sugar lactose—is especially common. By some estimates, between 70 and 90 percent of adults of African American, Hispanic, Asian, Native American, or Mediterranean descent are deficient in lactase, the enzyme that breaks down lactose. Even though yogurt and aged cheeses contain lactase, many people still have diarrhea and other digestive symptoms after eating them.

In our experience, patients who take carbohydrate digestive enzymes are able to break down lactose and other sugars, which inevitably clears up their diarrhea. Sometimes Dr. Ellen recommends treatment with BioSET, which desensitizes the body to a lactose or other carbohydrate intolerance.

DR. ELLEN'S PRESCRIPTION

If you're prone to frequent bouts of diarrhea, be sure to consult your doctor, who can help identify the underlying cause by ordering appropriate tests. Then try the following strategies.

- Take one capsule of a carbohydrate digestive enzyme before meals. If you're lactose intolerant, take one or two capsules before any meal that includes dairy foods.

- Take one capsule of the gastric enzyme formula twice a day between meals.

- Follow the diet for carbohydrate intolerance (see page 295).

- Steer clear of common food triggers, including refined sugar, grains, dairy products, and fruits. If you can't bear to forgo these foods, your best bet is to receive treatment to clear up your food sensitivities. Often this stops diarrhea and other digestive symptoms after eating foods to which you are sensitive.

If you're planning any foreign travel, especially in a country where the water supply is suspect, take a general digestive enzyme formula as well as a probiotic supplement that contains lactobacillus. The combination can be extremely helpful in preventing "traveler's diarrhea."

FROM DR. ELLEN'S CASE FILES *Two months before Alice came to the BioSET Clinic/Institute, she was a vibrant, active woman who played tennis, went walking with her girlfriends, and attended numerous social gatherings on a weekly basis. Then she developed chronic, explosive diarrhea, with episodes that often came on without warning, leaving her virtually housebound and very depressed.*

Alice sought help from her doctor, but he couldn't offer any solution except for over-the-counter medications such as Pepto-Bismol, Kaopectate, and Imodium. None of them worked for her.

Someone mentioned me and my work with enzyme therapy to Alice, so she scheduled a consultation. She was thrilled to learn that I had been successful in treating chronic diarrhea. I immediately started her on a carbohydrate digestive enzyme and advised her to limit sugars and dairy products in her diet. I was amazed that her doctor hadn't discussed any dietary restrictions with her.

Forty-eight hours after taking the enzyme for the first time, Alice's bowel movements were normal, and she hasn't experienced a problem with chronic diarrhea since. Understandably, she has been very committed to her enzyme regimen. She has also become a strong advocate of enzyme therapy and complementary medicine.

DIVERTICULAR DISEASE

Most people over age 60 and nearly everyone who reaches age 90 have diverticulosis, a condition in which small pouches called diverticuli form in the lining of the colon, or large intestine. Sometimes these pouches protrude through the colon's muscular outer wall.

In and of itself, diverticulosis is a rather benign condition; in fact, it rarely causes symptoms. Only when the pouches become inflamed does the situation progress to a potentially serious illness called diverticulitis. Its most common symptom is lower-abdominal pain.

People who develop diverticuli usually have longstanding issues with poor digestion, perhaps since birth. Many don't eat enough fiber-rich foods, so their intestines become irritated, and they strain during bowel movements. As colonic muscles contract, the pressure inside the colon rises, pushing out the colonic wall. This causes severe pain and muscle spasms, especially near the rectum.

Because their diets tend to be low in fiber, people with diverticular disease are also prone to high levels of blood fats such as cholesterol and triglycerides. Fiber plays a role in binding these fats and escorting them from the body.

In general, a high-fiber diet can be helpful for diverticulosis—but not in someone who can't break down fiber. In this case, the same diet may actually set the stage for diverticulitis.

Proper digestion of all foods—especially those that are rich in fiber—helps soften stools and improve regularity. It also reduces stress and strain on the colon by lowering pressure inside it so the contents can move through easily.

DR. ELLEN'S PRESCRIPTION

Diverticulitis is a serious condition that requires immediate medical care. Diverticulosis, on the other hand, should respond quite well to self-care. Here's what I recommend.

- Take two capsules of a carbohydrate digestive enzyme before meals, plus another capsule afterward.

- Take one capsule of the gastric enzyme formula twice a day between meals.

- Follow the diet for carbohydrate intolerance (see page 295).

- *Only with enzyme supplementation,* increase your consumption of fiber-rich foods, such as cabbage, cauliflower, brussels sprouts, turnips, beets, carrots, and apples (with peel).

HEARTBURN

The stomach is equipped with glands that churn out a number of substances, including highly potent hydrochloric acid, that help break down foods. To protect itself from this acid, the stomach lining produces mucus. Unfortunately, the esophagus doesn't have the same ability. So if stomach contents happen to slosh into the esophagus—a process known as gastroesophageal reflux disease (GERD), or simply acid reflux—you experience heartburn.

A number of foods can relax the lower esophageal sphincter, the valve that normally prevents stomach acid from backing up. Among the common culprits are alcohol, coffee, chocolate, spicy or fatty foods, peppermint, citrus fruits, tomatoes, and calcium supplements. The chemicals in tobacco can have the same effect, as can certain medications, such as theophylline, Valium, and oral contraceptives.

Heartburn may occur in tandem with other disorders, including asthma and chronic bronchitis. Sometimes it's a precursor to an ulcer, an erosion in the lining of the stomach or duodenum (the upper section of the intestine).

In GERD, the esophagus is under constant attack by stomach acid and can sustain permanent damage. If the acid reaches the upper esophagus and enters the airways, it can affect the lungs and larynx (voice box) as well, causing chronic laryngitis and a persistent cough.

Adequate predigestion of foods, especially proteins and fats, can have a profound effect on heartburn and GERD. It means that the stomach can do its job without undue stress. Because the environment inside the stomach remains healthy and stable, it consistently produces the correct amount of hydrochloric acid so normal digestion can occur.

A gastric enzyme formula will reduce stress on the stomach as well as initiate proper digestion in the remainder of the digestive tract. It also will help protect against food sensitivities. Sometimes a systemic enzyme formula can help heal the stomach and esophagus, but gastric enzymes are the pivotal treatment for heartburn and GERD.

DR. ELLEN'S PRESCRIPTION

If you are prone to flare-ups of heartburn and GERD, you may get relief with the following remedies.

- Take one capsule of the gastric enzyme formula before each meal, plus one capsule between meals as needed instead of an antacid. You also can use this formula for a flare-up of heartburn or indigestion. In general, you should notice improvement in your symptoms in about 30 minutes. For faster relief, open the capsule and mix the contents in water.

- If you've been following the basic plan with the general digestive enzyme formula, the protease supplement, and the probiotic supplement as outlined in chapter 3, discontinue these for the first 2 months that you use the gastric enzyme formula. Otherwise, you'll get too much protease, which can irritate the mucosa in cases of heartburn. After 2 months, you can resume the basic plan. Continue with the gastric enzymes between meals until you're completely symptom-free.

- Limit your consumption of the potentially irritating foods mentioned above. If you wish, you can test the foods one by one in combination with the gastric enzyme formula. If, over the course of 3 days, you don't experience a flare-up of heartburn or GERD after eating a particular food, you should be able to keep it in your diet.

- For short-term relief from heartburn, try honey or apple cider vinegar. Honey has a longstanding reputation for fighting infection and inflammation, improving circulation, and reducing pain. It also works fast. Be sure to use pure, unpasteurized raw honey in liquid form. Take 1 teaspoon anytime you feel the discomfort of heartburn coming on. You can also take honey before bedtime to soothe your esophagus and promote healing while you sleep. Apple cider vinegar is mildly acidic, and so can help digest food. Like honey, it provides relief quickly. You don't need more than 1 or 2 teaspoons. You may feel a slight burning sensation for about 5 seconds after taking it, but the sensation will go away.

HYPOCHLORHYDRIA

People who have hypochlorhydria are unable to secrete sufficient amounts of hydrochloric acid (HCl). HCl is critical for proper protein digestion not only because it breaks down food but also because it adjusts the pH of the stomach so that digestion can occur.

How can you increase the amount of hydrochloric acid in the stomach? The traditional, and perhaps logical, recommendation is to take a supplement like betaine hydrochloride. Unfortunately, this is only a temporary measure that doesn't correct the underlying problem of insufficient acid production.

The body's top priority is to maintain a blood pH of 7.4. If it's struggling to prevent the blood from becoming more alkaline, which can happen in the presence of poor digestion, it will want to hang on to its supply of acidic ions rather than lending them to the digestive system for production of hydrochloric acid. This is how hypochlorhydria occurs.[1]

Taking betaine HCl supplements may relieve the symptoms of hypochlorhydria, which include belching, bloating, gas, and a burning sensation immediately after meals. However, continued treatment can push too much acid into the blood, eventually exhausting the alkaline reserves that maintain a proper pH. This in turn jeopardizes the availability and effectiveness of alkaline enzymes, which support the digestion of carbohydrates, proteins, and fats in the small intestine.

DR. ELLEN'S PRESCRIPTION

The best way to correct hypochlorhydria is to maintain the proper pH balance in the blood while simultaneously reducing the demand for hydrochloric acid in the stomach. A general digestive enzyme formula, taken before a meal or with the first bite of food, can help the body accomplish both tasks.

If you haven't already, be sure to complete the questionnaire on page 53. This will help determine whether you're carbohydrate or protein/fat intolerant. You can use this information to choose the right enzyme formula for you—a carbohydrate digestive enzyme for carbohydrate intolerance, or a protein/fat digestive enzyme for protein/fat intolerance.

IRRITABLE BOWEL SYNDROME

Irritable bowel syndrome (IBS), also known as spastic colon, is one of the most common diagnoses made by primary care physicians. It affects 15 to 20 percent of the population in United States and Canada and is responsible for up to 40 percent of referrals to gastroenterologists.

In IBS, the intestinal tract seems unable to function properly, causing alternating bouts of constipation and diarrhea along with chronic bloating, gas, and painful abdominal cramps. Sometimes people with IBS pass mucus in their stools. But upon examination, the color appears healthy, with no inflammation of the lining. This is what distinguishes IBS from IBD, which involves inflammation.

To date, doctors have been unable to pinpoint a cause for IBS. Many believe that it may be triggered by emotional conflict, trauma, or stress. Research has shown that women with IBS are more likely to experience symptoms during their menstrual periods, which suggests a possible hormonal connection to flare-ups.

Not surprisingly, poor digestion—especially of proteins and fats such as meats, poultry, dairy products, and vegetable oils—may play a role in IBS. Chocolate and alcohol are also potential offenders. And caffeine, which commonly causes loose stools, is more likely to affect those with IBS.

Healing the digestive system and restoring proper digestion through enzyme therapy are the foundation of alleviating IBS symptoms. Together they ensure that the body receives adequate nutritional support, which allows every cell to function in a healthy, stable internal environment. This fosters the strength and resilience that enable us to survive and thrive in stressful situations. While we can't completely eliminate stress from our lives, we can minimize its impact on our bodies, particularly on the digestive tract.

One recent study established a link between an increase in physical activity—such as walking three or four times a week—with better quality of life among IBS patients. Exercise improves circulation, which in turn enhances peristalsis, the muscle contractions that move food along the digestive tract. This is why regular exercise is commonly recommended to IBS patients.

DR. ELLEN'S PRESCRIPTION

The following self-care strategies can make a dramatic difference in the frequency of IBS flare-ups and the severity of symptoms.

- Take one capsule of the gastric enzyme formula two or three times a day between meals. This helps ensure adequate absorption and delivery of gastric enzymes.

- Take one capsule of a carbohydrate digestive enzyme before each meal and one capsule of gastric enzyme formula between meals.

- Follow the diet for carbohydrate intolerance (see page 295).

- Avoid foods that may trigger IBS flare-ups. In addition to the ones listed above, be especially careful with high-fiber foods, such as whole grains, vegetables, and beans; raw fruits, including apples, citrus fruits, grapes, raisins, cantaloupe, and bananas; and fatty or processed foods. Taking a carbohydrate digestive enzyme with these foods may help prevent symptoms.

- Engage in some form of physical activity, such as brisk walking, for 20 to 30 minutes 3 days a week.

- Learn and practice stress-reduction techniques, such as deep breathing, meditation, and acupressure.

FROM DR. ELLEN'S CASE FILES   *Susan, a 63-year-old teacher, was referred to the BioSET Clinic/Institute by her physical therapist. At 5 feet 7 and 100 pounds, she appeared extremely unhealthy. She had been suffering from IBS as well as chronic fatigue for more than a dozen years.*

Depending on her digestive symptoms, Susan would rely on either Imodium or laxatives for relief. She also avoided milk, since she knew it could trigger a flare-up. Still, she felt bloated and distended, with chronic cramping and gas. There was practically nothing she could eat without developing symptoms. She was also prone to chronic infections, headaches, and dry skin.

Before Susan came to me, she had never taken enzymes. My approach appealed to her because it offered real hope for lasting relief from her symptoms.

An extensive evaluation revealed that Susan had what's known as an epigastric reflex, suggesting possible preulcerous inflammation of the esophagus, stomach, or duodenum. This helped explain why she experienced gas right after she ate. Susan also had trouble digesting carbohydrates. In fact, she couldn't tolerate most of the foods that she was eating regularly. Just by looking at her, I could tell that she wasn't absorbing most of the nutrients that she took in.

I immediately prescribed a carbohydrate digestive enzyme along with a gastric enzyme formula that contains marshmallow root and aloe vera juice extract. Both of these herbs help heal the mucous membrane along the digestive tract. In combination with the carbohydrate digestive enzyme, they can be tremendously effective in treating IBS.

Within 2 weeks of beginning treatment, Susan reported that her constipation and diarrhea weren't nearly as frequent as before. Most of her food sensitivities had subsided as well. She was thrilled.

Eight months later, Susan's bowel movements had returned to normal, and after gaining 10 pounds, she looked so different that I could hardly believe she was the same person. She had even begun taking a swing-dance class. "Dr. Ellen," she said, "I have been given a whole new life—one that I thought never would be possible."

A NEW VIEW OF DIGESTION

By now, you should recognize the importance of optimal nutrition to a healthy body. Too often, however, people don't understand just how the body gets its nutrients and how poor digestion can set the stage for nutrient deficiencies. Instead, they attribute these deficiencies to poor diet, which is why they take nutritional supplements—to make up for any suspected dietary shortfall.

The trouble with relying on supplements is that they won't correct any underlying imbalances that result from poor digestion, which hinders the body's ability to absorb and utilize nutrients—whether they come from food or from pills. Shifting our focus to restoring and maintaining the digestive process will have a monumental effect on the prevention of disease, not just the ailments discussed here but all manner of chronic health concerns.

To conclude this chapter, we want to share an e-mail from a patient of Dr. Ellen's. His name is Jeff, and he came to the BioSET Clinic/Institute because he had severe diarrhea and food sensitivities. His diet was very limited because most foods seemed to aggravate his symptoms. Physically, he was quite distressed.

Dr. Ellen hadn't spoken with Jeff for a few years. Just as we began writing this chapter, he wrote to say hello and talk about his progress with enzyme therapy. Here is his remarkable story, in his own words.

When I first came to see you, I was experiencing such severe digestive symptoms that I had curtailed many of the activities that I had enjoyed much of my life. My symptoms interfered with my work, my social life, and my spirit. All of that has improved significantly since our work together.

As a child, I felt fortunate that I could eat anything that I wanted without developing the allergic symptoms that affected my mother when she wasn't careful about what she ate. But by my teenage years, I was obese. At age 28, I went on an all-protein diet for a year, which helped reduce my weight. Around this time, I noticed that I would get diarrhea after eating dairy products. So I avoided them.

Over the years, I added more foods to my "off-limits" list, until it had about 35 items in all. Every one of them seemed to trigger diarrhea. One by one, I had eliminated these foods from my diet, which greatly restricted what I could eat. Whenever I went to a restaurant, I interrogated the waiter about the ingredients in every dish. Routinely, the waiter would assure me that all of my special dietary requirements would be met. Then my meal would appear, coated in a sauce made with something to which I was sensitive. If I'd eat it anyway, I'd experience bloating, cramping, gas, and diarrhea within 5 minutes.

For me, this was more than a minor inconvenience. I was the

top salesperson in my firm; my job required me to travel extensively and to treat clients to lavish meals. I soon realized the central role of food in my professional and social lives. When friends would ask me to a dinner party, I would arrive with my own meals. After a while, the invitations nearly stopped altogether. In a way, I was relieved. I no longer needed to explain my dietary restrictions to my hosts.

Traveling, whether for work or pleasure, became something to avoid. Imagine carrying an extra suitcase full of food to Europe just to feel secure about finding a meal. In each city, after I checked into the hotel, I would head for the nearest market and stock up on canned foods, which I would eat in my room rather than braving the restaurants.

When I was about 43, a business associate mentioned that she had worked with you to successfully treat her food sensitivities. Thinking that I had nothing to lose, I scheduled an appointment. When you assured me that I could resume eating many of my "forbidden foods" within a few weeks, I was incredulous. You performed some diagnostic exams and immediately prescribed digestive enzymes to take with meals. This was my first step on the path to recovery, from being a disabled person who refrained from so many activities to an ordinary person who enjoyed a normal diet. The journey was a surprising and fascinating one.

It has been several months since I ended treatments. For the most part, I can eat whatever foods I choose without any symptoms. I continue to take the digestive enzymes, because I've found that they're helpful for maintaining my health. I have far more energy than I did before, and my friends tell me how much better and healthier I look. Once again, I can fully participate in life.

CHAPTER 7

Reduce Cravings
and Lose Weight

I used to wear a size 8; I was so happy with myself! Then I started gaining weight, and now I'm up to a size 12. I tried working out, but it didn't help. I went on a diet. Again, no change. So I'm skipping breakfast and lunch.

My friends keep telling me that eating only one meal a day is bad for me. I know they're right. But I don't know how to lose weight, and I don't want to have liposuction. Maybe I can starve myself thin.

SELDOM DOES a day go by that a patient doesn't say something like this. Perhaps you've heard it from someone close to you, or perhaps you've said it yourself. It captures the ongoing, seemingly never-ending struggle between us humans and our waistlines.

Indeed, this struggle has spawned an entire lucrative industry that plays to our weight worries. Whether we're sitting at our computers, reading a magazine or newspaper, or watching TV, we're bombarded with advertisements that guarantee fast, effortless, fool-proof weight loss.

Overweight and obesity are among the most pressing public health issues in the United States. Over the past 20 years, the number of overweight adults has risen steadily, while the number of overweight adolescents has tripled. In a report published in the October 2002 issue of the *Journal of the American Medical Association*, the Centers for Disease Control and Prevention estimated that as much as two-thirds of the U.S. population is overweight. At the current rate, this figure could rise to 80 percent by 2010, and by 2040, nearly every American could be overweight or obese.

Weight gain, or the inability to maintain a normal, healthy weight, is more than just a cosmetic problem. Researchers have identified it as a risk factor for numerous chronic medical conditions, including cardiovascular problems, cancer, diabetes, and osteoarthritis.

Unfortunately, when we try to shed the extra pounds, we tend to go about it in unhealthy ways. For example, skipping meals and dieting may lower the number on the scale, but the effect is temporary. About 95 percent of people who slim down by dieting gain back what they've lost, and sometimes even more, within a couple of years.

Severely restricting food intake robs the body and mind of the fuel they need to operate at their best. What's more, because the body perceives the lack of food as a state of semistarvation, it conserves fat as a source of fuel—which means weight loss all but stalls. Sometimes the body takes over and triggers binge eating in an effort to get adequate nutrition. In the worst cases, extreme dieting leads to wasting illnesses such as anorexia nervosa, which can be fatal.[1]

Likewise, diet pills and cosmetic surgery don't offer permanent solutions to overweight and obesity. In fact, some weight-loss medications cause serious medical complications. You may recall how the pharmaceutical combination phentermine/fenfluramine, popularly known as phen-fen, was linked to heart and lung disorders in some people who took it.[2] What most of the American public doesn't realize is that even before the FDA approved phen-fen for weight control, European research had linked fenfluramine to brain damage in laboratory animals.

Fenfluramine is off the US market now, but some physicians still prescribe phentermine, an amphetamine, as an appetite suppressant. Amphetamines can be addictive, and it's possible to build up a tolerance to them. Plus, any suppressant effect ends when you stop taking the drug.

The reason none of these weight-loss methods works is that they don't address the underlying causes of overweight and obesity. In our experience, the primary reasons for excessive weight gain are poor digestion, a diet that's heavy on sugars and grains, food sensitivities that cause both food cravings and nutrient deficiencies, and toxicity. Once patients understand this, they invariably express relief. They realize that slimming down isn't about dietary deprivation or exhaustive exercise but about targeting overweight and obesity at their source.

FROM DR. ELLEN'S CASE FILES *Maureen, a 57-year-old woman who was 70 pounds overweight, came to the BioSET Clinic/ Institute on the advice of her psychologist, who believed that I needed to intervene. In the doctor's opinion, Maureen's addiction to certain foods—especially sugary ones—was somehow related to underlying intolerances.*

Because of her weight problem, Maureen had severe hip and knee pain. She worried that if she didn't make some changes, she would eventually need hip or knee replacement surgery. After trying every available diet with no success, she decided to seek professional help. She felt frustrated, and she needed answers.

I was eager to take on Maureen's case because I knew that I could make a difference. To begin, I ordered complete blood and urine workups to ensure that Maureen didn't have any underlying medical problems that might be contributing to her weight gain. She was already taking medication for hypothyroidism, or low levels of thyroid hormone. Her blood pressure was borderline high but seemingly under control.

Further examination and testing showed that Maureen had liver and bowel toxicity, and she wasn't able to digest sugars and starches. I prescribed a detoxifying systemic enzyme[3] to support liver and bowel regularity, along with a digestive enzyme to help break down carbohydrates. I also recommended following the diet for carbohydrate intolerance and adding brisk walking to her daily routine, gradually working up to 1 mile 3 days a week. Together, we practiced acupressure and emotional release techniques that would foster Maureen's sense of self-love.

As soon as she began taking the enzymes, along with homeopathic remedies for detoxification, Maureen lost 3 pounds. She was ecstatic. "It's only 3 pounds," I reminded her.

"It's a beginning," she replied.

Each week when Maureen came to the office, she was a little slimmer. Within 3 months, she had dropped 25 pounds.

I hadn't seen Maureen for about a year when she appeared in my office with her sister, Cecily, who had come in for a consultation. Maureen was transformed. At half her previous size, she looked absolutely beautiful. Most thrilling, she was pain-free for the first time in years. She was convinced that her food sensitivities had somehow contributed to her hip and knee pain.

Maureen lost all 70 pounds within 7 months. Since then, she has maintained a healthy weight with virtually no effort. She is very committed to enzyme therapy and her carbohydrate-intolerance diet, and her sugar cravings have vanished completely.

SLIMMING DOWN STARTS WITH PROPER DIGESTION

The number one reason both for gaining weight and for not being able to lose weight is poor digestion. When we don't properly

Keeping a Watchful Eye on Our Kids

Television is a major factor in the epidemic of overweight and obesity among our children. It isn't just the sedentary nature of TV viewing that's to blame. Our kids are being bombarded with ads for all kinds of junk food. By one estimate, the average child may see as many as 40,000 commercials a year. And these ads definitely have an impact. While children ages 6 to 8 are more likely to accept what they see and hear in commercials as true, even older kids—in the 8-to-10 range—don't question the validity of advertising claims unless they're urged to do so.

Of course, television isn't the only culprit. These days, ads are showing up in classrooms and gyms, on book covers and buses, and elsewhere. Many schools have even signed multimillion-dollar contracts with companies to sell fast food and soda in their cafeterias. Other countries are regulating this type of activity; Sweden, for example, does not permit advertisers to target children under age 12. Until the United States enacts similar legislation, parents need to be more mindful of commercials that market products, especially foods, to kids. Their weight, and their health, is much too important.[4]

---

break down foods, our bodies run low on key nutrients. In response, we begin to crave the foods that supply the missing nutrients. We eat more but are still undernourished, and we keep gaining weight.

Because poor digestion is at the root of our weight woes, no diet will be truly effective unless it involves enzyme therapy. We may drop some pounds, but the loss won't last. In the meantime, we won't feel healthy or vital, because we aren't getting the nourishment our bodies need. We weigh too much because we eat foods that are vacant nutritionally and aren't broken down thoroughly.

Which foods challenge the digestive system can vary considerably from one person to the next, based on individual factors such as metabolism, activity level, and genetic makeup. People who have trouble breaking down proteins and fats can gain weight on diets that contain an abundance of these foods, while others struggle with sugars and starches. Carbohydrate intolerance is a much more likely contributor than protein/fat intolerance to overweight and obesity.

As we've mentioned elsewhere, the vast majority of people are either carbohydrate intolerant or protein/fat intolerant. If you haven't determined which group you fit into, you may want to backtrack to the questionnaire on page 53. For both types of intolerances, the general prescription is the same: enzyme supplements to support proper digestion, plus the appropriate diet. Many patients report rapid, lasting weight loss with this combination of therapies alone, but choosing the right diet and enzyme supplements is crucial.

Enzyme therapy helps take off unwanted pounds by correcting the underlying deficiencies and imbalances that prevent adequate digestion of foods. Our bodies are better able to absorb and utilize nutrients, so they no longer prompt us to overeat to compensate for any nutritional shortfalls.

For example, patients with weight problems have an almost universal sensitivity to sugar—in other words, they can't digest it. Once we repair and restore this process through enzyme supplementation and diet, they no longer crave sugary foods. The results are consistent through hundreds of cases.

Craving Carbs

Patients with carbohydrate intolerance tend to share certain traits. You may be carbohydrate intolerant if:

• You feel "high" for a short time after eating carbohydrates.

• You need to increase your carbohydrate intake to get that same "high."

• You regularly experience carbohydrate cravings.

• When you don't eat carbohydrates, you develop withdrawal symptoms, such as irritability, restlessness, depression, and fatigue.

THE NOT-SO-SWEET
SIDE OF SUGAR

Structurally speaking, carbohydrates consist of various types of simple sugars, all linked together in a chain. The body uses these sugars to generate energy for cells. Any sugars that remain unused are saved as glycogen, which is basically a long string of glucose molecules. The body stores glycogen in two locations: the liver and the muscles. From there it can be broken down into glucose for release into the bloodstream, should the need arise.

Only the glycogen in the liver is available to the brain. It gets broken down into its component glucose molecules, which then can travel to the brain via the bloodstream. In response, the brain alerts the liver when it has enough glucose to satisfy its energy needs.

Once glycogen levels in the liver and muscles reach capacity, the body converts any remaining carbohydrates into fat for storage in adipose tissue. In other words, excess dietary carbohydrates end up as excess body fat.

By limiting carbohydrate intake, we encourage our bodies to tap into their fat reserves as optimal, efficient sources of almost unlimited energy. This is why Dr. Ellen advises her patients to get no more than 40 percent of their daily calories—and sometimes as little as 20 percent, if they're severely carbohydrate intolerant—from carbohydrates.

Most of us get a lot more than that, mainly in the form of sugar. The excessive amount of sugar in the typical American diet is behind not only our national weight crisis but also the many health problems for which overweight and obesity are risk factors. With table sugar and soft drinks ranking as two of the top four carbohydrate sources in the United States, most Americans seem to be in the dark about the health hazards of excessive sugar consumption.

The fact is, sugar is addictive. Food manufacturers capitalize on this by pouring sugar into their products, which we can't seem to resist buying. Even if we manage to avoid the obvious offenders, we may get sugar from less obvious sources such as ketchup, salad dressings, and even potato chips. While several countries have attempted to develop dietary guidelines for sugar intake, food industry groups routinely speak out against them.

The health effects of sugar overload are insidious and can take years to show up. Too much sugar is to some degree responsible for many of the ailments that plague the U.S. population, including diabetes, high blood pressure, cancer, osteoarthritis, migraines, attention deficit hyperactivity disorder (ADHD), and gynecological problems.

Research has shown that simple sugars can impair immune response for up to 6 hours. This can open the door to frequent infections, as well as autoimmune disorders such as fibromyalgia and rheumatoid arthritis.

From a purely nutritional perspective, sugar contains no fiber, no nutrients, and no enzymes. True, it does provide raw fuel for the body. But the body needs vitamins and minerals in order to convert fuel into energy. By taking the place of wholesome, nutritious foods in your diet, sugar robs your body of these necessary nutrients. And because it interferes with the absorption of the nutrients you do take in, it contributes to both malnutrition and weight gain.

For our bodies to function optimally, they require very little sugar—much less than the average American consumes. No wonder they so seldom last as long as the natural life expectancy of well over 100 years.

How Grains Cause Weight Gain

From both a clinical and a personal perspective, we have seen how sugars and grains—which biochemically function the same as sugars—contribute to a multitude of health problems for which people routinely resort to medications for relief. The real solution to their symptoms is to change their eating habits. Patients experience a complete health turnaround once they wean themselves from sugars and grains.

Thus, our advice is to steer clear of sugars, grains, and the foods that contain them—including cookies, candies, crackers, breads, cereals, pastas, and even energy bars, which can contain large amounts of carbohydrates. Instead, build your diet around vegetables, fruits (in moderate amounts), and proteins such as fish, poultry, beans, nuts, and oils. On a diet like this, patients have reported improvement in conditions as varied as arthritis, fibromyalgia, fatigue, hot flashes, headaches, asthma, and gastritis in as few as 10 days. The longer they refrain from sugars and grains, the better they feel.

Plant foods, including vegetables and especially fruits, contain modest amounts of natural sugars. With help from a carbohydrate digestive enzyme, your body can thoroughly process them. They're enough to satisfy your body's sugar "quota," so you shouldn't experience cravings.

Both patients and medical professionals express surprise when we suggest giving up grains. "But aren't grains nutritious?" they invariably ask. Their confusion is understandable. In the 1990s, when dietary fat bore the brunt of the blame for our expanding waistlines, grains and foods containing them emerged as healthy choices. While grains do have some nutritional value, the nutrients themselves aren't accessible, nor does the body assimilate them very well.[5]

Another issue with grains is that they contain secondary metabolic components that scientists commonly refer to as anti-nutrients. These chemical compounds evolved to protect plants from predators. Cooking and processing don't get rid of them completely, which means that we eat them. Research has shown that anti-nutrients can provoke an autoimmune response, actually mimicking molecules that prompt the body to react to its own tissues. This may set the stage for autoimmune disorders such as multiple sclerosis.[6]

Most important, grains cause a spike in blood sugar levels, which in turn triggers a rise in insulin. This hormone plays a major role in the accumulation of body fat.

The term *glycemic index* refers to the rate at which a particular food elevates blood sugar. A food with a low glycemic index, such as chicken breast or broccoli, raises blood sugar slowly. Foods with high glycemic indexes—including grains—have the opposite effect, increasing it quite rapidly. To compensate, the pancreas secretes more insulin into the bloodstream to escort glucose into cells, which lowers the amount in the blood.

Unfortunately, insulin is responsible for instructing fat cells not only to store fat but also to not release any fat. As a result, the body is unable to burn fat for energy. In order to make the body's fat reserves available for energy production, you need to moderate the body's insulin response. The best way to do that is to avoid grains, sugars, and all other high-glycemic foods.

It's interesting that we continue to view grains as dietary staples even though they may be behind many of the chronic illnesses for which conventional medicine can offer few effective treatments, much less a cure. Loren Cordain, PhD, author of *The Paleo Diet* and founder of the Institute of Paleolithic Nutrition, has studied and written extensively about the history of the human diet. He reports that grains are a relatively recent addition, having been introduced about 10,000 years ago—a mere blink by evolutionary standards. For this reason, Dr. Cordain theorizes, the body has not fully adapted to handle the digestion and metabolism of grains.

From our own research and clinical experience, we know that most people with chronic illnesses do much better once they eliminate grains from their diets. Grains are great for animals, but not for humans. Eliminating them can do wonders for your waistline, promoting rapid, significant weight loss. And because a carbohydrate digestive enzyme can minimize cravings for grains, among other sugars and starches, you won't feel as though you're missing anything from your diet.

What about Carb Blockers?

Perhaps you've been wondering about so-called carb blockers, which promise to stop the body from turning grains, sugars, and other carbohydrates into fat. The claims of these products vary, but typically, one or two tablets can prevent the absorption of about 400 calories' worth of carbs. It's an attractive option, especially for people who can't imagine giving up breads, pastas, and sweets. The question is, do these products deliver?

The main ingredients in most carb blockers are bean and wheat germ extracts, which supposedly work by inhibiting amylase, the digestive enzyme that breaks down starch. If starches pass through the intestines without being digested, the pounds should melt away—or at least that's the theory. In fact, the scientific research suggests otherwise.

In the 1980s, several studies found that bean extracts have no effect on carbohydrate absorption or body weight. More recently, researchers at the Mayo Clinic determined that megadoses of bean extract (4,000 to 6,000 milligrams) and wheat germ extract (4,000 milligrams) can slow carbohydrate digestion, but these larger doses aren't available in commercial carb blockers. Beyond that, no one knows whether slowing carbohydrate digestion is enough to take off pounds over time.

If carb-blocker products work as they say—by inhibiting enzyme activity, which in turn prevents carbohydrate absorption—then they undermine optimal digestion. Carbohydrates that aren't broken down instead ferment in the colon, possibly causing inflammation, irritation, and toxicity. This in turn can lead to a host of ailments, including constipation, diarrhea, skin problems, allergies, and joint pain. What's more, because the body doesn't recognize the undigested carbs, it continues to crave sugars and starches, which prompts excess consumption of these foods—and ultimately the accumulation of extra pounds.[7]

CRAVINGS, GO AWAY

While carbohydrate intolerance is a major risk factor for overweight and obesity, it's not the only intolerance that contributes to weight gain. By definition, a food sensitivity or intolerance is the inability to break down certain foods or food components. It's different from a food allergy, in which certain foods or components trigger an immune response.

Doctors can identify a genuine food allergy with a simple blood test for certain antibodies, but no comparable laboratory test is available for food sensitivities. Instead, diagnosis depends on monitoring and interpreting symptoms. People with food sensitivities may report a wide variety of symptoms, including abdominal pain, headaches, runny nose, chronic cough, asthma, mood swings, and ADHD. To complicate matters, the onset of symptoms can be immediate or delayed. Sometimes it's hidden—in other words, the symptoms never surface at all. Or they surface only with the convergence of multiple factors—for example, consumption of a particular food followed by exposure to heat, cold, or light.

Ironically, the foods to which we're sensitive are the ones that we most crave. Because our bodies can't properly break down these foods, they don't get the necessary nutrients, so they tell us to eat more in an effort to satisfy their nutritional requirements. Inevitably, the craving mechanism backfires. As long as the digestive process is functioning below par, our bodies continue to suffer the consequences of inadequate nutrition no matter how much food we eat—and how much weight we gain.

Food cravings are a major reason that most diets fail. They won't go away until we address their underlying cause. This is where enzyme therapy can have a dramatic impact, by supporting thorough digestion of foods and proper absorption of nutrients. Once patients begin enzyme therapy, they typically say something along the line of "I can't believe it—this is the first time in my life that I don't crave foods!" And they usually notice a difference within 48 hours.

Once you restore proper digestion and eliminate food cravings, you'll get better results with virtually any diet (although we recommend one for carbohydrate intolerance). Those pounds that seemed to be a permanent addition to your midsection will melt away and stay away for good as enzyme therapy coaxes your body toward a naturally healthy weight. As a bonus, you'll feel more vital and energetic than before because you're finally getting adequate nourishment—all because your body is breaking down food and assimilating nutrients. It can't be any simpler than this.

When Claire visited the BioSET Clinic/Institute for the first time, she was 67 years old and about 60 pounds overweight. The excess weight had already taken a toll on her knees and hips, which hurt almost constantly.

Claire had tried several weight-loss regimens over the years, none of them successfully. As we talked, she mentioned that she experienced voracious sugar cravings, a common sign of carbohydrate intolerance. She wondered aloud whether this intolerance might be contributing to her weight problem.

Sure enough, testing identified a number of food sensitivities, with carbohydrate intolerance by far the most severe. I recommended a carbohydrate digestive enzyme along with the carbohydrate-intolerance diet, which consists primarily of vegetables and proteins, with limited fruits and few or no grains. In Claire's case, I suggested giving up all grains immediately. I have consistently seen vast improvements in my patients with chronic joint pain once they eliminate grains.

After 10 days of enzyme therapy and the carbohydrate-intolerance diet, Claire's joint pain had improved noticeably. Just as important, her sugar cravings were all but gone, and she was pounds lighter. Encouraged by the results, she decided to undergo BioSET treatments to desensitize her to her trigger foods. I prescribed a regimen of homeopathic remedies to help detoxify her body, and she took up walking for exercise.

Just 2½ weeks later, Claire was completely pain-free, her joints functioning like well-oiled machines. She felt so good that she was walking 3 miles five mornings a week. As a bonus, she had lost a total of 13 pounds. She was ecstatic.

After 3 months of care, Claire had reached a healthy

weight and was feeling terrific. Encouraged by her success, her daughter and sister came to see me for help with their weight problems.

THE TOXICITY-OBESITY CONNECTION

Food sensitivities and cravings can affect weight and health in another, more indirect way. Because we can't fully break down the offending foods, we end up with undigested food particles circulating in our systems. Often, these particles trigger toxic reactions that can contribute to weight gain, not to mention other symptoms, such as headache, bloating, swelling, and skin problems.

Laboratory research has shown that undigested food can easily pass through a compromised intestinal lining—a condition known as leaky gut—and into the bloodstream. From there it travels to body tissues, where it causes irritation and inflammation. To dilute the effects of this toxic reaction, the body begins retaining water. As long as you continue eating foods to which you're sensitive, you will continue retaining water and gaining weight.

What's more, the chemicals involved in toxic reactions to everyday foods may slow metabolism. If the body isn't able to burn fat, weight control becomes even more of a challenge.

According to a study that appeared in the prestigious medical journal *Lancet*, particles left behind by undigested food allergens can act similarly to morphine-like opiate drugs. In other words, eating a food to which you're sensitive can produce a temporary "high." Then, as this feeling fades, you crave more of the same food, setting up a vicious cycle.

Other research, published in the *New England Journal of Medicine*, found that excessive amounts of partially digested food allergens increase appetite while decreasing metabolism.[8] The offending foods could be perfectly healthy, but the body just can't process them.

You may want to suspect toxicity as a factor in your weight prob-

More about Leaky Gut

The term *leaky gut syndrome* refers to a common medical condition in which the intestinal lining is more porous than usual. The large spaces between the cells of the intestinal wall allow toxic materials that would normally be eliminated from the body to pass into the bloodstream.

The primary cause of leaky gut syndrome is inflammation of the intestinal lining, usually brought on by one or more of the following factors.

• Antibiotics, which allow the overgrowth of harmful bacteria
  in the gastrointestinal tract

• Foods and beverages contaminated by parasites

• Deficiencies of enzymes such as lactase, which breaks down lactose
  (milk sugar)

• Nonsteroidal anti-inflammatory drugs, such as aspirin and ibuprofen

• Prescription corticosteroids, such as prednisone

• Prescription hormones, such as oral contraceptives

• Highly refined carbohydrates, such as candy bars, cookies, cakes,
  and soft drinks

• Mold and fungi in stored grains, fruits, and refined carbohydrates

Currently, the best way to identify leaky gut syndrome is to monitor symptoms. People who have the condition can help themselves by taking digestive enzymes; adding probiotic supplements to correct any imbalance among beneficial and harmful bacteria in the gut; steering clear of foods to which they're sensitive; and limiting consumption of fatty foods, caffeine, and alcohol.

Not everyone in the medical community buys into leaky gut syndrome as a diagnosis. For us, the controversy isn't a concern. Our recommendations can help heal the gut and restore optimal digestive function, and we believe that's an outcome doctors would want for their patients.

---

lems if you don't drop any pounds despite eating healthfully and exercising regularly, or you can't seem to get past a certain number on the scale. Water retention and bloating are also signs of a possible toxic reaction. By ensuring proper digestion, enzyme therapy can prevent the toxic reactions that lead to slow metabolism and other factors that interfere with weight loss.

Keep in mind that your body must fend off assaults from all kinds of toxins, not just undigested food particles. One of its "coping mechanisms" is to stash excess toxins—which include herbicides, pesticides, and chemicals in industrial waste—in its fat stores. Then, as the body burns fat, it releases these toxins, potentially reexposing tissues and organs to their damaging effects.

Fortunately, the body comes equipped with many natural detoxification processes, most involving the gastrointestinal tract, liver, kidneys, lungs, and skin. But these organs can become overwhelmed if toxins attack relentlessly. The solution is to limit toxin exposure as much as possible and to take enzymes that facilitate detoxification as necessary.

WHY DIETS DON'T WORK— AND ENZYMES DO

Successful weight loss has little to do with calorie restriction, deprivation, or sheer willpower. People who rely on these tactics are almost certain to fail in reaching their weight-loss goals. Or they may reach their goals, only to watch the pounds return. It doesn't have to be this way.

The real secret of successful weight loss is taking enzymes to ensure proper digestion and prevent cravings, along with adopting a diet that's tailored to any underlying intolerances. As long as you're careful about what you eat, you don't need to be overly concerned about how much you eat. Just limiting—or even better, eliminating—sugars and grains may be enough to melt away pounds without obsessively counting calories or grams of fat.

The following story perfectly illustrates that losing weight shouldn't be a challenge or a battle. It's all about understanding and adopting the principles covered in this chapter.

FROM DR. ELLEN'S CASE FILES *Jenny gained a lot of weight after her third pregnancy. She tried multiple diets, but none of them produced the results she expected. Sometimes she'd lose weight and then regain it—with extra pounds to boot.*

Other times, she'd break out in rashes or feel so exhausted that she'd sleep all day. She looked tired, with puffiness in her face and circles under her eyes. On a few occasions, she even developed heart palpitations.

This went on for 5 years, during which she continued gaining weight—no matter what she ate. People asked her if she was pregnant again, which left her even more embarrassed and depressed. It was a never-ending struggle.

Then one of Jenny's colleagues told her about my success with enzyme therapy for weight loss. Soon afterward, she came to see me. After testing her for intolerances and toxicities, I prescribed a carbohydrate digestive enzyme and a detoxification enzyme, along with the diet for carbohydrate intolerance. I told Jenny that she probably would lose some weight as soon as she started the enzymes. "I've heard that before," she said skeptically. " 'Just take this pill, and you'll be thin.'" Nevertheless, she decided to follow my advice.

Just 48 hours later, Jenny called me. Not only had she lost 3 pounds, she wasn't experiencing food cravings. She was ecstatic.

Jenny checked in again after several months, during which she had faithfully followed her enzyme regimen. "I've lost 40 pounds, and I haven't been exercising," she reported. "I know the enzymes are working." Within a year, she lost 75 pounds.

DR. ELLEN'S PRESCRIPTION

For patients who are carbohydrate intolerant and struggling with their weight, I typically recommend the following strategies.

- Take one capsule of a carbohydrate digestive enzyme either with each meal or no more than 10 minutes beforehand.

- Follow the diet for carbohydrate intolerance (see page 295).

- Consider substituting a meal-replacement drink for one meal a day. Look for a product that's made with soy or whey protein rather than rice protein, with no added ingredients. It should supply no more than 1 gram of carbohydrate per serving. Mix 2 level scoops in 8 ounces of water, which is one serving of most products. Remember to take your digestive enzyme with this drink just as you would with a meal.

- Avoid chewing gum, since even "sugarless" gums are packed with sugarlike substances.

- Brush your teeth with natural toothpaste. Many toothpastes contain sugars that can stimulate carbohydrate cravings.

As mentioned earlier, protein/fat intolerance is a less likely contributor to overweight and obesity than carbohydrate intolerance. Still, for people who are protein/fat intolerant, the following strategies can promote weight loss.

- Take one capsule of a protein/fat digestive enzyme with each meal or no more than 10 minutes beforehand.

- Adopt the diet for protein/fat intolerance (see page 307).

- Replace one meal a day with a soy protein or rice protein beverage that contains up to 15 grams of protein and up to 25 grams of carbohydrate. Mix two scoops of drink mix in 8 ounces of water or a half-and-half blend of water and juice.

Some people prefer to take both a carbohydrate digestive enzyme and a protein/fat digestive enzyme before meals that contain all three types of foods (carbs, proteins, and fats). This is perfectly fine, as it will further enhance digestion and nutrient absorption.

Beyond these recommendations, I suggest the following for people who are concerned about their weight. These measures can help take off the extra pounds for good.

- Take one capsule of a metabolic balance enzyme formula twice a day between meals (either 1 hour before or 2 hours after eating). This formula supports weight loss by boosting metabolism and preventing food cravings. It may be especially helpful if you've experienced severe cravings with past diets and are prone to overeating. If you can't find the primary ingredients (in bold) in a single formula, you can take them as individual supplements instead. For optimal absorption, pair the herbs and nutrients with a full-spectrum digestive enzyme blend.

Digestive enzymes: Look for a product that contains 40,000 to 80,000 HUT of protease.

Bladderwrack/kelp extract (60 to 300 milligrams). An underactive thyroid can contribute to weight gain. Bladderwrack contains high levels of iodine, which is important for proper thyroid function. *Note:* You should not use this herb or products containing it if you are allergic to iodine or have hyperthyroidism (overactive thyroid).

Guggulipid (60 to 200 milligrams). Studies show that guggulipid helps treat overweight and obesity by stimulating the production of thyroid hormone and increasing the rate at which the body burns calories.

Green tea leaf extract (250 to 400 milligrams). Green tea stimulates fat burning, among numerous other health benefits.

Chromium (200 to 400 micrograms). In studies, chromium—a trace mineral—supports fat burning and weight loss. Supplements take several forms, including chromium chloride, chromium nicotinate, chromium citrate, and chromium picolinate. Some animal studies suggest that chromium picolinate can damage the genetic material in cells, raising questions about the supplement's safety. But the problem appears to be the combination of chromium and picolinate, not chromium alone.

Banana leaf extract (64 to 128 milligrams). This herbal extract helps move sugar from the bloodstream into the cells, which use the sugar to produce energy. This action helps regulate blood sugar and insulin levels. It also aids in weight control.

***Rhodiola rosea* root extract (35 to 75 milligrams).** This little-known herb supports weight loss. In a study from the former Soviet Union, researchers gave *Rhodiola rosea* to one group of overweight patients, while a second group received a placebo. Over the course of 3 months, 92 percent of the rhodiola takers lost an average of 20 pounds, while those on the placebo lost just 7 pounds. Researchers theorize that the herb works by activating adipose lipase, an enzyme that's necessary to burn fat stores.

Zinc (15 to 30 milligrams). Zinc has a beneficial effect on a number of hormones, including thyroid hormone.

Selenium (100 to 400 micrograms). Selenium is a component of the enzyme that helps convert thyroid hormone into a more active form. A selenium deficiency may impair thyroid function and set the stage for hypothyroidism.

Alpha lipoic acid (20 to 40 milligrams): More commonly known as ALA, alpha lipoic acid pays a role in the metabolism of carbohydrates, proteins, and fats. It also helps clear glucose from the bloodstream.

Gymnema leaf extract (88 to 176 milligrams): Scientists first documented the blood sugar–lowering action of gymnema leaves in the late 1920s. The herb appears to work by raising insulin levels, possibly by supporting the regeneration of pancreatic cells that produce the hormone. Other research suggests that gymnema helps improve the transport of glucose into cells, which also would reduce blood sugar.

• Take one capsule of a liver detoxification enzyme formula two or three times a day between meals. As mentioned earlier, toxic reactions to food allergens can contribute to weight gain. With detoxifying enzymes, pounds melt away quickly and permanently. I recommend the following in a single formula, although taking individual supplements with a pH-balanced, full-spectrum digestive enzyme will work just as well. (The ingredients in bold are most important.)

Digestive enzymes. 60,000 to 90,000 HUT of protease is best.

Beet root extract (150 to 240 milligrams). Beet root improves liver function. In animal studies, it keeps fat from depositing in the liver, a sign that the organ isn't operating as efficiently as it could be.

Schizandra fruit extract (160 to 240 milligrams). This herb protects the liver from the damaging effects of toxins. Chinese research has determined that certain components of schizandra can regenerate damaged liver tissue.

Milk thistle seed extract (300 to 450 milligrams). Besides being a powerful antioxidant, milk thistle stimulates the liver's regenerative capacity.

Dandelion root extract (40 to 75 milligrams). Dandelion has a long history as a liver tonic, diuretic, and blood cleanser. It provides excellent support for the liver.

Turmeric root extract (40 to 60 milligrams). Curcumin, the active ingredient in turmeric, has a wide range of therapeutic properties. It protects the liver from a number of toxic compounds and is a potent antioxidant.

Phosphatidylcholine (1,000 to 1.500 milligrams). Once in the body, phosphatidylcholine breaks down into choline, a nutrient that helps move fats into and out of cells. This property makes choline very helpful in treating liver disease.

L-methionine (1,000 to 1,500 milligrams). An antioxidant, methionine improves liver function.

- For additional liver detoxification and support, try a homeopathic formula that contains berberis vulgarus, uva ursi, natrum carbonicum, bryonia, and lycopodium. A formula with this mix of ingredients will stimulate cells to release toxins. Follow the label directions for proper dosage.

- Take a multivitamin/mineral supplement that contains a broad spectrum of vitamins and minerals, plus other key nutrients. (For a list of recommended ingredients, see page 325.) The digestive enzyme will help ensure that you get optimal nutrient absorption.

- Avoid any foods to which you're sensitive. If you can't resist including them in your meals, you may want to consider desensitizing treatments such as those I administer through BioSET.

- If you use energy bars as meal replacements, look for brands that are grain-free and dairy-free, with minimal carbohydrates. Steer clear of ingredients that may interfere with weight loss.

- Try acupressure to curb food cravings and overeating. I developed what I call an acupressure balancing technique to help patients who are struggling with thoughts and feelings that may be an obstacle to healing. This technique has been especially helpful for weight loss as well as for anxiety, depression, and chronic pain. You'll find complete instructions on page 329.

CHAPTER 8

Revitalize Your Skin and Hair

O F ALL THE body's organs, the skin is the one that radiates inner health and balance to the outside world. It's easy to identify someone who is using enzyme supplements because the person's skin has a certain color, clarity, and vitality. When the body is properly digesting foods and absorbing nutrients, the skin shows it.

In this chapter, we'll explore how enzyme therapy can restore and maintain vibrant, youthful skin. Also, since proper nourishment is just as important for lustrous hair, we'll discuss how enzymes may help reverse even serious problems such as thinning and loss of hair.

SKIN IS THE WINDOW TO YOUR INNER HEALTH

The skin accounts for about 10 percent of the body's weight, making it the largest of the body's organs. It isn't there just for appearance's

101

sake, although it certainly plays a central role in how we look. Perhaps more important, it provides essential protection from the environment in which we live.

New skin cells form in the basal layer, the deepest layer of the epidermis. They start out perfectly round but flatten as they travel upward through the remaining layers. At the end of their journey, when they reach the skin surface, they slough off (desquamate) in a process known as exfoliation. Many people use exfoliating products to accelerate the shedding of cellular debris.

The primary component of skin is a structural protein known as collagen, which accounts for about one-quarter of all the protein in the body. Under a microscope, collagen looks like three chains wound together in a tight triple helix, with each chain consisting of more than 1,400 amino acids. Collagen fibers form short cables that give skin its smoothness, elasticity, and strength. They also support soft tissues, connecting them to the skeleton and internal organs.

A number of factors determine the tone, texture, and resiliency of your skin. Perhaps not surprisingly, much depends on genetics, hormone levels, and skin-care habits. But digestion, nutrient absorption, waste elimination, food sensitivities, and toxic reactions influence skin health as well. All of the latter can improve with enzyme therapy.

Actually, the skin is loaded with naturally occurring enzymes. While they all work together synergistically, each enzyme group serves a very specific function. For example, some are antioxidants that defend the skin against damage by free radicals, which are by-products of various biochemical reactions. Others support exfoliation by facilitating the shedding of dead skin cells.

It isn't just these skin enzymes that determine skin health, however. In fact, the combination of digestive enzymes, systemic (metabolic) enzymes, and food enzymes carries primary responsibility for nourishing skin and connective tissue. Without sufficient enzyme activity, for example, the body can't extract beta-carotene from foods and convert it to vitamin A, an essential skin nutrient.

Digestive enzymes are particularly important because they break down food and facilitate the absorption of nutrients into the bloodstream. The entire body receives optimal nourishment, and the skin glows with ageless radiance.

Unfortunately, the body's ability to produce digestive enzymes diminishes over time, and the enzymes themselves become less active. Without enzyme supplementation, neither the body nor the skin receives adequate nourishment. Many of the changes that we attribute to aging—including dry or discolored skin, sagging, and wrinkles—are actually by-products of enzyme deficiency or the collagen loss that it causes.

While a balanced, wholesome diet with plenty of fresh vegetables and fruits is important for skin health, even the most nutritious foods won't improve the skin's appearance if the body can't utilize the nutrients.[1] What's more, all of the body's tissues and organs suffer in the absence of adequate nourishment, which takes a toll on the skin, too.

We spend huge amounts of money on cosmetic products and procedures to restore and enhance the skin's appearance, but the real "secret" of fabulous skin is optimal digestion and nutrient absorption. By supporting both processes, enzymes help repair and rejuvenate skin from the inside out.

Enzymes also help minimize free radical damage, enhance detoxification, and preserve the proper balance of intestinal microflora. These are the cornerstones of radiant health and therefore radiant skin. Let's look at each one.

A Radical View of Skin Aging

Scientists first isolated free radicals some 3 decades ago. Since then, they've been studying the destructive effects of these unstable molecules, which steal electrons from healthy molecules and disrupt cell function in the process. Over time, this cellular damage can accelerate aging throughout the body. In particular, it robs the skin of elasticity and strength, leading to wrinkles, sagging, discoloration, dryness, and other "age-related" changes.

To restore normal cellular function and prevent further damage, we need antioxidant nutrients and enzymes. The only known purpose of antioxidants is to neutralize free radicals, converting them to harmless substances such as water and oxygen. While antioxidant nutrients come from foods, the body can make its own antioxidant enzymes, such as superoxide dismutase, glutathione peroxidase, and catalase. If free radical levels rise, enzyme production is stepped up accordingly. This is why athletes often have larger numbers of antioxidant enzymes than the general population: Their bodies compensate for the surge in free radicals that occurs after strenuous workouts.

Unfortunately, even nonathletes now generate more free radicals than ever before, largely because of the high-stress lifestyle that seems the norm these days. Environmental factors—such as industrial wastes, pesticide and herbicide residues, and air pollutants—also contribute to the free radical burden. The body does its best to keep up with the increased demand for antioxidant enzymes, but if production drops off—perhaps because of poor nutrition, environmental toxins, illness, or simple exhaustion—free radicals have free rein to continue their cellular assault.

Short of moving into remote caves and isolating ourselves from civilization, we can't escape from everything that generates free radicals. We can, however, minimize free radical damage by choosing to eat wholesome, organic foods and by taking digestive enzymes to break down these foods. Remember, antioxidant enzymes work synergistically with vitamins and minerals as well as with other enzymes (these companion nutrients and enzymes are known as cofactors). This is why we need to thoroughly digest our foods—to release and absorb the vitamins and minerals they contain.

Toxins Take Their Toll

Another strategy for minimizing free radical damage is to neutralize the toxins that trigger free radical formation. These toxins come from a variety of sources, including food additives and pesticide residues, nicotine, alcohol, medications, and environmental chemicals. Poor digestion adds to the toxin load by leaving undigested food particles to infiltrate the body's systems.

Fortunately, the body manufactures enzymes that are able to disarm or destroy all of these toxins. Most of these detoxifying enzymes inhabit the liver, although some exist elsewhere, such as on the surface of blood platelets, the cell fragments that support blood clotting. Much like antioxidant enzymes, detoxifying enzymes respond to what's happening inside the body. If the level of a particular toxin increases, so will the level of the appropriate enzymes.

To explore how this process works, let's use alcohol as an example. The more you drink on a regular basis, the more alcohol you need in order to feel inebriated. If you stop drinking for a few months, though, even a small amount of alcohol can make you tipsy. Your body is more sensitive to the effects of alcohol because your liver has scaled back its production of the necessary detoxifying enzymes.

The effectiveness of this process depends on the toxin. The body has a limited capacity to cope with certain toxins, and it may not be able to make more of the appropriate enzymes to handle an increased toxin load. Even alcohol comes with a limit: If the task of detoxification eventually becomes too much for the liver, it begins to fail.

When the toxin load exceeds the body's ability to churn out detoxifying enzymes, toxins are free to accumulate within tissues and cells. This sets the stage for a range of health problems, including skin disorders such as acne, eczema, and psoriasis. In fact, when the primary detoxifying organs—the liver and colon—aren't functioning as well as they should, the skin suffers even before enzyme production falters.

The liver plays a particularly important role in the elimination of toxic waste by filtering toxins from the blood. If this filtration process becomes overburdened or breaks down, the toxins begin assaulting the liver cells, causing damage and scarring. With the liver out of commission, unmetabolized toxins pummel the body, further raising the risk of skin disorders as well as other health problems.

Although perhaps secondary to the liver, the colon is critical to the detoxification process. Poor colon function affects the skin; it's a common cause of acne and discoloration.

Like virtually every other organ, a healthy colon depends on proper digestion. Thorough breakdown of food reduces the possibility of undigested food particles passing through the colon wall and triggering a toxic reaction. So efficient digestion greatly lightens the toxic load on the body in general and the colon in particular.

What's Going On in Your Gut?

Not all toxins come from outside the body; some come from internal sources, such as the bacteria that reside in the gut. Normally, these bacteria maintain a healthy balance among themselves. But once in a while, something—an enzyme deficiency, for example—creates ideal conditions for bacterial overgrowth. This overgrowth can take a toll on the skin; in fact, skin disorders can be a sign of an underlying bacterial imbalance.

The gastrointestinal tract is the most densely colonized region of the human body, with billions of bacteria residing in the large intestine alone.[2] Roughly 500 distinct bacterial species form a highly active society (or biomass) of organisms that have both positive and negative effects on their host—that is, the body.

Many factors can disrupt a healthy bacterial balance, including contaminated food and water, high-fat/low-fiber diets, and certain medications. Perhaps the most significant factor is the widespread, chronic use of antibiotics.[3] Because antibiotics don't distinguish between beneficial and harmful bacteria, they can cause significant upheaval among microflora in the intestinal and urinary/genital tracts.

Probiotic supplements help restore and maintain bacterial balance by introducing microorganisms that positively alter intestinal microflora. Healthy microflora reduce the risk of infections throughout the body, thereby reducing the need for antibiotics and helping to prevent the development of antibiotic-resistant strains of disease-causing organisms.

The idea of using beneficial microorganisms to prevent and treat diseases isn't new. Yogurt, perhaps the best-known source of probiotics, is a centuries-old remedy and tonic. Now, research is confirming many of these therapeutic benefits, with eczema being one of several active areas of study. Clinically, patients have shown dramatic improvement in all kinds of skin conditions once they begin taking probiotic supplements.[4] It's why probiotics are part of the basic plan (see page 32).

One factor to consider when choosing a supplement is which strain of beneficial bacteria possesses characteristics that will enable it to survive and establish itself in the current intestinal environment. *Lactobacillus acidophilus*, the type of bacteria in yogurt, has gotten the most research attention by far, but other strains of lactobacilli as well as bifidobacteria also appear to have healing powers.

Healing Troubled Skin

Everyone's skin is different, and it changes over the course of a lifetime, for a variety of reasons. Hormone fluctuations, sun exposure, allergies, and infections can cause skin to become oily or dry or break out in blemishes or rashes. As we've seen, these conditions can also point to an underlying imbalance or illness, which is why determining their cause is crucial to their treatment. The good news is, they respond quite well to enzyme therapy. Patients routinely report healthy changes in their skin even if they didn't have noticeable problems in the first place.

Dry Skin

Skin has its own natural moisturizer, a mix of water and oil known as sebum that helps keep the skin soft and pliable. As we get older, sebum production slows down, and as a result, our skin is more likely to become dry and lose its elasticity. It may also crack and peel.

An inability to digest fats and a deficiency of essential fatty acids can aggravate dry skin. When the body doesn't thoroughly break down fats, they form a coating over food particles. This interferes with hydrolysis, a process that uses water to split the chemical bonds in substances such as carbohydrates and proteins. Hydrolysis is vital to the decomposition of foods.

The breakdown of fats into a usable form is a two-step process. The first is digestion, which is largely the responsibility of an enzyme known as lipase (derived from *lipid,* another word for dietary fat). The second is absorption with the help of bile, which is produced by the liver and delivered to the intestines via the gallbladder. Lipase works with bile; if a shortfall of either can impair the breakdown of fats, leading to loose stools, diarrhea, and—more seriously—a deficiency of essential fatty acids.

These beneficial fats, also known as EFAs, are common in all life forms. For example, plant seeds are loaded with EFAs because they are the most efficient storehouses of energy. In fact, linoleic acid, alpha linolenic acid, and gamma linoleic acid—all EFAs—are the primary sources of energy for cells. They also build hormones and contribute to the integrity of nerve tissues.

Essential fatty acids are especially important to skin health because they not only lubricate the skin, they also protect against water loss from skin cells. The more water these cells retain, the more likely the skin will remain smooth and supple. Adequate absorption of EFAs is necessary to maintain the structure of cell membranes throughout the body, but especially in the skin and in the hair and nails.

Years of negative associations between dietary fat and weight gain and heart disease, among other health problems, have led to a general misconception that all fat is bad. As a result, modern diets don't supply nearly enough EFAs. The general public doesn't understand the negative health implications of low-fat diets and fatty acid deficiencies. Yet numerous reports have shown that when people take EFA supplements, their skin becomes soft and smooth, their nails harden, and their hair looks healthier, with more shine.

DR. ELLEN'S PRESCRIPTION

To heal and replenish dry skin, I recommend adding the following strategies to your self-care regimen.

- Take the skin, hair, and nail enzyme formula, the liver detoxification enzyme formula, and the thyroid support supplements, as described beginning on page 122. Be sure to include a full-spectrum digestive enzyme blend (see page 33), which helps the body assimilate all those nutrients.

- Increase your consumption of foods that contain zinc, which helps process essential fatty acids. Among the best sources of the mineral are oysters, crab, chicken, turkey, beef, and lamb.[5] Remember that proper digestion of these foods is necessary to free zinc for use by the body.

Oily Skin

Unlike dry skin, which produces too little sebum, oily skin produces too much. This skin type tends to have a shiny appearance with enlarged pores. If your skin looks shiny when you first wake up in the morning, it's probably oily. A sheen that develops later in the day may result from environmental or other factors.

The primary causes of oily skin are heredity and hormones. The good news about this skin type is that it doesn't show the signs of aging as quickly as dry skin. The bad news is that if you don't care for it properly, it's highly susceptible to clogged pores and acne.

While enzymes don't reduce sebum production, they do promote optimal digestion, which can help prevent acne breakouts. Efficient digestion also ensures optimal absorption of nutrients such as riboflavin (vitamin B_2), a deficiency of which can aggravate oily skin.

DR. ELLEN'S PRESCRIPTION

To keep oily skin healthy and acne-free, I recommend these strategies.

- Take the skin, hair, and nail enzyme formula (see page 122) and the liver detoxification enzyme formula (see page 124).

- Build your diet around nutrient-rich leafy green vegetables and fresh fruits.

- Increase your intake of riboflavin from sources such as beans, nuts, wheat germ, and nutritional yeast.

- Limit your consumption of fats, sugars, salt, and dairy products.

- Avoid junk food, especially chocolate and soft drinks, and alcoholic beverages.

- Refrain from cooking with oil and from consuming oils that have been subjected to heat, whether in cooking or processing. If you must use oil—in salad dressing, for example—choose cold-pressed canola or olive oil or flaxseed oil.

- Drink plenty of water, at least eight 8-ounce glasses a day, to hydrate the skin and flush out toxins.

Acne

For years, doctors and scientists have debated the role of diet and nutrition in acne. Some believe that certain foods are direct contributors to breakouts, while others contend that factors such as hormone fluctuations and stress bear most of the blame. We're inclined to agree with both camps. Blemishes can be a sign of an underlying imbalance or disturbance, which in turn may be driven by what we're eating—or more precisely, what we're digesting.

According to Loren Cordain, PhD, author of *The Paleo Diet* and founder of the Institute of Paleolithic Nutrition, as many as 60 percent of 12-year-olds and 95 percent of 18-year-olds in the United States have acne. But in a study to be published in the journal *Archives of Dermatology*, Dr. Cordain and his colleagues at Colorado State University point to the low incidence of acne among teenagers living in other parts of the world, where the traditional diets consist largely of unprocessed foods.[6]

In their natural state, plant foods, such as vegetables, fruits, nuts, and seeds, provide a wide range of nutrients as well as the necessary enzymes for digestion and absorption. If these foods aren't thoroughly broken down, the particles can pass through the intestinal wall into the bloodstream, where the immune system perceives them as foreign, or "enemies." In response, it sends out substances known as immune mediators to hook up with the food particles, creating circulating immune complexes (CICs). These complexes trigger an inflammatory allergic reaction, which in turn can lead to an acne breakout.

According to research, certain foods—such as milk and bread—are especially likely to form CICs. If bacteria also enter the mix, they can cause the more advanced and troublesome cystic acne, characterized by large, inflamed lesions that fill with pus.

Getting back to those wonderfully nutritious plant foods, let's suppose that we cook them before eating them. By doing so, we destroy virtually all of the nutrients as well as the enzymes. The high temperatures typical in cooking cause an exponential rise in the rate of chemical reactions that degrade and oxidize nutrients. As a result, very few nutrients are available to the body, and without crucial enzyme support, it must work even harder to process what few nutrients it can. Acne can be a symptom of this nutritional crisis. [7]

Some research suggests that eating too many cooked, enzyme-depleted foods—along with too many sugars and grains—increases production of a substance called insulin-like growth factor 1, or IGF-1. This opens the door to an excess of male hormones, which encourage the skin to secrete large amounts of sebum. As discussed earlier, too much sebum not only gives a shiny appearance to the skin, it also clogs pores and contributes to acne.

Sugars and grains are known to cause spikes in insulin, which is responsible for removing glucose from the bloodstream and escorting it into cells. Studies have identified a link between high levels of insulin and acne, a finding that appears consistent with claims that low-carbohydrate diets help clear up acne in some people.

Calorie restriction may also be beneficial in treating acne, since overeating can trigger hormone fluctuations—a common factor in breakouts. For adults prone to acne, low stomach acid may be behind the problem because too little acid interferes with the thorough digestion of foods, especially proteins. As we've seen, partially digested food particles can trigger an inflammatory immune reaction as the body tries to eliminate the invaders. This reaction can cause blemishes, among other inflammatory symptoms.

Low stomach acid is a natural by-product of age; the body simply doesn't produce as much acid as it gets older. Antacids, stress, and heredity can also contribute to low acid levels. (To learn more about the potential health impact of low stomach acid, or hypochlorhydria, see page 71.)

While it's controversial, some research has shown that people with acne tend to have a buildup of yeast (*Candida albicans*) in their bodies, which causes candidiasis, the most common fungal infection. Anyone who has been on repeated courses of antibiotics, such as ampicillin, tetracycline, and amoxicillin, is at high risk for candidiasis. Steroids, oral contraceptives, and hormone replacement drugs also encourage yeast growth. Sometimes the fungus passes from one person to another through sexual or skin-to-skin contact.

In order to survive, yeasts need to consume substances such as sugars and fats, which may be another reason that diets rich in sugary or fatty foods seem to increase breakouts. As the yeast microorganisms multiply, they produce toxins that can also cause blemishes, along with headaches, bloating, constipation, and fatigue.

DR. ELLEN'S PRESCRIPTION

Identifying precisely what is behind breakouts can be a challenge, which is why I usually recommend a broad-based treatment regimen like this one.

- Take the skin, nail, and hair enzyme formula (see page 122) and the liver detoxification enzyme formula (see page 124).

- Take 15 milligrams of zinc every day. This mineral may help reduce inflammation and heal skin problems such as acne. While some studies have used fairly high doses to obtain the therapeutic benefits, too much zinc can cause an imbalance with copper, which in turn can impair the immune system. Good food sources of zinc include raw pumpkin seeds, Brazil nuts, and brewer's yeast. A full-spectrum digestive enzyme blend will help ensure optimal absorption of the mineral, although bear in mind that it may take up to 3 months to see any noticeable benefit.[8]

- Take vitamin A in consultation with your doctor. Vitamin A is necessary for maintaining healthy skin and a balanced immune system. Some people have reported reductions in the frequency and severity of their acne flare-ups as well as overall improvements in their skin after taking large doses of vitamin A supplements. If you want to try this, be sure to work with your doctor, since too much of this vitamin can be toxic.

- Steer clear of acid-forming foods, which can trigger breakouts. Among the chief offenders are refined carbohydrates (such as sugars, breads, crackers, and chips), cooked fats (in fried foods, roasted nuts, and hydrogenated oils), meats, and dairy products. These foods also make for sluggish digestion. If foods move through the body too slowly, a buildup of toxins can result, and the body responds by forcing toxins to leave via alternate routes, including the skin. This causes clogged pores and acne.

- Avoid any foods to which you're sensitive. For example, many people have trouble digesting casein, the protein in milk and some other dairy products; for them, eating these foods could result in breakouts. Sometimes, taking a full-spectrum digestive enzyme blend is enough to minimize or completely eliminate the sensitivity. Try the enzyme supplements for 10 days while refraining from any problem foods. Then reintroduce these foods to your diet and see if any symptoms return.

- To reduce the frequency and severity of acne flare-ups, build your meals around fresh vegetables, fruits, nuts, and seeds. Remember that cooking and processing rob these foods of their nutrients and enzymes, so use heat sparingly, if at all.

- If you tend to break out after overeating, consider reducing your calorie intake. You should consume just enough calories to maintain your ideal weight. The digestive enzyme will support optimal digestion and nutrient absorption, which should defuse the urge to overeat. (The body uses food cravings and overeating as defense mechanisms to ensure that it's getting the nutrients it needs.)

- Hydrate your skin from the inside out by drinking plenty of water. A smart strategy is to fill a water bottle and take a sip every 30 minutes. Eating plenty of vegetables and fruits also helps hydration because these foods contain lots of water.

- If you're prone to cystic acne, be sure to take the protease enzyme that's recommended in the basic plan (see page 32). Protease clears up cystic acne quickly, and the results appear to be permanent.

- For low stomach acid, take two capsules of the general enzyme formula (see page 32) three to five times a day with every meal. This should restore acid to healthy levels.

- If you have yeast overgrowth or chronic candidiasis, take a probiotic supplement to restore balance to the internal microflora. The probiotic that's part of the basic plan should do the trick.

FROM DR. ELLEN'S CASE FILES *When 37-year-old Becky paid her first visit to the BioSET Clinic/Institute, she came with a laundry list of symptoms, including severe acne, chronic vaginal infections, constipation, and depression. She was also about 35 pounds heavier than normal for her height and age. Like many women, she had tried every diet, supplement, and alternative therapy she could think of. Any improvement in her symptoms was only temporary.*

With a thorough examination, I found that Becky was sensitive to sugar and dairy products. Unfortunately, her diet consisted primarily of carbohydrates, which are nothing more than long chains of sugars. She also drank a lot of diet soda and alcohol (three glasses of wine a night).

I prescribed digestive enzymes to help process sugar and fat, along with a protease enzyme to treat skin inflammation, detoxifying enzymes to cleanse the colon, and an herbal enzyme formula to nourish the thyroid. I advised Becky to give up dairy products at least until her symptoms subsided. Her other sensitivities—which included some vegetables, fruits, and oils—resolved quickly once she began enzyme therapy.

Within days, Becky reported that her acne was 50 percent improved, her vaginal infection had cleared up, and her weight was beginning to drop. She was sold on enzyme therapy; the fast results convinced her that her body finally would begin healing.

Becky decided to return to school to study acupuncture so she could receive her certification to administer BioSET, my system for desensitizing the body to certain foods. Today, she is one of the top BioSET practitioners in the country.

Eczema

Most cases of eczema, or atopic dermatitis, begin in infancy. In fact, 60 percent of children with eczema develop it before their first birthdays. It's most common in those who have family histories of allergies, asthma, or sinus infections.

Eczema is inflammation of the skin that causes chapping and intense itching. Some describe it as the "itch that rashes." If scratched too intensely, the rash may ooze and become infected.

Mainstream medicine has yet to pinpoint the cause of eczema. What's more, conventional therapies provide only temporary relief from symptoms.

Among my patients with eczema, there seems to be a distinct pattern of food sensitivities. The most common offenders are milk, eggs, and peanuts, although sugars, soy, wheat, tomatoes, citrus fruits, meats, chocolate, fats, and food additives also cause problems. Other factors that may set the stage for eczema include liver toxicity, low thyroid hormone, and emotional trauma or stress.

DR. ELLEN'S PRESCRIPTION

Since food sensitivities seem to crop up in virtually every case of eczema that I see, my typical treatment regimen includes one enzyme formula for detoxifying the liver and another for nourishing the thyroid. (For details on these supplements, see pages 124 and 125.) These, along with a pH-balanced, full-spectrum digestive enzyme, can reverse food sensitivities rather quickly. Once the sensitivities subside, the eczema symptoms invariably follow suit.

I also advise my patients with eczema to reduce or, even better, eliminate from their diets foods to which they're sensitive—at least until they're well into treatment. Then they may be able to experiment with reintroducing certain foods, although I certainly favor a permanent ban on sugars and grains, for a variety of health reasons.

FROM DR. ELLEN'S CASE FILES

Peter was just a little boy when he arrived at the BioSET Clinic/Institute with the worst case of eczema I had ever seen. I couldn't find even a tiny patch of skin that was free of the telltale rash. Peter scratched constantly, often to the point of bleeding. The itching worsened at night, which meant interrupted sleep for the boy and his parents.

In an effort to avoid overusing corticosteroids, the standard treatment for eczema, Peter's parents had tried many alternative and complementary therapies. Nothing seemed to work. In fact, Peter's condition seemed to get worse with every treatment.

Aware that certain foods seemed to aggravate his eczema, Peter's parents decided to remove some foods from his diet. Now his height and weight were far below average for a 4-year-old. His parents were desperate for a solution.

When we met for the first time, they mentioned that Peter had been experiencing frequent loose stools since birth. They were concerned that their son wasn't properly absorbing nutrients, and his slowed development was an indicator of this.

During my examination, I found that Peter's digestive system couldn't break down most foods. Further testing revealed some degree of sensitivity to almost all foods—which didn't surprise me, considering the severity of Peter's condition.

I decided to start Peter with a chewable enzyme supplement to restore and maintain normal, healthy digestion. After a while, we added other enzymes to help heal his skin, as well as a probiotic supplement. I also taught Peter's mother how to administer BioSET desensitization treatments so she could do them at home. [9]

Each time Peter returned to the clinic, he would point out new patches of skin that were free of eczema. He was eating more, and because he was sleeping better, he was happier and more energetic than before.

Peter's mother recently brought me a picture of her son on his last birthday. The improvement was astonishing. He still had very small patches of eczema on his arms, but the rest of his skin—including his face, scalp, and chest—was completely clear and healthy.

HEADING OFF HAIR PROBLEMS

Perhaps not surprisingly, many of the factors that affect how your skin looks and feels also determine how your hair looks and feels. Most patients who come in for other health concerns have dry, brittle, lifeless hair or are coping with hair loss. More often than not, these problems are manifestations of an underlying imbalance or illness. As the patients' bodies heal, their hair regains its natural softness and luster.

Chief among the factors that influence hair health is diet. People whose hair lacks body and shine aren't eating or digesting as well as they could be. Sometimes they're under extreme emotional stress, which can take a toll on hair, but usually diet is responsible for the damage.

For example, eating too many trans fats—the harmful fats that come primarily from hydrogenated oils—can wreak havoc on hair. The reason is that these fats cause an explosion in the number of free radicals floating around the body. As mentioned earlier, free radicals attack at the cellular level. Even hair cells are vulnerable to these renegade molecules.

Excessive amounts of sugar in the diet also threaten hair health. Sugar triggers a process known as glycation that leads to the breakdown of structural protein. Because glycation ages the skin, it no doubt affects the hair follicles in the skin.

When someone begins losing hair rather suddenly, we usually suspect some sort of dietary connection. Deficiencies of B vitamins and/or the minerals iron, selenium, and zinc can cause hair to thin and fall out. So, too, can toxicity and an underactive thyroid. (Sudden hair loss is distinct from male-pattern baldness, which is a hereditary condition.)

What many people don't realize is that before they begin any sort of diet or therapy, including enzyme therapy, they really should take steps to clear the toxins from their bodies. Otherwise, they won't experience genuine healing because the toxins continue to trigger immune reactions. These reactions can cause hair loss as well as more debilitating symptoms, such as back pain, insomnia, restlessness, dizziness, and depression.

DR. ELLEN'S PRESCRIPTION

The recipe for healthy hair is very similar to the one for healthy skin—a diet rich in vitamins, minerals, fiber, protein, and beneficial fats, along with enzymes that support proper digestion, detoxification, and thyroid function. (For more information about these enzyme formulas and their dosages, refer to pages 122, 124, and 125.) In addition, I recommend the following strategies.

- Take one capsule of an antioxidant supplement each day, either 1 hour before or 2 hours after eating. This can help repair and prevent free radical damage to hair cells. Look for a formula that contains the ingredients listed on page 322.

- Increase your intake of leafy green vegetables, berries, beans, eggs, salmon, raw nuts, flaxseed, and pumpkin seeds. Collectively, these foods offer an abundant supply of B vitamins, iron, sulfur, essential fatty acids, and essential amino acids—all vital for healthy, lustrous, manageable hair.[10]

- Limit your consumption of refined sugar, trans fats, and processed foods. Besides being nutritionally vacant, these foods fuel biochemical processes that can aggravate hair problems.

- For hair loss that results from a vitamin or mineral deficiency, take a full-spectrum digestive enzyme blend to restore optimal nutrient absorption. This can not only stop hair from falling out but also return it to its former thickness. Keep in mind that if you've been losing hair for some time, you may not notice results right away, so you'll need to be patient. After several months, you will see and feel a healthy change in your hair.

Hypothyroidism and Hair Loss

An underactive thyroid is a frequent contributor to sudden hair loss. The effect of a thyroid imbalance on hair follicles can be so dramatic that you may notice clumps of hair on your pillow or hairbrush or blocking your shower drain.

The most common cause of hypothyroidism is Hashimoto's thyroiditis, an autoimmune disorder in which the thyroid gland becomes inflamed. Sometimes thyroiditis produces transient hyperthyroidism (overactive thyroid), followed by transient hypothyroidism. Other times, it doesn't affect thyroid function at all.

Besides hair loss, symptoms of an underactive thyroid include dry skin, weight gain, facial puffiness, constipation, and depression. The only conventional treatment is thyroid hormone replacements, which people must take for the rest of their lives.

The BioSET system—which combines enzyme supplementation with other alternative therapies—has been enormously successful in treating Hashimoto's thyroiditis. Typical recommendations include a digestive enzyme, a detoxifying enzyme, and a thyroid-specific formula that provides nutrient support from foods and herbal extracts.

The late Broda Barnes, MD, studied enzymes extensively, documenting much of his work in the book *Hypothyroidism: The Unsuspected Illness*. Enzymes require proper body temperature in order to perform their jobs. Since the thyroid is the body's metabolic thermostat, regulating temperature and energy production, it has a direct impact on enzyme activity. We now know that an underactive thyroid is the basis of many disease states and that improving thyroid function is the key to optimal health.

- If you suspect that you have an underactive thyroid, be sure to take the supplements that support thyroid function (see page 125). An underactive thyroid, or hypothyroidism, can cause hair to fall out in clumps. It's distressing but very treatable. The supplements shouldn't interfere with any medication that your doctor may prescribe. (To learn more, see "Hypothyroidism and Hair Loss.")

THE REAL SECRET
TO SENSATIONAL SKIN AND HAIR

As you've seen, many of the problems that affect the health of skin and hair begin with poor nutrition. Even if we eat all the right foods and take all kinds of supplements, our bodies may not get the necessary nutrients because of incomplete digestion and absorption. This is why enzymes are essential comparisons to virtually all diet and supplement strategies: While nutritional interventions can repair cellular damage and restore vital biochemical processes, they can't do the job on their own. Enzymes help extract nutrients from foods so they're available to the rest of the body.

We make this point throughout the book, but it's so important that it bears repeating here: You are not what you eat; you are what you digest and assimilate. Enzymes are essential to optimal digestion and nutrient absorption. Many patients are amazed by the changes that occur when they add a digestive enzyme to, say, a calcium supplement. Their bone density increases measurably, their muscle cramps diminish, and they sleep better than ever.

With this in mind, certain nutrients—from either foods or supplements—are important to healthy skin and hair. We've seen how essential fatty acids and zinc can heal and prevent dry, rough skin. So, too, can magnesium, which seems to run low in people with skin and hair problems.

As science reveals more about the relationship between good nutrition, proper digestion, and healthy skin and hair, pharmaceutical companies and cosmetics manufacturers have been experimenting with topical formulations of nutrients, especially for skin disorders that result from nutrient deficiencies. Research has shown that vitamins and minerals taken orally don't always reach the skin in sufficient quantities because of poor absorption, suboptimal metabolic function, and the aging process itself. For example, the body absorbs just 20 to 40 percent of oral vitamin E. How much actually gets to the skin isn't known.

Of particular interest in cosmetics are vitamins A, C, and E and panthenol (a form of pantothenic acid, or vitamin B_5), as well as their derivatives. These nutrients are able to penetrate the skin (and, in the case of vitamin E and panthenol, the hair), so they work from within. In the proper amounts, they are safe and free of side effects.

DR. ELLEN'S PRESCRIPTION

Radiant skin and vibrant hair can be yours just by taking the supplements below. You'll see results immediately. Remember that if you can't find all of the ingredients in a single formula, the individual nutrients and herbs will work just as well. I've highlighted the most important of these in bold for your reference. Be sure to take them with a full-spectrum digestive enzyme blend to ensure optimal absorption.

- Take one capsule of a skin, hair, and nail enzyme formula three times a day, either 1 hour before or 2 hours after a meal. The ingredients in these products supply essential fatty acids, plus vitamins A and E, panthenol, and the mineral zinc—all vital to skin health. They also support immune and hormone function as well as toxin removal. Look for the following ingredients.

  Digestive enzymes. A good-quality formula will contain the enzymes lipase (150 to 300 LU) and protease (30,000 to 75,000 HUT).

  Safflower, black currant seed, and flaxseed oil (500 to 1,000 milligrams). These oils help moisturize the skin and heal bruises and wounds.

  Grapeseed extract (15 to 40 milligrams). Research has shown that grapeseed extract reduces the breakdown of collagen, the protein that maintains the structural integrity of the skin. It also minimizes the effects of dihydrotestosterone, a hormone that interferes with the growth cycle of hair follicles, thereby contributing to hair loss.

Calendula flower extract (75 to 180 milligrams). The compounds in calendula help heal the skin.

Oregon grape root extract (60 to 150 milligrams). This herb improves circulation, which is important for healthy skin.

Zinc (15 to 30 milligrams). Zinc stimulates the healing of skin irritations. It's a common remedy for acne and eczema. It also promotes healthy hair.

Vitamin A as beta-carotene (10,500 to 21,000 IU). This antioxidant can help reverse precancerous changes in the skin by inhibiting the growth of abnormal cells.

Bladderwrack/kelp extract (90 to 180 milligrams). This herb helps prevent and minimize hair loss.

Burdock root extract (75 to 225 milligrams). To treat skin conditions such as acne and eczema, some herbalists recommend a tincture from crushed burdock seeds. The herb is also effective for purifying the blood.

Foti root extract (30 to 60 milligrams). This herb detoxifies the liver, which is good for the blood as well as for the skin.

Horsetail extract (75 to 150 milligrams). The herb horsetail supports the regeneration of connective tissue. It's very helpful for healing dry skin and rashes as well as brittle nails and split ends.

L-lysine (1,000 to 1,500 milligrams). An amino acid, lysine is vital for the formation of collagen and the absorption of calcium.

L-methionine (1,000 to 1,500 milligrams). Research has linked low levels of methionine, an antioxidant, with skin and nail problems.

Gamma linoleic acid (GLA) from primrose or borage oil (25 to 50 milligrams). GLA helps skin maintain its youthful suppleness.

These dosages may seem lower than those some nutrition-ists recommend, but because you're taking the supple-ments in combination with a digestive enzyme, your body will be able to absorb and utilize them far more efficiently. Thus, you get the same therapeutic benefits from smaller doses.

- Take two capsules of a liver detoxification enzyme formula twice a day between meals. Here's a breakdown of ingre-dients.

Digestive enzymes. I recommend 60,000 to 90,000 HUT of protease.

Beet root extract (150 to 240 milligrams). Beet root im-proves liver function.

Schizandra fruit extract (160 to 240 milligrams). This herb protects the liver from the damaging effects of toxins.

Milk thistle seed extract (300 to 450 milligrams). A potent antioxidant, milk thistle also supports the liver's regenerative capacity.

Dandelion root extract (40 to 75 milligrams). Dandelion has a long history of use as a liver tonic as well as a blood cleanser and diuretic. It's also naturally rich in potassium.

Turmeric root extract (15 to 25 milligrams). Curcumin, the active constituent of turmeric, has a remarkable range of therapeutic benefits. A strong antioxidant, it prevents free radicals from disrupting cell function. It also protects the liver against a number of toxic compounds.

Phosphatidylcholine (1,000 to 1,500 milligrams). Once in the body, phosphatidylcholine breaks down into choline, a B vi-tamin. Choline facilitates the movement of fats into and out of cells, which is helpful for treating liver disease.

L-methionine (1,000 to 1,500 milligrams). Besides supporting skin and nail health, methionine bolsters liver function.

- As an alternative or adjunct to the liver detoxification enzyme formula, try a homeopathic detoxification remedy. In my experience, homeopathic remedies quickly and gently cleanse the body's systems—including the liver and colon—by stimulating cells to release toxins. And they work quickly, with few side effects. Look for a product that lists the following among its ingredients: berberis vulgaris, uva ursi, natrum carbonicum, bryonia, and lycopodium.

- Take each of the following supplements twice a day between meals to support thyroid function. A healthy thyroid is important for healing dry skin and eczema.

    Bladderwrack/kelp extract (60 to 300 milligrams). These herbs contain high levels of iodine, which triggers the production of thyroid hormone. Don't take either herb if you have hyperthyroidism (an overactive thyroid) or an allergy to iodine.

    Guggulipid (60 to 120 milligrams). Studies have shown that guggulipid not only supports the production of thyroid hormone but also increases the rate at which the body burns calories.

    Zinc (15 to 30 milligrams). Zinc exerts beneficial effects on various hormones, including thyroid hormone.

    Selenium (100 to 400 micrograms). This mineral is essential for converting thyroid hormone.

In addition to taking the above supplements, I suggest incorporating the following into your skin-care regimen.

- Exfoliate twice a week to get rid of dead skin cells. Some exfoliation products contain enzymes, which help induce the thousands of biochemical reactions necessary to maintain healthy skin. For aging complexions, enzymes can work wonders.

- Look for skin-care products that contain enzymes such as bromelain (from pineapple) and papain (from papaya) in a base that balances and/or inhibits xanthine oxidase. Also an enzyme, xanthine oxidase causes collagen production to shift into overdrive, producing thick, ropey fibers that rob the skin of elasticity and encourage the formation of wrinkles.[11] Products made with bromelain and papain help stabilize collagen production so skin stays soft and supple.

- Use a topical vitamin C serum to enhance enzymatic activity in the skin. This helps boost lipid production, which tends to decline with age, leading to dehydration and eventually fine lines and wrinkles.

- Be wary of products that contain mineral oil, a suspected carcinogen that may aggravate skin disorders rather than healing them. Mineral oil goes by many names, including paraffin and petrolatum.

CHAPTER 9

Recharge Your
Energy and Vitality

HEN YOU'RE in the presence of an active, vivacious child, do you ever say to yourself, "I remember myself at that age—so healthy, vibrant, and bursting with energy and ambition. Where did that spirit go? Why did I lose it? And how can I get it back?"

You certainly can get it back, and faster than you might expect—perhaps in as little as 2 weeks.

We're convinced that a diet of raw foods is the ticket to nonstop energy. As a bonus, you will probably maintain a healthy weight more easily, handle stress better, feel younger, and live longer. For most people, though, eating only raw foods is a challenge, for a variety of reasons. An excellent alternative is to eat *some* raw foods every day, choose organic foods whenever possible, and take digestive enzyme supplements. This is our prescription for a long, vital life.

THE MAIN ENERGY DRAINS

Lack of energy is the third most prevalent health concern among Americans, with more than 33 million citing it as their greatest challenge. (Depression and allergies rank first and second, respectively.) Of all the symptoms that send people to their doctors' offices, low energy and fatigue are probably the most common.

In fact, fatigue is a major issue for about half of the patients who come to the BioSET Clinic/Institute. Some say they feel tired when they wake up in the morning; others experience an energy crisis in the afternoon. Still others have chronic fatigue that persists through all their waking hours. For the most part, these energy crises result from one or more of the following factors: poor nutrition (from poor digestion and/or nutrient absorption), food sensitivities, toxicity, stress, hormone imbalances, certain medications—and of course, lack of sleep.

Your energy level is a clear indicator of the state of your vitality reserves—that is, your body's ability to remain healthy and resilient under physical or emotional stress. The good news is, you have more control over these reserves than you may realize—control that comes from maintaining an optimally functioning body. Enzyme therapy plays a critical role in restoring physical vitality and therefore energy.

As many as 85 percent of the patients who come to the clinic for help with sleep disorders improve dramatically once they begin enzyme therapy. Unfortunately, most people resort to drinking coffee, eating sugar, smoking cigarettes, and/or taking pharmaceutical stimulants for temporary energy boosts. These short-term solutions only mask the real problem, cause complications (addictions, headaches, weight gain, and toxicity), and aggravate existing medical conditions. A much healthier alternative for replenishing your energy reserves is to improve digestion and nutrient absorption, eliminate food sensitivities, and remove toxins from the body.

Poor Digestion

We've said it before, but it's so important that we'll say it again: You can eat the most wholesome foods, but unless you thoroughly digest them, you won't reap the benefits of all the nutrients they contain. Proper digestion frees those vitamins and minerals to support the body's many biochemical processes. This is the key to a high energy level.

People who attend Dr. Ellen's lectures routinely ask, "How can I be so tired when I'm eating all the right foods?" Well, they may have healthy diets, but the nutrients aren't getting into their bodies. As a result, they're starving nutritionally. They can't feel young and vital if their bodies' spark plugs aren't getting the necessary jump start.

If the body struggles to break down foods and assimilate nutrients, eating healthfully is something of a losing battle. What's more, when undigested food particles linger, they actually deplete energy reserves because the body musters all its resources to battle these "invaders."

When patients have what seem like symptoms of malnutrition even though they have excellent diets, we immediately suspect problems with digestion and nutrient absorption. These problems may account for many of the health concerns, including fatigue, that are prevalent in the United States.

The nature of poor digestion varies from one person to the next based on individual food choices, eating habits, and nutrient deficiencies. One solution that seems to work for everyone is to take digestive enzymes. Even though enzyme molecules are large, they can pass through the intestinal wall. From there, they enter the circulatory and lymphatic systems, where they disperse to every cell in the body.

For a long time, the mainstream medical community didn't buy into the claim that the body could absorb and utilize enzymes in supplement form. Many of our colleagues insist that the supplements can't survive in stomach acid. Although this argument may have some merit for enzymes from animal sources (as explained in chapter 3), it doesn't wash for enzymes from plant sources, which benefit from a process known as pinocytosis. In this process, the intestinal wall absorbs the enzyme and forms a protective covering or pouch around it. Then other enzymes intervene, breaking the pouch to release its contents into the bloodstream.

Once patients with poor digestion begin taking digestive enzymes, they finally experience the full benefit of the nutrients in their diets. Invariably, they report that they feel more energetic than they have in years. So if you feel as though you're running on empty, consider whether poor digestion could be to blame.

Keep in mind that in order to do their jobs, enzymes need certain vitamins and minerals to serve as cofactors. These nutrients adhere to the enzymes and facilitate enzymatic activity. If you're deficient in one or more cofactors, the enzymes won't work as they should, which compromises energy production.

Sometimes eating foods with the appropriate nutrients is sufficient. In other cases, concentrated food extracts and/or herbal extracts can supply the necessary nutritional reinforcement. The combination of enzymes and extracts paves the way to enhanced assimilation and utilization of nutrients and to fulfillment of the body's nutritional needs.

FROM DR. ELLEN'S CASE FILES *Mary, a 45-year-old flight attendant, had experienced severe fatigue for years. As she coped with the stress of a bitter divorce, her symptoms grew worse. Even though international flights had become unbearable for her, she was the sole provider for herself and her two children, and she couldn't afford to take time off from work. She found herself subsisting on six cups of coffee a day, along with fistfuls of supplements (B vitamins, adrenal supplements, and herbal stimulants). Eventually, even they didn't seem to help.*

Then one day, Mary fell asleep behind the wheel of her car. The incident made her realize that her constant fatigue

Extra Help for Low Energy

For fatigue or low energy, we recommend taking the following nutritional supplements for a specified period. These vitamins and minerals help provided balanced, complete nutrition for depleted bodies that require nutritional support to heal underlying imbalances or illnesses and return to optimal health.

The time frame for supplementation varies from one person to the next, but 2 months is usually sufficient. Taking these nutrients with a full-spectrum digestive enzyme will ensure their complete absorption and assimilation. Food sources appear here as well, in case you wish to get a little extra of the nutrients from your diet.

Biotin (2 to 4 milligrams). Assists in the breakdown of carbohydrates, proteins, and fats and the utilization of glucose; supports the production of various enzymes. *Food sources:* Soy products, nuts, legumes, cauliflower, fish, poultry, and yogurt.

Riboflavin (vitamin B$_2$; 2 to 4 milligrams). Supports the production of thyroid hormone as well as the conversion of carbohydrates, proteins, and fats into fuel. *Food sources:* Milk, cheese, yogurt, eggs, beef, fish, avocados, and mushrooms.

Niacin (vitamin B$_3$; 2 to 4 milligrams). Releases energy from carbohydrates. *Food sources:* Chicken, fish, beef, nuts, and other protein-rich foods.

Pantothenic acid (vitamin B$_5$; 2 to 4 milligrams). Improves resistance to stress; facilitates the utilization of vitamins and minerals; and stimulates the release of energy from carbohydrates, proteins, and fats. *Food sources:* Legumes.

Vitamin C (60 to 120 milligrams). Enhances the absorption of iron, an important mineral for energy. *Food sources:* Broccoli, raw cabbage, carrots, lettuce, celery, onions, tomatoes, citrus fruits, and orange juice.

Iron (2 to 4 milligrams). An essential ingredient in hemoglobin, the oxygen-carrying component of red blood cells. *Food sources:* Beef, clams, oysters, mussels, legumes, leafy greens, dried fruits (apricots and raisins), pumpkin, squash, and sunflower seeds.

Magnesium (20 to 40 milligrams). May be depleted in people with fatigue.[1] *Food sources:* Nuts, legumes, leafy green vegetables, and shellfish.

---

could have serious consequences not just for her but also for her children. That's when she came to the BioSET Institute/ Clinic on the advice of an acquaintance. She brought along her daughter, hoping that I could evaluate her as well. Coping with the stress of her parents' divorce may have con-

tributed to her chronic sore throats and swollen lymph nodes.

Through a complete examination, I determined that Mary was carbohydrate intolerant and had an array of sensitivities to foods, including fruits and grains. She also showed signs of liver, kidney, and lymph dysfunction.

Based on these findings, I advised Mary to begin taking a carbohydrate digestive enzyme, along with enzyme formulas for liver detoxification and adrenal support. We also began BioSET treatments to desensitize her to her problem foods.

Mary responded remarkably quickly. Only 2 weeks into her treatments, she noticed an increase in her energy level. She began exercising, reading, and scheduling more fun time with her children. Even her appearance changed; she bought new clothes and got a more stylish haircut.

One month later, Mary told me, "Dr. Ellen, my fatigue is gone, and I feel healthier than ever. I can't thank you enough." Her brilliant smile brought tears to my eyes.

As for Mary's daughter, she tested positive for sugar sensitivity. Once she began taking a carbohydrate digestive enzyme, her sensitivity cleared, as did her sore throats and swollen glands.

Food Sensitivities

Food sensitivities are a primary cause of fatigue. Caffeine, alcohol, sugars, and grains are common offenders, but any food can drain your energy reserves. As first explained in chapter 4, we tend to crave the foods to which we're sensitive. This is why we may feel tired after eating a favorite meal.

Actually, some sensitivities are not to foods but to substances in foods. Both of us have treated patients who seem to develop symptoms after consuming certain vitamins, minerals, or other nutrients. In these cases, they tend to be deficient in the nutrients to which they're sensitive. This can impair metabolism and immune function, which only worsens fatigue.

Food sensitivities are driven by a number of factors, from genetics to poor digestion and immune function. These "hidden" sensitivities may be responsible not only for fatigue but also for a host of symptoms for which modern medicine has yet to find a cause.

On the day 57-year-old Leonard first visited the BioSET Clinic/Institute, I was running behind in my appointments. My receptionist came to my office three times to tell me that a man was pacing back and forth in the waiting room, asking how long I would be. When we finally met, Leonard told me that he was always edgy and irritable, yet tired and depressed as well—a complex of symptoms that left him feeling as though he were at war with himself.

No doubt Leonard's back pain and insomnia were contributing to his symptoms. He described himself as being "eternally bloated and constipated." He also had a history of hepatitis, prostatitis, hearing loss, and tinnitus (ringing in the ears).

Leonard knew that he was sensitive to chicken, rice, eggs, and some dairy products. He suspected that his sensitivities might be contributing to the multitude of health problems that he was dealing with. At the same time, he hoped that he would be able to continue enjoying the foods that triggered his symptoms. That's why he sought my help.

When I evaluated Leonard, I found that he was sensitive to cheeses, vegetables, soybeans, string beans, lentils, nuts and seeds, soy sauce, coffee, tea, and chocolate. Food colorings and additives also triggered symptoms, as did nutritional supplements, such as calcium, magnesium, and B vitamins—all of which had been prescribed by his doctor. I explained that some of his symptoms might be the result of a calcium deficiency, which in turn could be a by-product of his protein intolerance.

Leonard was about to leave town for an extended pe-
riod, so we needed to take action immediately. I prescribed
a protein/fat digestive enzyme as well as an enzyme/min-
eral formula. Within a week, his energy level improved by
50 percent. He wasn't as irritable and anxious as he had
been, and he was sleeping more soundly than he had in
years. He was very pleased with the results of enzyme
therapy.

Free Radical Damage

Beyond improving digestion and correcting food sensitivities, enzymes fight fatigue by doing their part to repair and prevent free radical damage to cells. Free radicals are unstable molecules that steal
electrons from healthy molecules, disrupting normal cell function in
the process. In particular, they can attack the mitochondria, the energy powerhouses inside cells. Undermining the integrity of the mitochondria not only causes fatigue, it also contributes to disease and
accelerates aging.

While free radicals are natural by-products of the body's various biochemical processes, they come from external sources as
well, such as environmental and chemical toxins. One of Dr.
Ellen's patients, an artist, complained of extreme fatigue, which
turned out to be the result of repeated, prolonged exposure to the
chemicals in her paints. Other substances that can precipitate free
radical damage include dry-cleaning and industrial solvents; vinyl
chloride in plastics; adhesives; gaseous fumes from treated building
materials and home furnishings; radioactive waste; mercury in
dental amalgams; medications; food additives and preservatives;
and the minerals chromium, lead, cadmium, tin, and aluminum.
Free radicals also come from exposure to radiation and electro-
magnetic fields.

We Americans are repeatedly exposed to hazardous chemicals in
our food, water, and air. Each month, more new chemicals enter our

environment and threaten our health. Of particular concern is the effect of this chemical exposure on our children. According to a 1998 finding by the National Academy of Science, the average American child has received the maximum lifetime dose of eight pesticides by age 1.

Exposure to these chemicals and the resulting free radical damage may help to explain why the incidence of fatigue is on the rise among children. They have difficulty getting up in the morning, and they can't stay awake in class. They're prone to symptoms typical of allergies, such as runny nose, cough, and sore throat. They are probably reacting to environmental toxins in the building materials and cleaning supplies at their schools as well as the radiation emitted by TVs, computers, and microwave ovens.

By repairing and preventing free radical damage, we restore the optimal conditions for cellular metabolism and energy production, which are necessary to fend off fatigue. The first step is to eliminate the toxins generated by free radicals. This is the responsibility of antioxidant nutrients and enzymes, which include superoxide dismutase, glutathione peroxidase, and catalase.

The body generates its own antioxidant enzymes, whose only known purpose is to turn the toxins from free radicals into harmless substances such as water and oxygen. When the number of free radicals rises, the production of antioxidant enzymes also increases. Clinical research has shown that enzyme supplements, along with antioxidant nutrients from food sources, effectively reinforce this detoxification process.[2]

WHAT ELSE DRAINS YOUR BATTERY?

Other factors can deplete our energy reserves and leave us feeling less than our best. Some (such as sleep disorders) may be obvious, while others (such as an overactive immune system) may not be. This is why identifying the underlying cause of fatigue is so important: You need to treat the cause in order to experience true energy and vitality.

Adrenal Exhaustion

Many cases of fatigue are connected to poor adrenal function, or adrenal exhaustion. The adrenal glands, which sit atop the kidneys, are components of the endocrine system. They are responsible for producing several important hormones and are integral to the stress response.

Each adrenal gland has two parts: the cortex and the medulla. The cortex is the outer wrapping, or "shell," of the gland and produces cortisol, a powerful anti-inflammatory hormone. (Inflammation plays a role in a number of health concerns, including allergies, asthma, arthritis, and lupus.)

The medulla, which is inside the adrenal gland, pumps out adrenaline (epinephrine) and norepinephrine. These hormones are virtually a direct extension of the nervous system and govern the body's stress response, also known as the fight-or-flight response.

When the brain interprets a situation as a threat—which is what happens in cases of stress—the adrenal glands go to work, instructing the nervous system to prepare to fight the threat or flee from it. The nervous system mobilizes the circulatory and respiratory systems to take action, a process that not only diverts oxygen and blood away from normal body functions but also taps into the body's energy reserves.

Even when the fight-or-flight response switches off, the body remains on alert long afterward. If this "state of emergency" persists for an extended period, it further depletes the body's energy reserves. It also runs down the adrenal glands and kidneys, impairing immune function.

Unfortunately, the body has a tendency to react to both real and imagined stressors in the same way. For example, worrying about losing your job can overburden the adrenal glands and deplete energy reserves as much as actually losing your job. And stressors aren't just emotional or psychological. Other common causes of persistent, uncontrolled stress include overuse of caffeine, alcohol, nicotine, and drugs; poor nutrition; and deficiencies of the B vitamins and vitamin C. All of these factors can wear down the adrenal glands over time.

A person with weak or impaired adrenal function may have low blood pressure, low blood sugar, low body temperature, and a feeling of complete exhaustion. As the adrenal glands continue to weaken, other health problems, such as hypoglycemia and neuromediated hypotension (NMH), can set in. In NMH, the central nervous system instructs the heart to slow down, causing declines in the total volume of blood circulating per minute and in blood pressure. This allows blood to pool in the lower limbs, so less is available to nourish the brain.

If you are prone to fatigue and infections, it may be a sign that your adrenal glands aren't operating up to par. Other symptoms of poor adrenal function include depression, dizziness or lightheadedness, and memory lapses.

DR. ELLEN'S PRESCRIPTION

The adrenal enzyme formula on page 142 can help reinvigorate tired adrenal glands so you feel more energetic.

Hypoglycemia

Another common energy drainer, hypoglycemia, can result from a combination of protein intolerance and poor sugar metabolism. The body naturally strives to maintain an adequate supply of blood sugar, or glucose, in the brain. In hypoglycemia, though, the brain doesn't get enough. This leads to symptoms such as fatigue, depression, irritability, anxiety, mental confusion, and—in the most severe cases—convulsions and severe psychological disturbances.

Sometimes doctors mistake a serotonin deficiency for hypoglycemia, because the conditions produce very similar symptoms.

Adding to the confusion, people who have a serotonin deficiency tend to feel better after eating something—just as in hypoglycemia.

Serotonin is a neurotransmitter, a naturally occurring chemical that transmits messages between nerve cells. Usually, treating a deficiency involves taking amino acids, which the body can use to make neurotransmitters. This is where enzymes could play an essential role, supporting the digestion of proteins into their component amino acids for the purpose of neurotransmitter production.

DR. ELLEN'S PRESCRIPTION

In addition to the recommendations on page 142, I recommend taking one capsule of a carbohydrate digestive enzyme or one capsule of a protein/fat digestive enzyme with each meal. Which one you choose depends on what you're eating. If your meal contains both carbs and proteins, take one capsule of each enzyme. This can help correct low blood sugar so the brain gets the fuel it needs.

Hypothyroidism

The thyroid gland is responsible for regulating the body's metabolism and therefore its rate of energy production. As you might imagine, imbalances in thyroid hormones can have a profound effect on your energy levels. These imbalances can result from many factors, including nutrient deficiencies (especially of vitamin A, riboflavin, iodine, and selenium), enzyme dysfunction, chronic stress, and even aging.

Hypothyroidism—that is, an underactive thyroid—is among the most common contributors to fatigue. Physicians often overlook this condition because so many cases are subclinical, meaning that although patients have hypothyroidism, their laboratory tests come back normal.

Sometimes hypothyroidism coexists with other endocrine conditions. Thus, a person with low levels of adrenal or sex hormones, for example, may also be deficient in thyroid hormone. In a case like this, getting a proper diagnosis is critical since it will determine the appropriate course of treatment.

Hypothyroidism isn't the only thyroid disorder that depletes energy reserves. If fatigue occurs in conjunction with chronic insomnia, nervousness, and weight loss, the problem may be *hyper*thyroidism— that is, too much thyroid hormone rather than too little.

Other endocrine conditions can affect energy levels, too. For example, women and men can be sensitive to their own sex hormones, which can lead to deficiencies of the hormones and to symptoms such as fatigue. Often, people can't fathom being sensitive to substances that occur naturally in their bodies, but it's very prevalent. Over the years, Dr. Ellen has treated many patients who were sensitive to cortisol, adrenaline, and norepinephrine.

DR. ELLEN'S PRESCRIPTION

I've found the recommendations on page 142 to be especially effective in treating fatigue that results from thyroid imbalances. As I mentioned earlier, you should notice a dramatic difference in your energy level in 2 weeks, if not sooner.

Immune Dysfunction

According to several studies, people with severe fatigue have higher numbers of killer T cells, the white blood cells that fight viruses and other microorganisms. These people also have fewer suppressor T cells, another type of white blood cell that regulates immune reactions once infectious invaders are under control.

When this regulatory mechanism fails, the immune system continues to mount its defense, triggering the release of cytokines. These immune mediators may be responsible for symptoms such as fatigue and muscle aches. In other words, it's the effects of the cytokines that make you feel sick, not the infection itself.

You can help keep your immune system from going into overdrive by addressing any food sensitivities that you may have. Your body isn't able to thoroughly break down these trigger foods, leaving behind undigested particles. When the immune system recognizes these particles as invaders, much like the microorganisms that it usually targets, it responds accordingly. Clearing up food sensitivities prevents the reaction that can contribute to immune system hyperactivity and cytokine production, thus preventing fatigue.

DR. ELLEN'S PRESCRIPTION

In addition to following the recommendations on page 142, do your best to avoid any foods to which you're sensitive. If you're not certain which ones they are, think about what you crave. People tend to crave the foods to which they're sensitive.

If you haven't already, you may also want to complete the questionnaires in chapter 5. These can help determine whether you're carbohydrate or protein/fat intolerant. Carbohydrates, in particular, can sabotage energy levels; they're long chains of sugars, and sugars can cause fatigue by fueling spikes in glucose.

Sleep Disorders

Sufficient restorative sleep is essential for optimal energy, yet according to the National Sleep Foundation, more than 50 percent of American adults experience insomnia at least a few nights a week. When people don't get adequate rest, they rely on artificial stimulants to sustain them through the day. In the meantime, they run up an unhealthy, potentially dangerous sleep deficit.

Not everyone needs 8 or 9 hours of sleep a night. Generally, if you're able to wake up on time without an alarm clock, you're getting enough rest. If even an alarm clock can't rouse you, you probably aren't sleeping as much as you should.

What's behind our national sleep shortage? Stress, jet lag, and environmental factors such as noise and light certainly interfere with our natural sleep cycles. So, too, can poor digestion and impaired liver detoxification.

The liver and its enzymes are responsible for processing toxins in the blood and preparing them for elimination from the body. This process depends on certain nutrients, but as we've seen, they may not be available because of poor digestion and assimilation. Leaky gut can also be a factor, since it allows toxins to pass from the intestines into the bloodstream (for additional information, see "More about Leaky Gut" on page 93).

In the absence of adequate nutritional support, the liver must work even harder to process toxins. Eventually, it may not be able to keep pace, allowing toxins to build up. Some research has found a correlation between liver toxicity and insomnia. When toxins remain in the body, they deplete energy levels as well.

DR. ELLEN'S PRESCRIPTION

Of particular benefit for sleep disorders is the sleep-enhancing enzyme formula (see page 144), which stabilizes sleep patterns and improves sleep quality. If you use it in combination with the other supplements and strategies, you just may experience the best rest of your life.

RECLAIMING ENERGY— AND YOUR LIFE

Just as you choose your diet and lifestyle, you choose energy. You can have a direct impact on your energy levels simply by eating organic foods, taking nutritional and enzyme supplements, getting plenty of rest, and limiting stress. You can move beyond fatigue and discover greater productivity, pleasure, and passion for life.

Now is the time to achieve what you imagine: living to your full potential, with unlimited energy. That's the one side effect of enzymes. They give you more energy than you've ever known.

DR. ELLEN'S PRESCRIPTION

I have helped thousands of patients overcome fatigue and achieve optimal energy with one or more of the following enzyme formulas. As a reminder, the lists of ingredients are only suggestions of what to look for in enzyme products. If you can't find everything in a single formula, you'll get the same therapeutic benefits from taking individual supplements with a full-spectrum digestive enzyme blend (see page 33). In fact, if you pair a digestion enzyme blend with just two of the primary ingredients (in bold), it should work quite well.

The reason for taking the digestive enzyme is that it ensures thorough digestion and assimilation of the rest of the nutrients. Because you absorb more, you actually need less in supplement form. This is why the dosage ranges for the various herbs, vitamins, and minerals may be lower than you expect.

Over the years, many patients have come to me for help because they're taking many supplements but not seeing any results. As I remind them—and you—supplements can't do their job unless the body is able to use them. Digestion and absorption are the keys to the effectiveness of supplements, and enzymes are the keys to thorough digestion and absorption.

- Take two capsules of an adrenal enzyme formula twice a day, either with or between meals. This formula helps treat and prevent adrenal exhaustion by regulating the physical and mental response to stress. It contains the following ingredients.

  Digestive enzymes. The ideal formula will supply 60,000 to 90,000 HUT of protease.

  Panax ginseng root extract (320 to 500 milligrams). The Chinese have used Panax ginseng for thousands of years to enhance longevity and quality of life. The herb may provide support in situations of prolonged or intense stress or during recovery from extended illness. Herbalists believe that Panax ginseng can delay fatigue during exercise by enabling the muscles to use energy more efficiently.

Bupleurum root extract (200 to 600 milligrams). Also known as Chinese thoroughwax, this herb enhances adrenal function in addition to having a mild pain-relieving effect.

Vitamin C from acerola cherry extract (20 to 100 milligrams). Vitamin C enhances immune function and relieves fatigue.

Panthothenic acid (100 to 200 milligrams). Also known as vitamin B_5, pantothenic acid helps the body utilize carbohydrates, proteins, and fats. It fends off fatigue as well.

Rice bran (130 to 200 milligrams). Rice bran is a natural source of B vitamins, which are essential for building and maintaining the body's energy supply.

Siberian ginseng root extract (80 to 120 milligrams). This herb has a long history as a tonic for fighting fatigue and restoring energy. It also helps combat stress-related illness.

Riboflavin (25 to 50 milligrams). This vitamin, also known as vitamin B_2, supports the transformation of carbohydrates, proteins, and fats into fuel for the body. It also plays a vital role in the production of thyroid hormone, which speeds up metabolism and helps ensure a steady energy supply.

Niacin (25 to 50 milligrams). Niacin (vitamin B_3) is necessary to release energy from carbohydrates.

Biotin (100 to 200 milligrams). Like the rest of the B vitamins, biotin facilitates the breakdown of carbohydrates, proteins, and fats. It also enables the body to utilize glucose and contributes to the production of various enzymes.

Magnesium (100 to 200 milligrams). According to some studies, people with fatigue may have low levels of magnesium inside their cells.

Codonopsis root extract (300 to 600 milligrams). Some herbalists recommend codonopsis as an alternative to

Panax ginseng. It offsets the effects of stress and therefore fatigue.

- Take one capsule of a sleep-enhancing enzyme formula 1 hour before bedtime, plus another capsule right at bedtime. The ingredients in this formula promote sound, restorative sleep without causing daytime drowsiness. Just as important, they're safe and nonaddictive. If you have severe insomnia, I recommend taking all of the primary ingredients (in bold) with a full-spectrum digestive enzyme blend, at least to start. Otherwise, even one of the supplements plus a digestive enzyme may be enough. Experiment to see what works best for you.

  Digestive enzymes. The best sleep-enhancing formulas contain 16,000 to 50,000 HUT of protease.

  Valerian root extract (200 to 400 milligrams). Valerian is known for promoting restful sleep. It also alleviates the physical and mental effects of stress and anxiety.

  Passionflower root extract (120 to 240 milligrams). This herb is helpful whether you have difficulty falling asleep, are unable to sleep straight through the night, or wake up too early in the morning.

  Oat straw extract (30 to 60 milligrams). Oat straw helps improve sleep quality.

  Magnesium aspartate (60 to 120 milligrams). Magnesium enhances sleep.

  Calcium citrate (30 to 60 milligrams). Calcium promotes relaxation.

  Wild lettuce leaf extract (40 to 80 milligrams). Like oat straw, wild lettuce helps improve sleep quality.

  5-HTP (100 to 300 milligrams). A derivative of the amino acid tryptophan, 5-HTP helps treat insomnia through its conversion into serotonin. Most of the cells responsible

for this conversion reside in the lining of the gastrointestinal tract.

• Take two capsules of a multivitamin/mineral supplement twice
a day, either 1 hour before or 2 hours after a meal. Choose a
product that contains a broad spectrum of vitamins and minerals, plus other key nutrients. (For a list of recommended ingredients, see page 325.) The digestive enzyme will help ensure
that you get optimal nutrient absorption.

To round out your energy-enhancing efforts, you may want to
incorporate the following strategies into your self-care regimen.

• Enjoy an energy bar as a snack or a meal supplement. The best
bars are high in protein and low in carbohydrates, with no
grains or dairy products as ingredients. They should contain vitamins and minerals as well as the enzymes papain and bromelain. Take one capsule of a full-spectrum digestive enzyme
blend with your energy bar to ensure absorption of the nutrients.

• Engage in an aerobic activity such as brisk walking, jogging, or
swimming for at least 30 to 45 minutes at least 3 days a week.
Regular exercise raises energy levels by strengthening the circulatory system, which in turn increases the flow of nutrient-
rich blood to every cell. I have found that moderate activity
done consistently over a long period of time is more effective
than strenuous activity done in short bursts.

Usually, I recommend brisk walking to my patients since it
promotes cardiovascular fitness with minimal risk of injury. As
a bonus, it supports weight loss and encourages the elimination
of toxins through perspiration. Many patients report improvements in mood and declines in stress and anxiety once they
begin their walking programs.

CHAPTER 10

Enhance
Emotional Balance

W E TEND TO THINK of our moods as responses to situations that we encounter as we move through our lives. To some degree, though, what we feel emotionally is driven by what's going on physically. You've probably heard some experts talk about how the mind influences the body, but the opposite is just as true: The body has a tremendous impact on the mind, especially in terms of how well you break down foods and absorb nutrients.

Most people don't realize how poor digestion and nutrient deficiencies can undermine their emotional health, affecting their ability to respond to stress and contributing to mood swings, depression, and attention deficit hyperactivity disorder (ADHD). Once patients begin enzyme therapy, they invariably remark how much better they feel mentally and emotionally—less edgy or blue, more cheerful and relaxed. Some notice that they no longer struggle to stay calm and focused in the face of stress.

Just recently, Dr. Ellen met a 9-year-old boy named Michael, who had been throwing regular tantrums since he was 3. His mother described his behavior as physically aggressive. Once we treated his food sensitivities and began enzyme therapy, the change was astonishing. Even he said, "Dr. Ellen, I haven't screamed in 3 weeks."

By helping our bodies utilize key brain nutrients, enzymes profoundly affect our minds and moods. In combination with nutritional supplements, they even may eliminate the need for powerful prescription medications, which often have serious side effects yet don't resolve the underlying problem.

MOOD SWINGS

FROM DR. ELLEN'S CASE FILES

A friend whom I've known since childhood has had severe mood swings for as long as I can remember. Those of us close to her adored her, but we were reluctant to spend much time with her. Without warning, her normally sweet and gentle temperament would give way to an angry, mean-spirited, petulant alter ego. She seemed completely oblivious to these outbursts and couldn't understand why so many people avoided her company.

After years of tolerating my friend's behavior, I finally confronted her about her mood swings and offered help in the form of enzyme therapy. We spoke at great length about food sensitivities and eating habits. She was very amenable to trying enzymes.

Two years later, she was doing much better—running her own business, dating, and expanding her circle of friends. As a bonus, she lost 23 pounds during the first 6 months of treatment. She still has occasional mood swings, but they are few and far between. She is more relaxed and at peace—and she has become a vocal advocate of enzyme therapy.

Chronic mood swings are a common sign of food sensitivities, in which the body can't completely digest certain foods. While virtually any food can trigger sensitivity, the most common culprits are those that contain nitrites, glutamates, aspartic acid, tyrosine, caffeine, brewer's or baker's yeast, or sugar. Soy, wheat, corn, peanuts, milk, eggs, citrus fruits, and tomatoes are also frequent offenders.

Once undigested food particles pass through the intestinal wall into the bloodstream, they act as antigens. In other words, they trigger an immune response, prompting immune cells to produce and release immunoglobulins (antibodies). The immunoglobulins confront the antigens like the defensive unit on a football team, attacking the opponents while guarding their teammates.

If enough antigens are present and enough antibodies form, they join to create larger molecules. These are known as circulating immune complexes, or CICs. Under normal circumstances, CICs serve an important purpose, recognizing and eliminating infectious microorganisms such as viruses, bacteria, and fungi as well as toxic chemicals.[1] The CICs immobilize the invaders and then stimulate other immune system cells called macrophages to gobble them up and get rid of them.

Although CICs are beneficial in small numbers, in excess, they trigger the release of immune mediators. These messenger chemicals alert the immune system to attack and destroy the CICs. The presence of too many immune mediators in the body can cause an array of symptoms, including mood swings.

People who have food sensitivities may not connect them to emotional symptoms or to common physical symptoms such as increased heart rate and respiration. They also may not recognize how sensitivities can cause cravings—usually for the very foods to which they're sensitive. Thus, if they indulge those cravings, they only add to the load of circulating immune complexes, which ultimately worsens their symptoms.

One of the primary roles of enzyme therapy is to break down CICs. Then the macrophages clear away any remaining debris. This limits the number of CICs in the bloodstream, which in turn prevents the release of immune mediators. Immune function returns to normal, and as a bonus, your mood stabilizes.

Both of us have seen this phenomenon in patients. Many of them have reported immediate, positive changes in mood and spirit once they began using enzyme therapy.

Keep in mind that food sensitivities are quite different from food allergies, although both involve an overzealous immune system. In general, allergic reactions occur immediately after exposure to the food, although sometimes symptoms—which include wheezing, nasal congestion, itchy or teary eyes, and hives—appear hours or days later. Food allergies can be quite serious and may require medical attention.

The Role of Low Blood Sugar

Protein intolerance is a form of food sensitivity. People who are protein intolerant have trouble breaking down the proteins in foods. This may be a factor in mood swings because it deprives the brain of the amino acids necessary to produce key neurotransmitters such as serotonin and dopamine. Futhermore, the liver should convert up to 57 percent of the proteins from any given meal into glucose for the brain.

When poor protein digestion leads to a decline in glucose—a condition known as hypoglycemia, or low blood sugar—the adrenal glands respond by releasing cortisol and adrenaline. In turn, the two hormones prompt the liver to release stored glucose. Although this helps ensure adequate glucose for the brain, the increased levels of cortisol and adrenaline also lead to emotional arousal. In this way, the hypoglycemic cycle can feed into mood swings, among other emotional symptoms.

Since mood swings can be a symptom of low blood sugar, you might think that a high intake of dietary sugar would help stabilize mood. In fact, people with hypoglycemia tend to instinctively eat a piece of candy or another sweet if they feel dizzy or lightheaded—a sign of falling blood sugar. The sweet provides a quick fix because refined sugar enters the bloodstream quickly. But too much can trigger a sharp spike in blood sugar, followed by a precipitous plunge. This is why people who get lots of sugar from their diets often feel as though they're riding an emotional roller coaster, vacillating along with their blood sugar levels between the highs of anxiety and irritability and the lows of sadness and depression.

The Hormone Connection

Women's hormones are generating big business these days. Millions of menopausal women flock to their doctors' offices each year seeking relief from mental fuzziness, mood swings, irritability, and anxiety attacks, among other complaints. The usual prescription for these emotional symptoms is antidepressants and/or hormone replacement therapy.

While hormone replacement has come under scientific scrutiny because of serious concerns about its long-term health effects, it remains the treatment of choice among many in the medical community who assume that every woman of a certain age who reports a certain set of symptoms is premenopausal or menopausal. For these women, declining estrogen is the problem, so replenishing the hormone should be the cure.

We believe that a woman's menopausal symptoms aren't always about hormones and that other possible physiological causes don't get the attention they should. Too often, women receive prescriptions for hormone replacement and other medications with potentially serious side effects. In effect, they're taking drugs that only mask the symptoms rather than addressing the real cause and may pose significant health risks as well.

For most women, the onset of menopause just happens to coincide with the time in life when unhealthy habits—such as poor diet, lack of exercise, and uncontrolled stress—begin taking a toll. Menopause only adds to the tremendous physiological burden of past "transgressions." So while declining estrogen may contribute to symptoms, other long-term lifestyle factors bear much of the blame. This is why treating symptoms with hormone replacement doesn't always help. In fact, depending on what's behind the symptoms, it may aggravate them.

DR. ELLEN'S PRESCRIPTION

Since mood swings can be a sign that the brain isn't getting sufficient glucose or neurotransmitters from protein sources, I advise everyone who's prone to this mood disorder to eat high-quality proteins such as fish, nuts, and seeds and take a protein digestive enzyme. The enzyme will ensure that protein is thoroughly broken down and available for glucose or neurotransmitter production.

While I generally advocate steering clear of sugars, you can eat complex carbohydrates (which consist of long chains of sugars) in moderation, provided that you also take a carbohydrate digestive enzyme. This will help slow the absorption of sugar into the bloodstream, which in turn will help stabilize blood sugar levels and prevent mood swings.

If you tend to experience mood swings when you haven't eaten for a while—a sign of hypoglycemia or a possible serotonin deficiency—I suggest choosing one of the following beverages rather than candy or another sweet to help stabilize your blood sugar.

- For protein/fat intolerance: Mix two scoops of soy protein or rice protein drink powder in 8 ounces of water. If you wish, you can replace half of the water with freshly squeezed orange juice. The drink powder should contain about 15 grams of protein and 25 grams of carbohydrate.

- For carbohydrate intolerance: Mix two scoops of soy protein or whey protein drink powder into 8 ounces of water. The ideal product will be almost pure protein, with no more than 1 gram of carbohydrate per serving.

Be sure to take one capsule of a full-spectrum digestive enzyme blend with your protein drink. Even with liquid protein, you need the extra enzyme support to facilitate thorough digestion and nutrient absorption.

In addition to a digestive enzyme and the enzyme formulas on page 160, I recommend a number of nutritional supplements, including B-complex vitamins (60 to 90 milligrams), chromium (50 to 100 micrograms), copper (3 to 6 milligrams), and zinc (6 to 9 milligrams). These support glucose metabolism and pancreatic function, two processes that are crucial for preventing hypoglycemia and the mood swings associated with it. You might also consider taking an essential fatty acid formula that supplies 90 to 180 milligrams of eicosapentaenoic acid (EPA) and 60 to 120 milligrams of docosahexaenoic acid (DHA). Both are omega-3 fatty acids, which protect against mood swings as well.

FROM DR. ELLEN'S CASE FILES *When Victoria, a 21-year-old aspiring model and actress, first visited the BioSET Clinic/Institute, she reported several symptoms typical of hypoglycemia, including mood swings, anxiety, and periods of fatigue and fainting. She also had severe acne.*

Victoria was meticulous about her diet. She ate three to five meals every day, each consisting of lean protein, organic vegetables and fruits, and small amounts of complex carbohydrates. She limited her consumption of sugar and simple carbohydrates because she had linked them to the headaches she used to get after indulging in sugary desserts and other sweets. Still, her other symptoms persisted, disrupting her life and career.

A thorough evaluation revealed that Victoria had difficulty digesting protein and was sensitive to some amino acids (the building blocks of protein). Considering the amount of protein in her diet, including drink powders and energy bars, she needed basic treatment. I recommended a protein digestive enzyme followed by an adrenal support enzyme. (As I mentioned earlier, the adrenal glands release cortisol and adrenaline in response to low blood sugar.)

I expected these two enzymes to produce results quickly. Victoria showed improvement in just 4 days. Her skin began to clear, along with the rest of her symptoms. She felt more energetic, more focused, and less moody than before, and she had fewer bouts of depression.

Victoria's improvement continued over time. Now an accomplished fitness teacher and photographer, she continues to take her enzymes, just as she has for years.

DEPRESSION

Of all the illnesses for which people seek medical advice online, depression ranks as one of the most common. Certainly, part of the reason is the perceived social stigma that surrounds depression and discourages some from seeking help, even from their doctors. But many more are looking for alternatives to powerful antidepressants and other psychiatric drugs, with their potentially serious side effects.

Depression affects not only a person's mood but also thoughts and behaviors. Among its more common symptoms are low self-esteem, a sense of worthlessness, social withdrawal, lack of satisfaction with life, disrupted sleep patterns, physical inactivity, and difficulty focusing and concentrating. In the United States, depression is the number one mental health problem. More than 20 million Americans (twice as many women as men) will experience an episode of depression at some point in their lives.[2]

In Dr. Ellen's practice, virtually every female patient who experiences persistent fatigue is battling depression, too. It seems especially common among middle-age women, who often must juggle the demands of raising children with the responsibility of caring for aging or ill parents. Being tugged in so many directions—family, home, career—leaves very little for rejuvenation time. Grief over the perceived loss of youth and fertility may also be factors—especially in our culture, which tends not to value older women as much as other cultures do.

Sometimes depression has a genetic component, which means the condition passes from one generation to the next. It can affect anyone at any age, from children to the elderly, although it doesn't always produce the same symptoms. Older people, for example, may experience insomnia, low energy, impaired memory, and a decline in weight. Teenagers may become uncommunicative and withdrawn in addition to displaying physical symptoms such as fatigue, headaches, bedwetting, and diminished appetite.

Traditionally, most physicians and psychiatrists have treated depression with a variety of psychiatric drugs. Now, though, a growing number of mental health professionals are concerned about the emphasis on drug therapy for mental and emotional disorders. They worry that some medications are psychologically and physically addictive and/or may cause brain damage.

We have found that the symptoms of depression often improve once patients begin taking a full-spectrum digestive enzyme blend. For this reason, we're convinced of a correlation between depression and food sensitivities, which arise from poor digestion and nutrient absorption. In fact, many people who appear to have symptoms of depression instead may have massive food sensitivities. Clearing up these sensitivities with enzyme therapy can profoundly improve mood.

This is why we're such believers in enzymes—because they work in harmony with our bodies to correct any underlying imbalances and restore a naturally healthy state. They are safe for all ages, and they produce results quickly. Best of all, they don't have side effects.

DR. ELLEN'S PRESCRIPTION

Of the recommended enzyme formulas that begin on page 165, the mood/depression formula is especially helpful for alleviating depressive symptoms. Be sure to take it with a full-spectrum digestive enzyme blend (see page 33) for optimal digestion and nutrient absorption.

For depression, as for mood swings, I recommend an essential fatty acid formula that supplies 90 to 180 milligrams of EPA and 60 to 120 milligrams of DHA. Both of these omega-3's help alleviate depression by restoring and maintaining key biochemical processes.

Because food sensitivities have such a strong connection to depression, you may want to do a little investigating to identify any

Depression in the Elderly

The high incidence of depression among the elderly probably has some connection to poor nutrition, since declines in enzyme production that occur with aging can inhibit nutrient assimilation from foods. Just as significant, older people may not eat as well as they should—and it often goes unnoticed.

When researchers from the University of California, San Francisco, School of Medicine evaluated food and fluid intakes among 56 residents of one nursing home, they found that the staff overestimated actual intakes by 22 percent. The staff also failed to identify 53 percent of the residents who ate less than 75 percent of most meals.

Prompted by this study, David Bayley, ND, a naturopathic physician in North Vancouver, Canada, began looking for nutrient deficiencies in his elderly patients. Among those who were low in key nutrients, depression and lethargy were quite common.

Based on his observations, Dr. Bayley theorizes that the elderly are especially prone to poor nutrition because they eat many packaged and processed foods, which contain few nutrients or enzymes. While those who reside in nursing homes and assisted living facilities have little control over their meals, even those who live on their own tend to skimp in the kitchen. They may not get to the supermarket very often, or they may have a hard time using certain kitchen tools and appliances. So they choose convenience foods, which have little nutritional value but are easy to prepare and keep longer than fresh produce.

The less efficient digestive process in the elderly complicates matters even further. What's more, the food supply isn't as nutritious as it was 60 years ago. Today, fruits and vegetables are grown in poor-quality soil, and they're harvested before they ripen, which cuts off their enzyme supply.

Everyone, especially the elderly, ought to adopt a wholesome, balanced diet to ensure optimal nutrition.[3] Since this may be a challenge for a variety of reasons, taking a multivitamin/mineral supplement (see the list of recommended ingredients on page 325) in combination with a full-spectrum digestive enzyme blend can help prevent a nutrient shortfall. In fact, this is my standard "prescription" for all of my elderly patients.

---

trigger foods. An easy way to go about this is to make a list of your food cravings. People tend to crave the foods to which they're most sensitive. Once you've zeroed in on the potential troublemakers, eliminate them from your diet and see if you notice any improvement in your symptoms. As I mentioned earlier, taking a full-spectrum digestive enzyme blend should help clear up any sensitivities, so you can enjoy your trigger foods without symptoms.

Of course, you mustn't overlook the significance of lifestyle factors in depression. I routinely advise patients with depressive symptoms to carefully assess each aspect of their lives for people and situations that may be depleting their mental and emotional energy and to make changes that can help minimize the impact of these energy drains. It's also important to take steps to reduce stress, which can trigger depressive episodes. Stress generally results not from what is but from the *perception* of what is. Unfortunately, our perceptions are often inaccurate, which makes our lives more stressful than they need to be. (We'll discuss stress in more detail a bit later in the chapter.)

I have also noticed how so many of us tend to focus on the future rather than living in the present. If only we would stop running, breathe, and awaken to the moment, we might be able to truly embrace and enjoy life. Then depression would fade away gradually and naturally.

FROM DR. ELLEN'S CASE FILES

Ted, a 25-year-old patient of mine, had been diagnosed with a form of depression known as dysthymia. The symptoms surfaced every 2 to 3 months, usually starting with a decline in immune function that left him vulnerable to cold and flu viruses. During these periods, he became irritable and impatient, straining his relationship with his longtime girlfriend. He lost interest in exercising, which only aggravated his fatigue and poor outlook on life. At work, his performance suffered.

Ted had noticed occasional digestive upsets during his bouts of depression, so he hoped that enzyme therapy might provide some relief. A thorough evaluation pointed to a number of potential problems, including liver congestion, difficulty digesting proteins and fats, and deficiencies in the amino acids tyrosine, phenylalanine, and taurine, which play a role in hypoglycemia.

Because he couldn't digest proteins and fats well, Ted was sensitive to a variety of foods. His dietary staples—eggs, milk, beef, chicken, fish, soybeans, baked beans, and cottage cheese—also happened to be major protein sources. In other words, his body wasn't able to break down most of what he was eating.

I immediately prescribed a liver detoxification enzyme formula, along with a protein/fat digestive enzyme. Within 2 months of beginning enzyme therapy, Ted's depression and mood swings subsided. Follow-up testing found no amino acid deficiencies (a sign of poor protein digestion) or food sensitivities.

Because Ted's energy level was so much higher, he began to exercise on a daily basis. He played tennis and resumed skiing, his favorite sport. Gradually, his life returned to normal.

STRESS

An ever-growing body of research is shedding new light on the myriad ways in which persistent, chronic stress whittles away at our health. In a nutshell, stress gradually depletes our reserve capacity to cope with extreme emotional and physical challenges. Over time, even seemingly minor stressors begin to have a major impact on us because we lack the emotional and physical resilience to manage them effectively.

Of course, our reserve capacity also depends on adequate nutrition. In the worst-case scenario, we're stressed out and nutrient deficient—an almost certain recipe for illness. This is when enzyme supplements become especially important. Even if we can't avoid a particular stressor, we can take enzymes to ensure thorough food digestion and nutrient absorption. This increases our chances of avoiding illness even in the face of stress.

Stress isn't all bad. It alerts us to the presence of a threat, then enables us to respond to the threat appropriately. Problems arise when the stress doesn't let up, whether because of ongoing circumstances or some longstanding, unresolved emotional trauma or distress. Poorly handled stress can be just as devastating.

During periods of stress, the adrenal glands work overtime, pumping out large quantities of the hormones adrenaline (epinephrine) and norepinephrine. Overworked adrenals eventually crash, leading to adrenal exhaustion, in which the glands can't produce hormones at normal, healthy levels. Adrenal exhaustion wreaks havoc on the endocrine system by disrupting the body's natural hormone balance. This, too, opens the door to illness.

To prevent adrenal exhaustion and maintain adrenal function, some physicians recommend vitamin C supplementation. Irwin Stone, MD, one of the pioneers in vitamin C research, was able to establish the connection between the nutrient and human physiology by tracking its genetic history. As Dr. Stone discovered, at one time, the human body could manufacture its own vitamin C. Over the millennia, humans lost this ability, even though the vast majority of animals did not.

For his research, Dr. Stone chose to focus on goats. He found that when a goat is under stress, its body will churn out 1,000 or more milligrams of vitamin C. This discovery led Dr. Stone to describe C as a stress vitamin, which we humans need in sufficient amounts in times of stress. Since we can't make our own, we must rely on other sources, such as foods and supplements.

Over the years, both of us have treated hundreds of patients who were coping with stress and the health problems that result from it—including fatigue, chronic pain, colitis, ulcers, sinusitis, eczema, and acne. Enzyme therapy not only helps resolve many of these conditions, it also enables people to maintain their inner balance and outer vitality, even in the face of stress.

Once you begin enzyme therapy, your ability to resist the emotional and physical effects of stress will improve dramatically. Your energy level and stamina will explode. And you won't get sick.

DR. ELLEN'S PRESCRIPTION

To enhance your emotional and physical resilience—and your disease resistance—during times of stress, I recommend taking a full-spectrum digestive enzyme blend along with the following supplements.

- One capsule of an antioxidant supplement each day, either 1 hour before or 2 hours after eating. Ideally, you should choose a product with vitamin C as one of its primary ingredients. It may also contain acerola cherries and/or quercetin, extracts that are commonly included in antioxidant enzyme formulas with vitamin C. (For a full list of recommended ingredients, see page 322.)

- Two capsules of an adrenal enzyme formula three times a day, either 1 hour before or 2 hours after a meal. This formula helps protect against adrenal exhaustion, a common by-product of chronic stress. It contains the following ingredients.

  Digestive enzymes. Look for a product that contains 60,000 to 90,000 HUT of protease.

  Panax ginseng root extract (320 to 500 milligrams). Panax ginseng has been a staple of Chinese medicine for thousands of years. It may be helpful in situations of prolonged or severe stress as well as for people who are experiencing fatigue or recovering from long-term chronic illness.

  Bupleurum root extract (200 to 600 milligrams). Known for enhancing adrenal function, this herb—which sometimes goes by the name Chinese thoroughwax—also has a mild sedative effect.

  Vitamin C from acerola cherry extract (20 to 100 milligrams). Vitamin C is essential for protecting against the effects of stress and supports immune function.

  Panthothenic acid (100 to 200 milligrams). A B vitamin, pantothenic acid (vitamin B_5) helps alleviate fatigue.

Rice bran (130 to 200 milligrams). Rice bran is a natural source of B vitamins, which are essential for building and maintaining the body's energy supply.

Siberian ginseng root extract (80 to 120 milligrams). This herb has a long history as a tonic for fighting fatigue and restoring energy. It also helps combat stress-related illness.

Riboflavin (25 to 50 milligrams). Also known as vitamin B_2, riboflavin assists in the production of thyroid hormone, which revs up metabolism and supplies vital energy.

Niacin (25 to 50 milligrams). Niacin, or vitamin B_3, helps release energy from carbohydrates.

Biotin (100 to 200 milligrams). This B vitamin enables the body to utilize glucose, an important energy source.

Magnesium (100 to 200 milligrams). According to some studies, people who are prone to fatigue tend to have low magnesium levels.

Codonopsis root extract (300 to 600 milligrams). Sometimes recommended as an alternative to ginseng, codonopsis is an effective remedy for stress and fatigue.

Remember that if you can't find all of these herbs and nutrients in a single formula, you can take them as separate supplements. In fact, a formula with just the primary ingredients (in bold) will work fine as long as you combine it with a full-spectrum digestive enzyme blend.

ATTENTION DEFICIT HYPERACTIVITY DISORDER

People who have attention deficit hyperactivity disorder, or ADHD, exhibit degrees of inattention or hyperactivity/impulsivity that interfere with optimal mental performance. Their behavior can strain their relationships with others and undermine their success at work, in school, and in other situations.

Although diagnoses of ADHD are becoming more common among adults, they're alarmingly frequent among school-age children. Some experts estimate that between 3 and 5 percent of children in the primary grades are taking methylphenidate (Ritalin) for ADHD symptoms.[4] About 1 to 3 percent of the school-age population has full-blown ADHD, while another 5 to 10 percent has only certain symptoms or related problems, such as anxiety and depression. Between 15 and 20 percent show behaviors consistent with ADHD but are not diagnosed with the disorder because the behaviors occur only in specific situations, do not cause disruptions at home or at school, or are symptoms of another medical condition.

Researchers have noticed a correlation between gender and age and the frequency of ADHD diagnoses. Boys are about three times more likely than girls to have ADHD symptoms. The symptoms tend to decline with age, although for 30 to 50 percent of children with ADHD, they persist into adulthood.

Understandably, parents whose kids develop ADHD first want to know "Why *my* child?" Family history seems to be a strong indicator of who gets the disorder, since usually at least one close relative has it. In fact, one-third of all fathers who were diagnosed with ADHD in their youth have children with the condition. Among pairs of identical twins, if one twin exhibits ADHD symptoms, the other usually does as well.

Food sensitivities also play a role in ADHD. Among the foods that seem especially likely to trigger symptoms are wheat, corn, yeast, chocolate, cinnamon, peanut butter, and dairy products. Additives such as food colorings, sulfites, and MSG can also cause problems.

Levels of essential fatty acids tend to run low in children with ADHD, leading some researchers to speculate that a deficiency of these beneficial fats may be a factor in the disorder. They're important to the structure and integrity of nerves, but they must come from foods because the body can't manufacture them. Thus, if a child has a fat intolerance—that is, he can't properly digest or absorb fat—he may be at higher risk for ADHD.

Dr. Ellen has gotten excellent results by treating ADHD and similar behavioral disorders with enzyme therapy. We hate to see so many children on Ritalin when dietary changes and digestive support may be all that's necessary to reduce hyperactivity and improve focus, concentration, and behavior.

DR. ELLEN'S PRESCRIPTION

In addition to the enzyme formulas on page 165, I recommend an essential fatty acid formula that supplies between 90 and 180 milligrams of EPA and 60 to 120 milligrams of DHA. The usual dosage is two capsules twice a day, either with or between meals—whichever you prefer.

You can also increase your intake of essential fatty acids by eating more fish, leafy greens, flaxseed and flaxseed oil, pumpkin and sunflower seeds, walnuts, cashews, almonds, Brazil nuts, and evening primrose oil—all top-notch sources of the good fats. Be sure to take a good-quality protein/fat digestive with these foods as well as with your supplements to ensure thorough fat digestion and absorption.

FROM DR. ELLEN'S CASE FILES

When Justin's parents first brought him to the BioSET Clinic/Institute, they told me that their son had always been small for his age. He was 7 at the time, but his height and weight were more typical of a 4-year-old. He was astonishingly aggressive and hyperactive. Within the first half hour of his visit, he scribbled on the walls with crayon, punched his mother in the face for no apparent reason, overturned a cabinet, emptied his mother's purse and wallet all over the carpet, and damaged the treatment table.

When I feel overwhelmed and perplexed by a patient, I step back and sit for a while—watching, listening, and trying to imagine what it would be like to step into that person's shoes. The only way I can really help is if I truly empathize with, instead of react to, the person's situation. I asked myself, "What is Justin feeling, and what can I do for him?"

I also asked Justin's parents what their son ate every day. I wasn't surprised when they said, "Whatever he wants." Practically every one of his meals consisted of Chicken McNuggets, a milkshake, and maybe an apple. His snacks of choice were ice cream and cookies. As his mother explained, "Because Justin is so small and because he's very picky about his food, we're just happy that he eats so he will continue to grow."

I explained to Justin's parents that their son could be sensitive to just about everything in his diet, and it could be affecting his behavior. Sure enough, when I tested him, I discovered that he couldn't tolerate chicken, dairy, wheat, fruits, or foods containing sugar, yeast, vitamin C, or minerals—in other words, most of what he was eating. Further evaluation revealed severe carbohydrate intolerance, along with kidney and liver toxicity and mineral deficiencies.

I immediately started Justin on a carbohydrate digestive enzyme, a kidney/liver detoxification formula, and a mineral absorption formula. I also recommended some dietary changes, and I administered BioSET treatments to help clear up his food sensitivities.

About a month after our first appointment, Justin walked into my office and handed me a flower. Then he announced, "I would like you to retest me for my food sensitivities. I think they are less." He was so calm and focused—much different from the little boy I had met the month before. I was very pleased.

GOOD MOODS START WITH GOOD NUTRITION

Your emotional health very much colors your perception of every aspect of your life. It also influences other people's perceptions of you. Even when outside factors threaten your emotional balance, you can take steps to resist their effects and remain calm and clear-headed.

At the top of the list, of course, are eating nutritious foods and taking enzyme supplements. Together, these strategies ensure that your brain—like your body—gets the necessary nutrients so it can continue performing at its best no matter what life throws your way.

We're continually educating our patients about how important healthy eating habits and proper digestion are to their emotional well-being. We hope that you will take this lesson to heart as well. Your mood and emotions depend on it.

DR. ELLEN'S PRESCRIPTION

The following two enzyme formulas can do wonders to foster emotional balance and resilience as well as general mental function. The ingredients that I've listed for each formula are what I consider ideal. If you can find a pH-balanced, full-spectrum enzyme formula with just the primary ingredients (in bold), it should work just fine. Another option is to take separate supplements of these ingredients along with a full-spectrum digestive enzyme blend.

- Take two capsules of a mental focus enzyme formula twice a day, either 1 hour before or 2 hours after a meal or as needed for extra mental sharpness—perhaps before an important business meeting, for example. Look for the following ingredients.

  Digestive enzymes. A good-quality product will contain 16,000 to 50,000 HUT of protease.

  Ginkgo biloba leaf extract (200 to 360 milligrams). Ginkgo has a number of active compounds, including bioflavonoids and terpenoids, to help enhance memory and concentration.

  Gotu kola herb extract (50 to 300 milligrams). Gotu kola helps prevent mental fatigue while improving memory and concentration. The herb also appears to stimulate the central nervous system and support circulation—both beneficial for mental function.

Panax ginseng root extract (150 to 240 milligrams). This form of ginseng has a longstanding reputation for enhancing energy and concentration.

Water hyssop herb extract (80 to 100 milligrams). Water hyssop improves mental sharpness.

Schizandra fruit extract (100 to 150 milligrams). Like water hyssop, schizandra enhances mental acuity.

Phosphatidylserine (300 to 500 milligrams). An amino acid, phosphatidylserine may improve mental function and fight depression.

Acetyl-L-carnitine (1,500 to 2,000 milligrams). This amino acid appears to boost cellular energy as well as the activity of memory-enhancing chemicals.

Vitamin B$_{12}$ (3 to 6 micrograms). This B vitamin may support memory and mood.

- Take two capsules of a mood/depression formula twice a day with or between meals, or as needed to relieve mood swings and depression. All of the following ingredients are beneficial.

  Digestive enzymes. The formula should contain 21,000 to 42,000 HUT of protease.

  Rice bran (30 to 60 milligrams). Rice bran is a natural source of B vitamins, which are beneficial for mood.

  Ginkgo biloba leaf extract (75 to 150 milligrams). The compounds in this herb help alleviate anxiety and depression.

  St. John's wort extract (450 to 900 milligrams). Studies have found this herb to be helpful in treating depression.

  GABA (500 to 1,000 milligrams). This amino acid prevents nerve cells from overfiring. In combination with niacinamide and inositol (see below), it can mimic the calming effects of prescription tranquilizers without the risk of addiction. GABA also stimulates alpha wave activity in the brain, reducing anxiety while increasing mental alertness. In fact, GABA appears to act on the same receptors in the brain as drugs such as alprazolam (Xanax) and diazepam (Valium).

Niacinamide (6 to 10 milligrams). A B vitamin, niacinamide relieves anxiety while improving mental alertness and focus.

Inositol (30 to 50 milligrams). This compound plays an important role in preventing anxiety and reducing stress.

Folic acid (400 to 800 micrograms). A B vitamin, folic acid can relieve depression and enhance the effectiveness of antidepressants.

Valerian extract (75 to 150 milligrams). With its calming effects, valerian can ease stress and anxiety.

Oat straw extract (60 to 120 milligrams). This herb enhances blood flow to the brain and nervous system.

To round out your self-care regimen, consider these relaxation techniques, which can balance mood and sharpen mental function.

- Schedule an appointment for a massage, which can release tension and improve your ability to cope with stress. All massage techniques work by stimulating specific receptors in the surface of the skin. They're great for distracting the brain and body from stressful situations. Your doctor or local hospital may be able to provide a referral to a qualified massage therapist. Keep in mind that some medical conditions preclude vigorous or deep massage, so if you're receiving medical care, be sure to consult your doctor first.

- Practice meditation, which has numerous benefits for mood and mental function. To start, try this simple exercise.

Find a quiet room in your home where you won't be disturbed. Sit on a pillow with your back straight, either cross-legged on the floor or against a wall with your legs extended in front of you. Slowly and deeply inhale and exhale, allowing your body to completely relax. Feel the breath permeate your entire body, from the top of your head to the tips of your fingers and toes. As you inhale and exhale, allow thoughts to float through your mind, but let go of them without dwelling on them. Continue concentrating on your breathing.

Practice this exercise for about 10 minutes once or twice a day at first. Before long, you'll be able to sit for up to 30 minutes straight without feeling the slightest bit restless. The sense of calm and centeredness that grows from meditation will carry through to other aspects of your life.

• Sign up for a yoga class. An ancient discipline that combines deep breathing and postures, yoga has grown in popularity over the past decade. It not only brings tranquility to mind and body, it also releases tension, improves flexibility, and increases nourishing blood flow to tissues and organs.

Yoga takes many forms. Perhaps the best known is hatha yoga, which emphasizes movements that stretch and tone the body. Kundalini yoga concentrates on strengthening and balancing the nervous system, while pranayama yoga targets breathing and the respiratory system. Try various classes to choose the best yoga technique for you. Many health clubs offer yoga instruction; you also may be able to find an instructor who teaches independently.

CHAPTER 11

Maintain a Healthy Immune System

FROM DR. ELLEN'S CASE FILES *Richard, age 45, scheduled an appointment at the BioSET Clinic/Institute on the advice of a good friend of his, whom I had treated for food sensitivities. Richard explained that he wanted to strengthen his immune system and alleviate the sluggishness and chronic eczema that had plagued him since he had been diagnosed with HIV. He also had asthma and frequent bouts of bronchitis.*

I have gotten good results in treating people who are HIV positive. In these cases, the most important objectives of enzyme therapy are to improve digestion and to regulate or reduce the number of circulating immune complexes in the body. This relieves stress on the immune system, which in turn minimizes autoimmune activity.

Richard's nutrient and enzyme evaluations showed carbohydrate intolerance and mild to moderate liver/gallbladder toxicity. Based on these results and Richard's health history, I immediately prescribed enzymes for carbohydrate digestion and for immune, respiratory, and adrenal support.

Once Richard began taking the enzymes, his immune function improved, as did his digestion and elimination. His energy no longer dipped after eating, and his asthma attacks subsided. He did so well with enzyme therapy that he began referring others to my clinic.

Those of us in medicine and health care recognize the importance of the immune system and its influence over other body systems and processes. The immune system is unique in that it doesn't have one central regulating organ. The circulatory system has the heart; the respiratory system, the lungs; and the digestive system, the stomach and intestines. In comparison, the immune system's components are spread throughout the body and communicate with one another through immune cells and chemicals known as cytokines.

The primary function of the immune system is to stay alert for invasions by disease-causing microorganisms and to distinguish them from the body's own cells. By its standards, anything foreign to the body is a potential enemy. Once the immune system homes in on an invading substance, called an antigen, it sets in motion a highly complex response.

The immune system is responsible for maintaining our health when we're well and healing us when we're sick. It is overbuilt to ensure its effectiveness, with hundreds of control mechanisms and backup lines of defense, many of which we're still learning about. Much of the immune system is not yet understood, but we know enough about it to harness it and regulate it to our advantage.

For this reason, everyone should do what they can to maintain healthy immune function. Enzyme therapy is one means to this end. Ever since Dr. Ellen began taking enzymes 22 years ago, she rarely gets sick—a sign of an efficient, effective immune system. Patients who take enzymes report similar results.

HOW FOOD CAN WEAKEN
THE BODY'S DEFENSES

A decline in immune function often begins with the one-two punch of food sensitivities and poor digestion. When you're sensitive to a food, it means that your body can't thoroughly process it. The undigested food particles find their way into the bloodstream, where they trigger an immune response.

For a long time, it was thought that the intestinal wall would block food particles from getting into the bloodstream. Now we know this isn't the case. Some evidence suggests that people with food sensitivities have leakier intestinal linings than those without sensitivities, which means that more food particles can pass into the bloodstream. What's more, the inflammation that occurs with the immune response can make the intestinal linings even leakier.

Once the immune system spots the food particles, it sends in a cellular "search party" to check out the foreign substances. How the searchers determine whether a particular substance poses a threat is a rather complex mechanism. But with a signal from them, other immune cells begin pumping out cytokines that in turn initiate production of antibodies. They're responsible for marking the food particles, or antigens, as targets for destruction and removal. Depending on the type and number of antibodies, they attach to the antigens to form circulating immune complexes (CICs).

This is one method the body uses to deal with foreign substances—it forms CICs. The trouble is, immune complexes are inflammatory. They can wreak havoc on the body even if they linger for only a brief period of time. The body recognizes this, and it takes action to extract CICs from the bloodstream. In fact, certain cells in the liver and spleen exist for the primary purpose of attaching to and disposing of CICs. After one pass through the liver or spleen, the blood should be largely free of immune complexes.

Problems arise when the liver and spleen find themselves facing more CICs than they can remove from the bloodstream. The immune complexes tend to congregate in certain tissues and organs, such as the kidneys, joints, and blood vessel walls, where they trigger inflammatory conditions that eventually lead to illness.

Where the CICs settle depends largely upon heredity. This is why symptoms of food sensitivities can vary so greatly from one person to the next. Some people become prone to migraines; others develop joint pain; and still others experience kidney disease. Left untreated, inflammation can cause scarring so severe that the affected tissue no longer can function.

According to the medical literature, the tissue damage caused by CICs is present in a number of conditions that affect many organs. It can lead to lung disease, chronic pancreatitis, ulcerative colitis, and Crohn's disease.[1]

At their worst, CICs confuse the immune system so it loses its ability to distinguish between what belongs in the body and what doesn't. It starts attacking perfectly healthy tissues and organs as if they were antigens. This process sets the stage for serious autoimmune diseases, such as multiple sclerosis (MS), rheumatoid arthritis, lupus, and thyroiditis.

Because they are active participants in the immune system, enzymes can help prevent, reduce, or reverse the immune response when it threatens to backfire on the body. For example, the enzyme protease helps break down viruses and other infectious microorganisms, which eases the immune system's workload and keeps it from becoming hyperactive.[2] In autoimmune disease, enzymes help not only by interrupting the inflammatory cascade but also by breaking down CICs and activating the macrophages to gobble up and get rid of them.[3]

FROM DR. ELLEN'S CASE FILES *Sharon, a 46-year-old accountant, had multiple sclerosis. Her most severe symptoms were migraines and fatigue, although she also experienced frequent bouts of numbness, dizziness, fainting, heart palpitations, and lower-back pain. This seemed consistent with my other MS patients, many of whom reported concurrent lower-back pain, sciatica, and leg weakness. Sharon's med-*

ical history also included digestive problems, such as occasional gas and irregular bowel movements.

When she came to see me at the BioSET Clinic/Institute, Sharon already knew that she had many food sensitivities. Her severely distended abdomen, which I noticed during her physical examination, seemed to confirm this. Further evaluation revealed carbohydrate intolerance, along with specific sensitivities to fish, dairy products, wheat, beans, animal and vegetable fats, chocolate, coffee, certain alcoholic beverages, yeast, and food colorings and other additives. Sharon also had liver/gallbladder toxicity and mild kidney dysfunction, which contributed to her back pain.

Based on these findings, I prescribed five enzyme formulas—one to improve her digestive function; another to heal her apparently leaky gut; the third to detoxify her liver, gallbladder, and kidneys; the fourth to counteract her bloating; and the last to enhance assimilation of calcium, magnesium, and trace minerals. Soon after she began following this regimen, Sharon noticed a dramatic decline in her digestive symptoms and bloating. Her migraines and lower-back pain subsided; in fact, her back was so much better that she felt more flexible than before, with greater range of motion.

Sharon continues to do very well. With the help of enzyme therapy, she's better able to resist infections that previously would have made her sick. Although she continues to have occasional bouts of fatigue, she can work full days without problems. Also, to her delight, she can eat pretty much whatever she wants.

GUT HEALTH AFFECTS IMMUNE HEALTH

As you might imagine, the integrity of the intestinal lining and the coating of mucus that protects it is a major factor in determining whether food particles get into the bloodstream in the first place. In fact, the mucus serves as an important communication center for the immune system. When harmful substances, such as bacteria, parasites, allergens, and toxins, find their way into the gut, the mucus alerts the immune system to send in forces to defend the rest of the body against damage.

If the coating sustains damage or scarring, the intestinal lining becomes too permeable to prevent food particles from passing through. This sets in motion the chain of events that activates the immune system and prompts production of CICs.

Perhaps the most important strategy for maintaining a structurally sound gut is to support proper digestion. As long as food is thoroughly broken down, fewer food particles travel through the intestinal lining and stimulate what's known as the gut-associated lymphoid tissue. If food particles never reach this tissue, they can't penetrate and damage it, worsening an already leaky gut. Nor can they venture into the bloodstream and trigger an immune response.

Another protective measure is to increase production of secretory immunoglobulin A, or IgA. This antibody binds with food particles in the gut, keeping them from adhering to and passing through the mucous coating. If IgA runs low—which can happen when the intestinal wall is damaged—food particles are more likely to lodge in the gut-associated lymphoid tissue. You can step up IgA production by taking a probiotic supplement, [4] which is one reason that Dr. Ellen includes probiotics in her basic plan. (For a refresher on the basic plan, see page 32.)

Some experts believe that we humans would live longer if we took steps to improve our digestion and intestinal microflora. Several hundred species of bacteria—some 2½ to 3 pounds of living microorganisms—reside principally in the large intestine and to a lesser extent in the small intestine. Collectively, they far outnumber the cells in the rest of the body. They can have a tremendous impact on our health, for better or for worse.

This is why maintaining balanced intestinal microflora is so important: Any imbalance (a condition known as dysbiosis) can have a systemic effect on the body and cause all manner of illnesses. By the same token, a healthy gut supports a healthy body—one that is less vulnerable to serious ailments such as heart disease, cancer, diabetes, and arthritis.

Taking probiotics is a fundamental strategy for maintaining an optimal intestinal environment. They work with the bacterial species in the gut to create less hospitable conditions for harmful microorganisms and substances. The benefit is twofold: First, the intestinal wall and its coating are less vulnerable to damage; and second, the immune system is less likely to switch on and intervene.

WHILE WE'RE ON THE SUBJECT . . .

Despite the central role of intestinal health in determining immune health and general well-being, few people feel comfortable talking about this particular area of human anatomy—even with their physicians. Yet bowel problems affect a majority of Americans. And if your bowels don't function properly, the rest of you won't, either. After all, this is where nutrients are absorbed from foods and waste collects for excretion.

When something goes awry in the intestine, it can hamper the nutrient absorption process. Furthermore, it permits the toxins that congregate there—such as cellular debris, biochemical waste, hormones, and bile—to pass into the body. These toxins damage tissue and divert disease-fighting white blood cells. The overall result is a weakened immune system and increased susceptibility to a variety of health problems.

Because of this, irregular bowel movements are more than an inconvenience; they can signify much bigger problems. The question for most people is, What constitutes "regular" bowel movements? "Basically, you should have a soft, well-formed stool that exits without much straining," according to Stephen Holt, MD, author of

Natural Ways to Digestive Health.[5] Stools that appear as small pellets usually indicate insufficient fiber in the diet, which you can easily correct by eating more vegetables and other fiber-rich foods. As for frequency, "regular" can range from three bowel movements a day to three a week, Dr. Holt says.

Flatulence is another sign of intestinal distress that, while embarrassing, may not seem to have major health implications. Every day at least one patient says, "Do you mean passing gas isn't normal?" When we eat or drink, we swallow small amounts of air, which we usually release as burps. This is perfectly normal. Flatulence, however, is not.

Among the most common causes of gas is undigested foods in the small intestine. Usually they're carbohydrates—sugars and starches—that don't break down because of insufficient enzymes. When this undigested food passes into the large intestine, it turns into a feast for the bacteria that reside there, which is what produces gas.

FROM DR. ELLEN'S CASE FILES

Thirteen-year-old Lori came to the BioSET Clinic/Institute for help with chronic bloating and gas, which came on immediately after eating. According to her mother, none of Lori's siblings had this problem. To aggravate matters, Lori's skin had begun breaking out, and she experienced frequent dizzy spells throughout the day—a possible indicator of hypoglycemia, or low blood sugar.

Usually, bloating and gas immediately after eating occur because of poor protein/fat digestion. It can contribute to acne and hypoglycemia as well.

Based on a thorough evaluation, I thought that Lori might benefit from a protein/fat digestive enzyme. I recommended that she take two capsules with heavy or high-protein meals and one capsule with the rest of her meals. Almost as soon as she started enzyme therapy, Lori's bloating and gas disappeared. Her acne cleared up, too.

ANOTHER REASON
THAT SUGAR IS NO GOOD

Sugar consumption compromises immune function. Reports point to a correlation between a diet high in sugar and declining numbers of white blood cells.[6] The cells that remain aren't as effective at sweeping up and disposing of harmful microorganisms and substances.

What's more, sugar robs the body of many vitamins and minerals, such as zinc, which is vital for immune function. And since bacteria and yeast thrive on sugar, the more of it you eat, the harder time you'll have fighting bacterial and yeast infections. [7]

Eating foods that are low in sugar—and minimizing carbohydrates generally—establishes a solid foundation for good immune function. It also prevents highs and lows in energy and mood by helping to stabilize levels of blood glucose. When you do eat carbohydrates, you want to make sure that you thoroughly digest them. Enzyme supplements can help with this, in addition to reducing cravings for these foods.

We may not be able to control all of our health risk factors, but we are responsible for making our food choices. By avoiding sugar and restricting refined and complex carbohydrates, we improve our immune function and overall health.

TOXINS AND
IMMUNE RESPONSE

Nutritionally depleted foods, such as sugar, and undigested food particles are the most common toxins to challenge the body. Exposure to radiation, air and water pollutants, household chemicals, and medication residues only adds to the toxin load.

When toxins assault or build up in the body, the immune system must make an effort to eliminate these harmful substances. Otherwise, it loses its ability to protect against other offenders, such as viruses and bacteria. We end up getting sick more often—and even when we're "well," we may not feel as strong and resilient as we could.

Because food and environmental toxins and food sensitivities manifest themselves in very similar ways, distinguishing between them can be a challenge, at least at first. This is why patients who show signs of toxicity begin treatment with a combination of detoxification and enzyme therapy. Once their bodies are free of toxins, we can work to isolate and clear up the source of any lingering symptoms. Typically, the symptoms that persist after detoxification and enzyme therapy are much milder and respond well to desensitization treatments.

Making sensible dietary changes and taking a pH-balanced, full-spectrum digestive enzyme plus a systemic enzyme help detoxify the body and return it to a state of balance, or homeostasis. The prescription that begins on page 181 includes a list of dietary recommendations that can help minimize toxin exposure and reduce the burden on your immune system. Then it can save its resources to fend off the real enemies—the harmful microorganisms and substances that can set the disease process in motion.

FROM DR. ELLEN'S CASE FILES   *Joseph—a 14-year-old with asthma, chronic bronchitis, and acne—came to the BioSET Clinic/Institute with his parents, who were concerned that their son's health was getting worse. They hoped that a combination of enzyme therapy, detoxification, and allergy desensitization would improve his situation.*

I decided to begin by learning more about Joseph's eating habits. Like many teenagers, he lived on fast foods such as hot dogs, hamburgers, and sausage—all toxin-laden meats—as well as sugary soft drinks. He skimped on fruits and vegetables, which meant he was probably running low on key vitamins and minerals. In short, he seldom ate a wholesome, nutritionally balanced meal.

Next, I asked Joseph to complete a detoxification questionnaire. Based on his responses, I recommended an enzyme for gentle cleansing. I also advised him to forgo soft drinks at least 3 days a week and to replace his fast-food lunches with packed lunches consisting of organic turkey or another organic protein source, vegetable sticks, a piece of fresh fruit, and spring water. I recommended a pH-balanced, full-spectrum digestive enzyme to ensure optimal nutrient absorption.

Joseph agreed to try everything that I suggested. When he returned to my office 3 weeks later, I could tell right away that his immune system was functioning much better. His asthma flare-ups weren't as frequent or severe, his bronchitis was much better, and his skin had cleared up. He was a completely different boy.

STRESS HAS TOXIC EFFECTS

In any discussion of toxins and their impact on immune function, we mustn't overlook how emotional and psychological stress adds to the toxic burden and how enzymes can help reduce our physical vulnerability to these toxic effects. We see it every day, in patients of all ages.

The medical literature has explored at length how the suppressed emotions that often accompany stress can contribute to toxicity and set the stage for physical illness. The conscious mind may be able to ignore stressors, but the subconscious mind—and our cells—remembers. These subliminal memories wear down the body, specifically the immune, nervous, and endocrine systems. The physical impact is very real.

Since suppressing your emotions can be so harmful, you need to find appropriate venues for expressing them. Build opportunities for release into your life. We encourage patients to practice relaxation techniques, such as meditation and yoga; to contemplate nature; and to listen to music or play it. Laughter is another powerful tool for cleansing and healing, as Norman Cousins discussed in his book *Anatomy of an Illness*.[8] So is writing about your life experiences in a journal, where you can say what you like and be who you really are without fear or embarrassment.

Dr. Ellen routinely recommends enzyme therapy and homeopathic remedies to help restore a mind and body that are under stress. When the toxic effects of negative emotions make us sick, enzyme therapy can make us well again.

OPTIMAL IMMUNITY, OPTIMAL HEALTH

The immune system is a complex system that affects our health in ways that science has only begun to explore. In turn, it is affected by almost everything we do—which means that we can control how it performs, at least to some degree.

A healthy lifestyle is essential to restoring and maintaining optimal immune function. Literally thousands of studies have documented the beneficial effects of lifestyle on immunity. The centerpiece of a healthy lifestyle is good nutrition. It is relevant to every cell, tissue, and system of the body, including the immune system.

Good nutrition depends on sensible food choices and, of course, proper digestion and nutrient absorption. The body's systems can't possibly work optimally if they aren't receiving adequate nutritional support. When it comes to immunity, we are dealing with a system that prevents not only everyday ailments such as colds and flu but also more serious conditions, such as heart disease, cancer, and autoimmune disease.

With optimal immune function, your body can defend itself against pretty much anything that comes its way. Enzyme therapy is the key.

DR. ELLEN'S PRESCRIPTION

For patients who are especially prone to illness or in a generally weakened state of health, I recommend one or more—or sometimes all—of the following enzyme formulas and nutritional supplements to bolster immune function. They are also your first choice if you simply want to make sure that your immune system is as strong as it can be.

Please don't feel daunted by the number of ingredients in each formula. I realize that you may not be able to find one product with everything that I've listed, and that's okay. As long as it contains at least the primary ingredients (in bold) along with a full-spectrum digestive enzyme blend, it will work just as well.

Another option is to take these ingredients as individual supplements. If you go this route, be sure to combine them with a digestive enzyme formula.

- Take one capsule of an immune health enzyme formula two or three times a day on an empty stomach. After about 4 months, take a break for a month or two, then resume treatment. The ingredients in this formula will help restore and maintain immune function.

  Digestive enzymes. Look for a product with 80,000 to 225,000 HUT of protease.

  Astragalus root extract (320 to 525 milligrams). Astragalus appears to be especially effective at enhancing resistance to illness. It may have antiviral and antibiotic properties as well.

  Reishi mushroom extract (120 to 240 milligrams). In Japan, people who undergo chemotherapy for cancer take reishi mushrooms to strengthen their immune systems. Studies have shown that mushroom extracts boost the effectiveness of chemotherapy treatments, allowing for lower dosages while protecting healthy cells from the potent drugs. Some research indicates that reishi mushrooms may be powerful enough to help enhance immune function in people with HIV and AIDS.

Shiitake mushroom extract (120 to 240 milligrams per day). Shiitake mushrooms contain lentinan, a compound that promotes production of T cells.

Cat's claw herb extract (120 to 240 milligrams). Cat's claw helps support the immune systems of cancer patients, which may be weakened by chemotherapy, radiation, and other conventional cancer treatments. The herb's root and inner bark contain compounds called procyanidolic oligomers, which work in part by stimulating immune cells to engulf viruses and bacteria. According to research reports, cat's claw may even be of value in combating stubborn infections such as sinusitis.

Burdock root extract (80 to 160 milligrams). Burdock root is well known for inhibiting tumors and destroying bacterial and fungal cultures. Japanese researchers found in the herb a new type of desmutagen, a substance that is uniquely capable of reducing cell mutation.

Echinacea angustifolia *root extract (120 to 240 milligrams) and* E. purpurea *root extract (120 to 240 milligrams).* Perhaps best known for reducing susceptibility to colds and flu, echinacea also limits the duration and severity of infections.

Goldenseal root extract (120 to 240 milligrams). Herbalists often recommend goldenseal to treat recurrent middle-ear, respiratory, urinary, and vaginal infections.

Vitamin C from acerola cherry extract (100 to 200 milligrams). A well-known immune enhancer, vitamin C also minimizes cold symptoms and reduces asthma flare-ups.

Beta-carotene (10 to 15 milligrams). This vitamin A precursor is a potent immune booster and antioxidant. It may also reverse certain precancerous conditions.

Zinc (10 to 15 milligrams). Zinc helps fend off colds and flu and builds disease resistance generally.

Coenzyme Q_{10} (10 to 20 milligrams). This nutrient is essential to a cell's ability to produce energy. It also may help alter the course of cancer and AIDS.

Quercetin (30 to 50 milligrams). Quercetin is excellent for fighting viral infections.

- Take one capsule of a gastric enzyme formula three times a day, 1 hour before or 2 hours after a meal. This particular formula strengthens the immune system by healing the gut, which reduces leakage of undigested food particles and other toxins into the bloodstream. It should contain the following ingredients.

  Digestive enzymes. A good-quality product will contain a mix of enzymes in the following dosages: amylase (3,000 to 9,000 DU), lipase (150 to 450 LU), cellulase (200 to 600 CU), lactase (75 to 225 ALU), invertase (75 to 300 SU), peptidase (1,000 to 3,000 HUT), alpha galactosidase (10 to 30 GalU or 25 to 75 AGSU), glucoamylase (2 to 12 AGU), and malt diastase (75 to 300 DP). Make sure the product also contains pectinase, xylanase, hemicellulase, phytase, and/or beta-glucanase; these enzymes help process the nutrients from foods.

  Marshmallow root extract (50 to 100 milligrams). Marshmallow root may have antiviral, antibacterial, and antifungal properties in addition to enhancing immune function and soothing the gastrointestinal tract.

  Deglycyrrhizinated licorice root extract (100 to 200 milligrams). This form of licorice can help rebuild the protective mucous coating in the gut. It also reduces inflammation.

  Aloe vera juice extract (10 to 30 milligrams). Beyond its antiviral, antibacterial, and antifungal properties, aloe vera may improve immune function. Be careful not to exceed the recommended dosage, as too much aloe vera juice extract can cause cramping.

- Take one capsule of an antioxidant supplement a day, 1 hour before or 2 hours after a meal. Antioxidants help prevent and repair cellular damage by harmful free radical molecules. Look for a product with the ingredients listed on page 322.

- Take one capsule of a protease enzyme three to five times a day on an empty stomach. A systemic enzyme, protease is beneficial for detoxification, hormone balance, and general healing. Please note that the dosage for immune enhancement is slightly higher than the one in the basic plan (see page 32).

- Take one capsule of a probiotic supplement once a day, at least 40 minutes before or after a meal, as recommended in the basic plan. Probiotics such as *Lactobacillus acidophilus* produce antimicrobial compounds that help minimize levels of parasitic bacteria in the gut. This suggests that the supplements not only decrease the risk of intestinal problems but also support a healthy gastrointestinal tract and therefore a healthy immune response.

- Take two capsules of an essential fatty acid formula twice a day. Essential fatty acids play an important role in immunity, among numerous other bodily functions and processes. Look for a formula that supplies 90 to 180 milligrams of eicosapentaenoic acid, 60 to 120 milligrams of docosahexaenoic acid, 60 to 80 IU of vitamin E from d-alpha tocopherol succinate, and amylase, protease, and lipase enzymes.

- Take two capsules of a multivitamin/mineral supplement twice a day. (For a complete list of ingredients, see page 325.)

For additional immune support, you may want to incorporate the following strategies into your self-care regimen.

- Adopt a wholesome, balanced diet of primarily organic foods.

- Restrict or eliminate sugars and other refined carbohydrates, high-sodium foods, caffeine, alcohol, artificial sweeteners, and food colorings and additives.

- Practice meditation and yoga to defuse stress, which affects gastrointestinal health and therefore immune function. The gastrointestinal tract contains so many nerve cells that some experts refer to it as the body's second brain. As you might imagine, it's exquisitely sensitive to stress. Anything that helps short-circuit the body's stress response will protect the gastrointestinal tract against the effects of stress.

  Both meditation and yoga are excellent for calming the emotions and fostering inner strength and balance. While I recommend signing up for a yoga class to learn proper form and technique, meditation doesn't necessarily require such formal practice. The simplest exercises can be done while you're standing in line at the supermarket, waiting in a line of traffic, or sitting at your desk. For a sample meditation, see page 167.

CHAPTER 12

Lower Your Risk
of Heart Disease

HEART DISEASE is the number one killer in the United States, responsible for 41 percent of all deaths each year. This figure includes more than 500,000 women, challenging the conventional wisdom that heart disease is a "man's problem."

It's estimated that nearly 60 million Americans are living with the condition.

The good news is that heart disease readily responds to dietary and lifestyle changes. What's more, research and clinical evidence have shown that enzyme supplements can be an important component of heart disease treatment and prevention.

While this chapter is not meant to offer every solution for the vast spectrum of heart problems, it covers the most important clinically proven strategies for correcting them. It also explores the value of optimal digestion and thorough absorption of key nutrients in maintaining a healthy heart and blood vessels, which are vital to general good health.

ANGINA

Angina pectoris is a medical term for chest pain that results from coronary heart disease. It is a symptom of myocardial ischemia, a condition in which the heart muscle doesn't receive sufficient blood for a given level of work.

Typically, angina occurs because of a heart attack, atherosclerosis, or inflammation of the sac that surrounds the heart. Not all chest pain is angina, however. Sometimes it's a symptom of heartburn, a panic attack, a pinched nerve, inflamed ribs, swallowing disorders, shingles, gallbladder or pancreatic problems, sore chest muscles, or cancer.

Each year, about 600,000 people go to hospital emergency rooms because of chest pain. Of this number, more than 100,000 turn out to have heartburn, or gastroesophageal reflux disease (GERD), rather than angina. Both chest pain from heartburn and severe angina can occur after a heavy meal. In general, though, the pain probably is a result of heartburn if it is worse at night or after lying down.

Heartburn and heart disease often coexist. In fact, one theory suggests that in patients with coronary artery disease, acid reflux may be responsible for triggering angina flare-ups. In these cases, experts believe, acid in the esophagus may activate nerves that temporarily impair blood flow to the heart.[1]

Interestingly, Dr. Ellen has noticed that many patients with fibromyalgia report chest pain that's similar to angina. Usually, they come to the BioSET Clinic/Institute after they receive a clean bill of health from their physicians, who perform thorough workups but find no signs of heart trouble. In fibromyalgia, much of the discomfort is in the upper body, which certainly could be mistaken for angina or a heart attack. Patients have gotten very positive results with enzyme therapy.

If you ever experience unexplained chest pain, do not attempt to self-diagnose; it's vital to seek emergency medical care without delay. Even if it turns out that the pain is unrelated to a heart problem, you don't want to take the chance. In this case, it really is better to be safe than sorry.

DR. ELLEN'S PRESCRIPTION

Conventional medical treatment for angina pectoris includes aspirin, which inhibits blood clotting; nitroglycerine, which dilates blood vessels and improves blood flow to and from the heart; and beta blockers, drugs that help relax the heart muscle, slow the heartbeat, and lower blood pressure. Sometimes doctors recommend angioplasty, a surgical procedure to open any blocked blood vessels that are responsible for the chest pain.[2]

While you should never discontinue or alter the dosage of a heart medication without consulting your physician, you may want to ask about adding the following supplements to your self-care regimen.

- Take two capsules of a full-spectrum digestive enzyme blend (see page 33) twice a day, either 1 hour before or 2 hours after a meal. Supporting proper digestion may help prevent angina flare-ups. Look for a formula that contains amylase, protease, lipase, cellulase, and bromelain enzymes.

- Take 25 to 50 milligrams of magnesium twice a day. Recent research indicates that this mineral is beneficial for treating and preventing heart disease. It appears to lower blood pressure and support recovery after a heart attack by inhibiting blood clots, widening arteries, and stabilizing dangerous heart arrhythmias.

- Take 200 to 500 milligrams of hawthorn berry extract a day. This herb relieves angina, lowers blood pressure, and helps the heart pump blood more efficiently.

- Take 30 to 60 milligrams of coenzyme Q_{10} (CoQ_{10}) a day. An established heart tonic, CoQ_{10} not only relieves angina but also stabilizes heart arrhythmias, strengthens the heart muscle, and improves circulation in people with congestive heart failure.

- Take 60 to 300 milligrams of garlic a day. It may reduce blood clotting and lower cholesterol, both of which contribute to angina.

- Take 50 to 100 IU of vitamin E from d-alpha tocopherol succinate a day. Research suggests a modest dosage of this antioxidant vitamin can help protect against heart disease.

FROM DR. ELLEN'S CASE FILES

Pearl developed angina while still in her forties. Over the years, she underwent three balloon angioplasties, which didn't bring the lasting relief she had hoped for. She was 67 by the time she came to the BioSET Clinic/Institute. By then, she had noticed that her angina flare-ups occurred in combination with heartburn after she ate certain foods. She was certain that somehow her symptoms were related.

After thorough testing, Pearl and I were convinced that certain food sensitivities were contributing to both her angina and her heartburn. I also determined that Pearl had trouble digesting proteins and fats and was deficient in magnesium. Based on her test results, I recommended a protein/fat digestive enzyme, a cardiovascular enzyme formula, and a magnesium supplement. I also administered BioSET treatments to help clear up some of her food sensitivities.

As with virtually all of my angina patients, I advised Pearl to make some dietary changes. She switched to a mostly vegetarian diet with few carbohydrates and a moderate amount of fats. Her new diet consisted primarily of vegetables and fruits; modest amounts of nuts, seeds, and fish; and a minimum of dairy products. At my suggestion, she avoided all foods containing sugar, white flour, artificial sweeteners, additives, and preservatives. I also recommended steering clear of tobacco smoke, alcohol, chlorinated water, and fluoride in all forms (including toothpaste).

Pearl began working out for 1½ to 2 hours 4 days a week, engaging in both aerobic activity and weight training. I advised her to work with a personal trainer who specialized in cardiac rehabilitation. I also suggested trying meditation and yoga, which would help relieve stress while improving her physical fitness.

With treatment, Pearl has experienced very few angina

episodes. She is faithful to her enzyme supplement program and her exercise routine. While her eating habits have waxed and waned, she remains committed to a low-carbohydrate, mostly vegetarian diet.

HIGH CHOLESTEROL

Part of the standard bloodwork for heart disease risk is a lipid panel that measures total cholesterol and triglycerides. Usually, total cholesterol includes numbers for the two primary cholesterol subclasses: high-density lipoprotein, or HDL, and low-density lipoprotein, or LDL. You probably have heard that the lower your LDL cholesterol and triglycerides, the lower your heart disease risk. It's true, but as we'll discuss in a bit, it's not the whole story. Nevertheless, among people with heart disease, elevated cholesterol (especially LDL) and triglyceride levels are quite common.

People who run low in lipase, the fat-digesting enzyme, may be especially prone to cholesterol problems. In the intestines, fat coats food particles and interferes with their breakdown into other food components, including carbohydrates and proteins. As the food particles find their way into the bloodstream, they take their fatty coatings along with them, which is one way that fat elevates total cholesterol levels.

Because fat isn't water soluble, it must undergo a special digestive process in order to break down into end products that the body can use. This is where lipase enters the picture, splitting fat into its component fatty acids plus glycerol by adding water (a process known as hydrolysis). Lipase gets an assist from bile, which breaks down the large fat molecules into tiny droplets that are more water soluble. Bile and lipase work together to ensure complete, thorough fat digestion.

While proper fat digestion can help prevent high cholesterol, it's equally important to thwart the process by which LDL cholesterol—the unhealthy kind—can harm blood vessels and set the stage for atherosclerosis. According to one prominent theory, the atherosclerotic disease process begins when LDL undergoes oxidation by free radicals. In this modified form, LDL becomes sticky. If a blood vessel becomes injured—because of infection or high blood pressure, for example—the exposed protein in the vessel wall can serve as a binding site for lipoprotein(a). This fatty substance acts like Velcro, grabbing LDL and attaching it to the vessel wall. In response, the immune system releases immune cells known as macrophages, which rush to the wound site and gobble up the LDL. They also trigger the inflammation that leads to atherosclerosis.

The notion of plaques depositing on blood vessel walls, causing atherosclerosis and coronary heart disease, is simplistic and somewhat outdated. Over the past 20 years, scientists have devoted considerable attention to defining and understanding the role of inflammation in the disease process. The most potent of the body's immune defenses, inflammation occurs when immune cells release specific mediators that control localized circulation and cellular activity. Typically, this can produce symptoms such as pain, swelling, redness, and heat in the affected tissues.

The inflammatory response evolved as a means for the body to make war on invading microorganisms. Many of modern civilization's serious medical conditions, especially autoimmune diseases, are manifestations of chronic inflammation. We absolutely believe that chronic inflammation bears at least some responsibility for the prevalence of heart problems in the United States.

According to research, antioxidant compounds—including certain enzymes—may help prevent atherosclerosis by reducing the production of free radicals, which are by-products of poor digestion and elevated toxin levels as well as normal biochemical processes. Fewer free radicals mean a lower risk of oxidized LDL cholesterol, which in turn means a lower risk of inflammation of the blood vessel walls.

Enzyme therapy may have a more general effect on cholesterol levels as well. Through years of treating other chronic health problems by customizing enzyme regimens and clearing up food sensitivities, we have noticed considerable reductions in total cholesterol. With lower total cholesterol, there's less LDL available for oxidation in the first place.

DR. ELLEN'S PRESCRIPTION

The cardiovascular enzyme formula that appears on page 202 is especially beneficial for maintaining healthy cholesterol levels. The following strategies can help as well.

- Take 60 to 300 milligrams of garlic a day. In laboratory studies, garlic reduces cholesterol production by 40 to 60 percent. It also prevents blood fats from sticking to blood vessel walls.

- Take 50 to 100 milligrams of manganese a day. This mineral appears to elevate HDL cholesterol, the beneficial kind that helps keep blood vessels clear.

- Take 100 to 200 milligrams of alpha lipoic acid twice a day. A powerful antioxidant, alpha lipoic acid inhibits the oxidation of LDL cholesterol, which triggers the inflammatory response.

- Eat plenty of foods that help lower cholesterol, such as pecans, peanuts, spinach, sweet potatoes, pineapple and pineapple juice, oatmeal, shredded wheat and raisin bran cereals, rice, and beans.

FROM DR. ELLEN'S CASE FILES   *Judy, age 51, was referred to the BioSET Clinic/Institute because of extremely high cholesterol as well as menopausal symptoms such as hot flashes, insomnia, and frequent mood swings. Her internist had prescribed medication and recommended dietary changes, which she followed to the letter. She was very active and fit, but her cholesterol remained high.*

Perplexed by the whole matter, Judy decided to explore other options to help rein in her cholesterol readings. She had heard about my work with enzyme therapy and wondered whether it might help.

Upon examination, I discovered that Judy had extreme difficulty digesting proteins and fats. Since she still showed signs of inflammation from prior neck and shoulder injuries, I wondered whether she might be prone to an inflammatory response, which could increase her risk for atherosclerosis.

I advised Judy to take a protein/fat digestive enzyme as well as an enzyme formula with vitamin E, coenzyme Q$_{10}$, hawthorn leaf, and large amounts of lipase to ensure complete fat digestion. No significant dietary changes seemed necessary, since she already was eating quite healthfully. The digestive enzyme was her most basic requirement.

At my suggestion, Judy waited 4 months before having another cholesterol test. When she did, she was astonished: Her cholesterol had dropped 50 points, from 260 to 210. Her internist was just as surprised—and quite pleased. Judy is living proof of the powerful connection between enzyme therapy and heart health.

HYPERHOMOCYSTEINEMIA

Among the possible causes of atherosclerosis is a condition known as hyperhomocysteinemia, which involves an elevated level of the amino acid homocysteine. In excess amounts, homocysteine can irritate blood vessels and contribute to blockages. In fact, physicians consider it a significant risk factor for heart disease—perhaps more significant than high cholesterol.

Homocysteine forms during the metabolism of another amino acid, methionine. In hyperhomocysteinemia, something disrupts the metabolic process, shifting homocysteine production into overdrive. That something appears to be an enzyme deficiency,[3] although research suggests that certain medications—such as chemotherapy drugs, diuretics, and anticonvulsants—and cigarette smoke can aggravate matters. (Incidentally, an enzyme deficiency is also responsible for homocysteinuria, a genetic disorder that causes premature atherosclerosis, among other serious medical complications.)

DR. ELLEN'S PRESCRIPTION

To prevent homocysteine levels from climbing too high, you need to maintain adequate levels of three B vitamins—B$_6$, B$_{12}$, and folate. Just as important, you need to thoroughly digest and absorb these nutrients. This is where a full-spectrum digestive enzyme blend can help.

INFLAMMATION

You've seen how oxidized LDL can attach to an injured blood vessel wall, launching an inflammatory response. This damage can also occur with immune system by-products known as circulating immune complexes, or CICs. The formation of CICs begins when poor digestion allows food particles to gain entry to the bloodstream. There, the immune system recognizes them as invaders, or antigens, and sends in antibodies to fight them. The antigens and antibodies combine to produce CICs, which play a major role in inflammation.

An overabundance of CICs can trigger a cascade of biochemical events that eventually lead to tissue damage. Generally, this damage won't occur unless injured blood vessels allow the immune complexes to get between layers of otherwise healthy tissue. The influx of CICs, in combination with immune mediators, could punch enough holes in a cell to kill it. This is precisely what you want to happen if the cell happens to be a virus, a bacterium, or another infectious microorganism. But if the cell is one of your own, the CICs can set in motion an inflammatory response.

Nature has provided a wonderful defense mechanism in inflammation, but sometimes it goes too far or lasts too long. Then it can do more harm than good.

DR. ELLEN'S PRESCRIPTION

Enzyme therapy helps inflammation not by disrupting the inflammatory process but by supporting and quickening it so the body isn't in an inflammatory state for a prolonged period. What's more, because enzymes occur naturally in the body, they won't produce the side effects that pharmaceutical anti-inflammatories can cause.

The protease enzyme that is a component of the basic plan (see page 32) is quite effective at easing inflammation. I do recommend a somewhat higher dosage, though—one capsule three to five times a day, either 1 hour before or 2 hours after a meal. You may also want to add the following supplements to your self-care regimen—along with a full-spectrum digestive enzyme blend to support nutrient absorption.

- *Bromelain (25 to 50 milligrams):* reduces swelling and inflammation

- *Vitamin C from acerola cherry extract (60 to 120 milligrams):* speeds healing and prevents bruising

- *Grapeseed extract (5 to 10 milligrams):* blocks the release of prostaglandins, chemicals that play a key role in the inflammatory process

- *Quercetin (10 to 20 milligrams):* reduces inflammation and prevents bruising

HIGH BLOOD PRESSURE

Current federal guidelines define high blood pressure, or hypertension, as consistent blood pressure readings of 140/90 mmHg (millimeters of mercury) or higher. An optimal reading is under 120/80 mmHg.

Hypertension directly increases the risk of coronary heart disease (which can lead to a heart attack) and stroke, especially when it occurs in combination with other risk factors. While it can affect virtually anyone, it's most prevalent among middle-age African-Americans; the elderly; and people who are obese, drink heavily, or have diabetes or kidney disease. Those who are prone to anxiety or depression commonly develop high blood pressure as well.

Many people who have hypertension don't even realize it. It causes no specific symptoms and no warning signs, which is why it has earned a reputation as a "silent killer." The good news is that hypertension responds quite well to dietary and lifestyle changes in combination with enzyme therapy.

DR. ELLEN'S PRESCRIPTION

Virtually all of my patients with hypertension take the cardio-vascular enzyme formula that appears on page 202. For optimal blood pressure control, I also recommend these dietary strategies.

- Limit your sodium intake to 2,400 milligrams a day, the equivalent of about 6 grams of salt.

- Eat plenty of bananas, cantaloupe, potatoes, and other fruits and vegetables that are rich in heart-healthy potassium.

- Snack on tree nuts—almonds, brazil nuts, cashews, hazelnuts, macadamia nuts, pecans, pistachios, and walnuts—and peanuts. All of these contain compounds that are good for the heart.

- Increase your consumption of flavonoid sources, such as legumes, soy products, nuts, green tea, and citrus fruits (oranges, tangerines, and grapefruit). These phytonutrients may help protect and strengthen blood vessels, among numerous other health benefits.

FROM DR. ELLEN'S CASE FILES *Ken, age 47, came to the BioSET Clinic/Institute seeking relief from his hay fever symptoms. During his initial consultation, he mentioned that he had been dealing with hypertension for the previous 2 years. He saw no improvement with any natural therapy, which concerned him since he wasn't ready to take medication.*

As we spoke, Ken admitted to experiencing quite a bit of stress in his life. His wife had been diagnosed with cancer, and his job was demanding. He really didn't know how I could help him with his hypertension, but he hoped that I could at least clear up the chronic sinusitis brought on by his hay fever.

I explained my ideas about the relationship among hypertension, food sensitivities, and poor digestion. I was confident that enzyme therapy would clear up his sinusitis, and I suspected that it would improve his blood pressure as well.

When I did my workup, I found Ken to be carbohydrate intolerant and hypoglycemic—that is, he had low blood sugar. I recommended an enzyme regimen for cardiovascular health, along with the diet for carbohydrate intolerance (see page 295). Each time Ken returned to my office for BioSET treatments to clear up his hay fever, I checked his blood pressure as well.

Over the course of 6 months, Ken's sinusitis subsided, and his blood pressure gradually returned to normal. He continues to limit his carbohydrate consumption and to take his enzyme supplements; he's noticed that if he slacks off, his blood pressure creeps up a bit. His doctor—who's open to natural therapies—is pleased with the results of his treatment.

STROKE

A stroke is a cardiovascular event that affects the blood vessels supplying blood—and therefore oxygen and nutrients—to the brain. If one of these blood vessels bursts or becomes blocked, the area of the brain that the vessel nourishes doesn't get the blood that it needs. Nerve cells die within minutes, and the part of the body controlled by these cells can no longer function properly. Because the cells can't be replaced, the devastating effects of stroke often become permanent.

Perhaps the most important measure for preventing stroke is maintaining a healthy endothelium, the cell layer that forms the surface of blood vessel walls. As long as the endothelium remains smooth and intact, it won't invite the plaque deposits or inflammation that can lead to blockages.

In the past couple of years, research has shown that nitric oxide—a small molecule that's released by the endothelium—may be helpful not only for preventing new arterial plaques but also for removing existing ones. As a bonus, when nitric acid enters a cell, it triggers a biochemical reaction that ultimately relaxes and dilates the blood vessels. Under certain conditions, it also reduces the production of free radicals. All of these benefits add up to a reduced stroke risk.

The amino acid arginine is a precursor of nitric oxide; it, too, can help shrink arterial plaques. Studies suggest that arginine supplements not only improve endothelial function but also slow the progression of atherosclerosis, which is a risk factor for stroke. What's more, the improvement in endothelial function appears to be associated with improvements in cholesterol levels and blood pressure readings.

To prevent the blockages that can lead to stroke, it's also important to reduce the risk of blood clots. New research shows that many people have hypercoagulation—that is, a tendency to form clots more quickly or more aggressively than normal. One of the by-products of an overactive coagulation system is fibrin. In the brain, fibrin deposits in small blood vessels can set the stage for mini-strokes.

Enzymes can help reduce clotting. They are fibrinolytic, which means they can prevent fibrin from sticking to blood vessel walls. They also help separate blood platelets, which improves blood flow and minimizes clotting.

DR. ELLEN'S PRESCRIPTION

The cardiovascular enzyme formula on page 202 is critical to stroke prevention. In general, I don't recommend arginine supplements because this amino acid is so readily available from foods, such as meats, poultry, fish, dairy products, and nuts. To ensure thorough digestion of these foods and optimal absorption of their nutrients, I do recommend a full-spectrum digestive enzyme blend.

Arginine supplements may help some cases of mildly elevated blood pressure by enhancing the synthesis of nitric oxide in the endothelial cells. This dilates blood vessel walls and improves blood flow around the heart. In fact, nitric oxide is the body's most potent blood vessel expander. If your cardiologist prescribes arginine supplements, I would combine them with the full-spectrum digestive enzyme so your body fully assimilates the arginine.

CIRCULATORY DISORDERS

Certain circulatory disorders respond quite well to enzyme therapy. Enzymes reduce edema (excess accumulation of fluids in body tissues) and prevent fibrin deposits on blood vessel walls. This helps ease swelling and pain while improving blood fluidity and flow.

Back in the 1960s, Max Wolf, MD, and his colleagues concluded that certain enzyme formulas are superior for treating phlebitis,[4] a circulatory disorder that involves inflammation of a vein, usually in the leg but sometimes elsewhere. Phlebitis and its sibling condition, thrombophlebitis (which refers to formation of a clot in an inflamed vein), commonly occur as a result of hypercoagulation of the blood or trauma to the blood vessel wall. Standing or sitting for long periods—as on an airplane, for example—can also cause inflammation and possibly a clot. The telltale symptoms include pain, swelling, and possibly skin discoloration.

Since Dr. Wolf's pioneering research, numerous studies have borne out the effectiveness of enzyme therapy, even in advanced cases of post-thrombotic syndrome, in which a persistent blood clot produces myriad symptoms, such as calf pain, swelling, nighttime leg cramps, venous ulcers, and skin disorders.[5] In one such study, leg swelling diminished by more than 50 percent after 7 to 14 days of treatment, allowing patients to cut back on their diuretic medications.

DR. ELLEN'S PRESCRIPTION

For phlebitis, varicose veins, and other circulatory disorders, I recommend taking two capsules of the following enzyme formula twice a day, either 1 hour before or 2 hours after a meal. If you can't find a single formula with at least the primary ingredients (in bold), you can take separate supplements with a full-spectrum digestive enzyme blend for optimal nutrient absorption.

Digestive enzymes. Ideally, the product you choose will contain 30,000 to 100,000 HUT of protease and 200 to 1,500 LU of lipase. Another important enzyme for cardiovascular health is natokinase, in a recommended dose of 1,500 to 2,000 FTU. Natokinase protects against the effects of fibrin, which builds up on blood vessel walls. The only caveat is that if you're taking a blood thinner such as warfarin (Coumadin), be sure to talk to your doctor before beginning supplementation.

Vitamin C from acerola cherry extract (60 to 120 milligrams). An antioxidant, vitamin C helps strengthen blood vessel walls.

Vitamin E from d-alpha tocopherol succinate (50 to 100 IU). This vitamin also has antioxidant properties and can relieve the severe leg pain caused by circulatory problems.

Collinsonia root (400 to 600 milligrams). By reducing pressure inside blood vessels, this herb keeps varicose veins from worsening.

Horse chestnut (300 to 600 milligrams). Horse chestnut reduces inflammation and swelling in blood vessels.

Grapeseed extract (50 to 100 milligrams). This extract supports blood vessel integrity.

Gotu kola herb extract (200 to 400 milligrams). The herb gotu kola strengthens veins and supports vein health.

Ginkgo biloba leaf extract (100 to 200 milligrams). Like gotu kola, ginkgo strengthens veins and supports vein health.

Bilberry fruit extract (300 to 600 milligrams). This herb has a time-honored reputation for relieving varicose veins.

Butcher's broom (30 to 50 milligrams). Butcher's broom helps shrink varicose veins.

Quercetin (20 to 40 milligrams). An anti-inflammatory, this nutrient helps repair and maintain blood vessels.

FROM DR. ELLEN'S CASE FILES

Tim, the 42-year-old husband of one of my BioSET practitioners, developed phlebitis during a long flight from Australia to New York. His legs became extremely swollen. A doctor immediately prescribed Coumadin, which works by inhibiting vitamin K–dependent coagulation factors. Tim's wife contacted me, hoping that I could offer some additional suggestions.

I mentioned how successful enzymes have been in treating circulatory disorders and inhibiting clot formation. So Tim began taking large amounts of protease enzyme, which works systemically to prevent clots and reduce inflam-

matory reactions in blood vessel walls.[6] *I advised him to take a higher dose for the first 2 months, then taper off to a maintenance dose.*

Tim has been following this enzyme regimen ever since. He is doing very well, with no circulation problems. He reports that his energy and immune response are much improved as well. He is so enthusiastic about enzyme therapy that he has become an associate BioSET practitioner, helping his wife in her practice.

THE BEST MEDICINE FOR HEART HEALTH

The advances in heart disease treatment and prevention are so remarkable that cardiologists all over the world should learn about them and their lifesaving benefits. Enzyme therapy, in particular, can reduce the enormous number of prescriptions that doctors pass out to patients with angina, high blood pressure, and high cholesterol. It is also an effective preventive measure.

This is not meant to downplay the importance of diet and lifestyle in cardiovascular conditioning. Perhaps taking pills seems much easier than making changes in personal habits, but in order for enzyme supplements to do their job, they require good working conditions. This means wholesome foods from which to assimilate nutrients and a lifestyle that supports optimal health rather than challenging it.

We can live to a ripe old age without depending on potent medications, with their often serious side effects. Enzymes are the medicine for the 21st century. While heart disease can kill, enzymes—the spark of life—can restore, repair, and revive.

DR. ELLEN'S PRESCRIPTION

For several of the conditions in this chapter, I've recommended a general cardiovascular enzyme formula. This formula is also an excellent choice if you simply want extra protection and support for your cardiovascular system. It helps regulate blood fats, minimizes clotting, and ensures healthy blood flow throughout the body. The suggested dosage is one capsule twice a day, either 1 hour before or 2 hours after a meal.

Remember, you can take the individual herbs and nutrients if you can't get all of them in a single product. Actually, if you pair just of the primary ingredients (in bold) with a full-spectrum digestive enzyme blend, it should meet your needs.

Digestive enzymes. Look for a formula that contains 30,000 to 100,000 HUT of protease, 200 to 1,500 LU of lipase, and 1,500 to 2,000 FTU of natokinase. (*Note:* Be sure to consult your doctor before taking natokinase in any form if you're already on a blood thinner such as warfarin, or Coumadin.)

Hawthorn leaf and flower extract (200 to 500 milligrams). Hawthorn leaf improves blood flow and acts as a diuretic, but it's much less toxic than its pharmaceutical counterparts.

Garlic bulb concentrate (60 to 300 milligrams). Garlic's history as a therapeutic agent dates back thousands of years. Some current research is exploring the herb's potential to inhibit hardening of the arteries and reduce the stickiness of blood platelets so they're less likely to attach to each other and to blood vessel walls.

Vitamin E as d-alpha tocopherol succinate (50 to 100 IU). D-alpha tocopherol is the most common and most potent form of vitamin E. Research has shown that vitamin E helps protect against heart disease, including heart attack and stroke, by reducing the harmful effects of LDL cholesterol and preventing blood clots. It may also intervene in the inflammatory process that contributes to heart disease.

Coenzyme Q_{10} (25 to 50 milligrams). The primary purpose of CoQ_{10} is to serve as a catalyst, speeding up vital metabolic processes that enable cells to digest food and use it for energy. CoQ_{10} is especially abundant in the energy-intensive cells of the heart, helping it beat its normal 100,000-plus times each day. As an antioxidant, CoQ_{10} helps to repair and prevent free radical damage.

Grapeseed extract (20 to 40 milligrams). This herb treats blood vessel disorders and lowers heart disease risk.

Alpha linolenic acid (30 to 50 milligrams). An important source of essential fatty acids, alpha linolenic acid helps protect against heart disease.

Vitamin B$_6$ (6 to 12 milligrams); vitamin B$_{12}$ (175 to 250 micrograms); and folic acid (25 to 50 micrograms). This trio of B vitamins reduces the risk of heart disease and stroke.

Potassium (50 to 100 milligrams). Potassium is important for lowering blood pressure and stabilizing heart rhythm.

Acetyl L-carnitine (50 to 100 milligrams). A natural enzyme from soybeans, L-carnitine successfully removes fibrin deposits from blood vessel walls. It also strengthens the heart and supports recovery after heart attack.

Guggulipid (80 to 160 milligrams). Guggulipids are known to lower cholesterol.

To round out your self-care regimen, I suggest the following strategies.

- Take one capsule of a multivitamin/mineral formula twice a day. (For a list of recommended ingredients, see page 325.)

- Engage in regular aerobic activity—such as brisk walking, jogging, or swimming—for at least 30 minutes 3 days a week. In my experience, moderate exercise done consistently over a long period is much more effective than strenuous exercise done in short bursts. If you have hypertension or any other heart problem, be sure to check with your doctor before beginning any fitness program.

- Maintain a healthy weight. (For advice on weight loss, see chapter 7.)

- Manage stress by practicing meditation, tai chi, yoga, or another relaxation technique. It helps short-circuit the body's stress response, which raises blood pressure.

CHAPTER 13

Treat and Prevent Diabetes

THROUGH YEARS OF clinical practice, Dr, Ellen has identified one characteristic shared by 80 percent of her patients: carbohydrate intolerance. They're unable to thoroughly break down sugars and starches, which makes them susceptible to cravings for carbohydrates and can lead to myriad chronic health problems, from skin conditions and mood disorders to heart disease and obesity.

Because people who are carbohydrate intolerant tend to overeat carbs, they are also at risk for high blood sugar, insulin resistance, and eventually type 2 (non-insulin-dependent) diabetes. In this form of diabetes, the pancreas is able to produce insulin, but the hormone can't do its job, either because the blood contains too much fat or because the cells don't allow insulin to unload sugar from the bloodstream. In response, the pancreas secretes even more of the hormone. This is why people with type 2 diabetes tend to have both high insulin levels and high blood sugar levels. If they continue to fill up on carbohydrates, they push their insulin and blood sugar even higher.

Type 2 diabetes accounts for 90 percent of all diagnosed diabetes cases. According to the National Institute of Diabetes and Digestive and Kidney Diseases, as many as 16 million Americans have type 2 diabetes, and the number is rising at an alarming rate. What's more, while the disease generally comes on at middle age, it's becoming increasingly common in kids.

In type 1 (insulin-dependent) diabetes, the pancreas loses its ability to produce insulin, leading to a deficiency of the hormone. This form of diabetes is beyond the scope of our respective practices. We refer patients with type 1 diabetes to an endocrinologist, who specializes in diseases of the endocrine system, which includes the hormone-producing glands and organs. In the following discussion, any mention of diabetes refers to type 2.

Diabetes is a formidable illness because a high concentration of sugar in the bloodstream is very dangerous to the body. Specifically, it causes an accumulation of sorbitol, a by-product of blood sugar, which in turn triggers the swelling of body tissues, especially in the eyes and nerves.

Blood sugar also binds with and chemically alters proteins. The modified proteins can accumulate in cells and set the stage for complications that affect the eyes, kidneys, and cardiovascular system. Excess blood sugar can also increase production of free radicals, which cause damage that leads to other chronic health problems, such as heart disease and cancer.

For people who have diabetes, enzyme therapy is more than just nutritional support. Enzymes can restore balance and resilience to a body that's facing challenges on a variety of fronts because diabetes affects so many organs and systems. Even for those who don't have diabetes, enzymes can safeguard against the disease by ensuring proper digestion, which is important for stabilizing blood sugar.

Before we get too far into the discussion of enzyme therapy, let's take a closer look at how diabetes happens. While it has a number of risk factors, diet usually bears much of the blame.

Not Just an Adult Disease

For the first time in our nation's history, doctors are seeing children who have type 2 diabetes. Among kids with diabetes, between 20 and 30 percent had type 2 in 2002, compared with fewer than 5 percent in 1994. The change is occurring because this generation has a steady diet of foods and beverages with lots of sugar but very little nutritional value. Even though children are eating more than ever, their bodies are starved for nutrients.

Dr. Ellen has done many interviews in which the host points out how the media bombard our kids with ads for junk food and how this phenomenon has contributed to poor eating habits and health problems.[1] While this is true, to some degree we're using the media as an excuse. Placing blame is easier than taking responsibility.

The bottom line is that good nutrition begins at home. If parents are willing to teach their children about proper nutrition and to set a good example by preparing healthy meals of wholesome foods, all those ads for junk food will have less impact. More than likely, we'd also see a corresponding decline in the incidence of type 2 diabetes among our kids.

SUGAR SETS THE STAGE

The diabetes disease process often begins with excessive sugar consumption and poor sugar digestion. Sugar is a form of carbohydrate; in fact, carbohydrates consist of sugar molecules joined together by chemical bonds to form long chains.

When you eat a food rich in carbohydrates—which includes grains, fruits, and vegetables, among a wide variety of foods—the digestive process splits the carbohydrates into their component sugars. This process begins in the mouth with thorough chewing, which activates the food's own enzymes as well as amylase, a salivary enzyme. Amylase breaks down starches into fragments, most of which are disaccharides—that is, molecules with two sugars.

From the mouth, the food travels to the upper stomach, where amylase continues to do its job until the stomach acid deactivates it. Then the food passes out of the stomach into the small intestine, where even more powerful enzymes break down any remaining carbohydrate into disaccharides and eventually into monosaccharides—molecules with a single sugar. The monosaccharides are small enough to absorb rapidly and easily into the bloodstream.

Once they cross over the intestinal lining, the sugar molecules enter the portal vein, which carries blood to the liver. The liver cells take up any molecules that aren't already glucose and convert them. Because the liver can't use all of the glucose, the body stashes away any leftovers as glycogen. Then, if glucose runs low, the body can tap its glycogen stores.

This is a very important protective pathway because while the body uses glucose for energy, it seldom needs the entire supply right away—only in cases of extreme physical exertion, such as running a marathon. If all that glucose headed directly into the bloodstream, blood sugar levels would skyrocket.

In the meantime, the absorption of sugar through the intestinal lining prompts the pancreas to release insulin, which is responsible for escorting the sugar from the bloodstream into the cells. The amount of insulin should be proportionate to the amount of sugar entering the portal vein at any given moment. If you eat a high-carbohydrate meal, for example, a lot of sugar floods the portal vein at once. In response, the pancreas churns out more insulin and continues to do so until the amount of sugar in the bloodstream returns to normal.

Insulin serves several important functions in the body. First and foremost, it helps balance blood sugar, thus protecting the body and brain from the effects of excessive blood sugar. It's the most important nutrient transport hormone, delivering not only sugars but also proteins and fats into cells. And it alerts the liver when there's too much sugar in the body so the liver can step up the conversion of sugar to fat to help stabilize blood sugar levels.[2]

Each cell has numerous receptors that open up to insulin, allowing the hormone to deliver its load of sugar for use as fuel. Actually, insulin works in conjunction with another hormone, glucagon, to regulate the distribution of nutrients. As with insulin, the pancreas is responsible for the release of glucagon into the bloodstream. The difference is that glucagon is a response to proteins, while insulin is a response to carbohydrates and some amino acids.

Glucagon mobilizes nutrients through three primary actions. It directs the liver to send glucose into the bloodstream so it's available to the brain and body; it instructs cells to free up fats for use as fuel; and it signals cells to release proteins, which serve as building materials for muscles, bones, skin, hair, and fingernails.

The ratio of insulin to glucagon determines how the body utilizes and stores the various nutrients. For example, when you eat carbohydrates alone, they enter the bloodstream quickly, prompting a rise in insulin and a corresponding decline in blood sugar. In response to this elevated ratio of insulin to glucagon, the body stores the excess sugar as fat. Conversely, eating a protein-only meal increases glucagon while reducing insulin. Fats and nonstarchy vegetables, meanwhile, have no effect on the ratio of the two hormones.

To maintain a balanced ratio, then, you should build your meals around a healthy mix of carbohydrates; proteins; fats; and nonstarchy vegetables, such as asparagus, broccoli, celery, cucumbers, leeks, and onions.[3] With insulin and glucagon in proper proportion, the body uses carbs and proteins to replenish cellular energy and repair structural components rather than storing them as fat.

A measurement known as the glycemic index (GI) reflects the ratio of insulin to glucagon in a given food. The GI is an indicator of how quickly insulin rises in response to sugar entering the portal vein. The faster insulin rises, and the more sugar entering the portal vein, the higher the glycemic index of a food.

As a rule of thumb, simple sugars such as refined grains have higher GI ratings. Because these grains have been stripped of their fiber, their sugars enter the bloodstream quickly. Whole grains retain their fiber, which slows the rate at which their sugars enter the bloodstream. For this reason, whole grains have lower GIs.[4] (As mentioned in chapter 7, however, we still have reservations about eating any grains, even whole ones.)

Keep in mind that when you eat a meal largely made up of refined carbohydrates, the corresponding rise in insulin signals the liver to convert more sugar into fat. This helps stabilize blood sugar levels but results in fat storage and weight gain.

WHEN INSULIN
CAN'T DO ITS JOB

Years of eating high-carbohydrate meals translates into years of excessive, cumulative sugar buildup in the body. Cells become so saturated that they can't admit any more sugar molecules. They respond by reducing the number of insulin receptors that dot their surfaces, which prevents insulin from dropping off its load of sugar. This is what's known as insulin resistance,[5] a forerunner of type 2 diabetes.

Actually, insulin resistance may be something of a defense mechanism. Cells become insulin resistant because they're trying to protect themselves from the toxic effects of high insulin levels. They reduce their receptor activity so they aren't subject to all that stimuli all the time. In the meantime, the pancreas keeps churning out more and more insulin because it's trying to clear the bloodstream of all the excess sugar. But it can't sustain such a high level of insulin production forever. As it begins slowing down, or as cellular resistance picks up, blood sugar continues to climb (what doctors call hyperglycemia). Eventually, diabetes sets in.

Other factors besides eating too many carbohydrates can trigger or aggravate insulin resistance. For instance, if you reduce the number of calories that you take in, or if you don't properly digest the foods you eat, your body may need to manufacture its own supply of sugar in order to feed your brain. It accomplishes this by converting any glycogen that's stored in liver cells and muscle into glucose. This process can contribute to insulin resistance. So, too, can skipping meals, drinking lots of caffeinated beverages, smoking cigarettes, dealing with persistent stress—and, of course, running low on key enzymes.

Insulin resistance is on the rise in this country, especially among the younger segments of our population. It's the primary symptom of metabolic syndrome, or syndrome X, which the federal government now recognizes as a major risk factor for type 2 diabetes, among other serious medical conditions. (For more information, see "Taking the Mystery Out of Metabolic Syndrome.") Enzyme therapy and lifestyle changes are the best answers to this epidemic, which can seriously compromise our health and longevity.

FROM DR. ELLEN'S CASE FILES
Nancy, age 34, came to the BioSET Clinic/Institute seeking help for her food sensitivities and environmental allergies. At the time, she was also struggling with her weight. She felt very frustrated with her health and her health care.

During our initial consultation, Nancy mentioned that she was monitoring her blood sugar on a daily basis on her doctor's recommendation. She had gotten some very high readings after eating, and her doctor was concerned. He was considering prescribing medication to control her blood sugar, but Nancy preferred to find a natural solution instead.

Taking the Mystery Out of Metabolic Syndrome

According to the American Heart Association, as many as 47 million Americans may have metabolic syndrome, or syndrome X. It's a constellation of symptoms that includes insulin resistance as well as high blood pressure, high blood fats (total cholesterol and triglycerides), and excessive abdominal fat.

While some people have genetic predispositions to metabolic syndrome, lifestyle factors such as overweight and physical inactivity also raise the risk. Over time, it can set the stage for type 2 diabetes as well as heart disease and stroke.

To treat metabolic syndrome, the most important strategies are to shed any extra pounds—especially in the abdominal area—and exercise regularly. Coincidentally, the same strategies can help correct insulin resistance by stabilizing blood sugar levels and preserving insulin sensitivity so the hormone can deliver sugar into cells.

I performed a complete enzyme evaluation and food sensitivity testing, which showed that Nancy was highly sensitive to most starches and sugars as well as to most fruits and some starchy vegetables. The enzyme evaluation also revealed that she was carbohydrate intolerant.

Based on these results, I advised Nancy to follow my diet for carbohydrate intolerance (see page 295). I also recommended a trio of enzyme formulas: one to help digest carbohydrates, another with chromium to stabilize Nancy's blood sugar levels and control her sugar cravings, and a third to alleviate her environmental allergies and improve her liver function.

Nancy tracked her weight, blood sugar, and allergy symptoms for the next month. When she came back to the clinic, she had lost 5 pounds, and her blood sugar had stabilized. Her environmental allergies were improving as well.

Nancy remained a patient for 2 years. To this day, she has not needed to take any medication. She knows that when she goes off her diet and eats too many carbohydrates, her blood sugar level rises, so she remains dedicated. The enzymes definitely have helped with her cravings and mood swings. She is one of hundreds of patients with similar health histories and results.

OTHER DIABETES RISK FACTORS

While insulin resistance is a precursor of type 2 diabetes, other factors can elevate your risk. Actually, the latest research suggests that being overweight or obese is the single most important predictor of diabetes. If you weigh more than you should, following the advice in chapter 7 can help take off those extra pounds.

Poor diet, lack of exercise, smoking, and excessive alcohol consumption also significantly increase your chances of developing type 2 diabetes. These risk factors support the hypothesis that a majority of cases of diabetes could be prevented if people adopted healthier lifestyles.[6]

With this in mind, let's take a closer look at a few of the lesser-known diabetes risk factors. You'll want to consider these as you shape your self-care regimen.

Sugar Sensitivity

The prevalence of sugar in the standard American diet is a major reason for the epidemic of type 2 diabetes in this country. The problem isn't just that we're eating too much sugar, it's also that we aren't digesting it properly. When the digestive process goes awry—because of an enzyme deficiency, for example—it can cause cravings for sugary foods such as candy, baked goods, and ice cream.

Enzyme therapy can correct sugar sensitivity by restoring and supporting proper digestion. This not only eliminates carbohydrate cravings but also prevents sugar from bypassing the liver and seeping directly into the bloodstream. A carbohydrate digestive enzyme can be tremendously successful in treating sugar sensitivity.

Even in the absence of sensitivity, sugar is highly addictive, and its potential impact on our bodies and our health is overwhelming. It inhibits not only healthy digestion but also optimal immune function. The vast majority of doctors' visits each year are for symptoms and conditions that begin with excessive sugar consumption and poor sugar digestion. Diabetes is chief among them.

FROM DR. ELLEN'S CASE FILES

On 5-year-old Eric's first visit to the BioSET Clinic/Institute, he was wearing dark sunglasses and a large baseball cap that sat low on his forehead. He walked with stooped shoulders, like a 90-year-old man with arthritis. My receptionist accompanied him to our "kids' room," where I observed him for a while.

As soon as Eric entered the room, he turned off the light and sat cross-legged on the floor with his head down and his eyes fixed on the floor. Was he autistic? I wondered. Or was he wearing some sort of costume? Both of my guesses were wrong. As his mother, Joan, explained, Eric was extremely sensitive to light. Even when inside a building on a cloudy day, he could not function without wearing sunglasses. His classmates laughed at him, and his teachers were upset by what they described as "his shenanigans."

Joan told me that her son had been given a variety of treatments, from antihistamines and steroids to homeopathy, herbs, and nutritional supplements. Some of the treatments provided some relief, but they worked for only short periods.

When I tried to strike up a conversation with Eric, he didn't respond. Although he wouldn't remove his glasses or his cap so that I could look into his eyes, I could tell from his mannerisms that he was depressed. How could I help him?

I stepped out of the room for a moment and took a deep breath. When I returned, I sat cross-legged on the floor next to Eric. I was barely able to engage his eyes, but nonetheless, I spoke to him from the heart. I told him that I didn't understand exactly how he felt but that a lot of sick children who came to see me got well. "Maybe you can get well," I said. "I can't be sure without testing, but I think your eyes might bother you because you're sensitive to certain foods."

Eric thought for a moment before lifting his head as if to look me in the eyes. Then he took off his hat and removed his glasses. His eyes were so red and sore that they were almost fully closed. I knew that I had to help this child.

Testing confirmed my suspicion that Eric was sensitive to many foods. We immediately scheduled a series of twice-weekly appointments to try to clear up his sensitivities with BioSET treatments. I also advised his mother to start him on a general digestive enzyme.

Over time, Eric became more comfortable with me. Since my daughter was 5 at the time, I was able to relate to him very well. He actually seemed to enjoy his office visits, and I must say that I looked forward to seeing him.

Then came the Friday afternoon when we had planned treatments for Eric's sugar sensitivities. As he walked into my office, I immediately noticed that his demeanor had changed. He was holding on to his mother, and he seemed withdrawn. I asked Joan what had happened. "Well," she replied, "he doesn't want to be treated for sugars."

As I was about to ask why, I suddenly realized that Eric was probably addicted to sugar. He may have reached a turning point in his recovery. With his mother's consent, I decided to administer the BioSET treatment anyway. I also recommended a carbohydrate digestive enzyme, thinking that sugars and starches might be a source of digestive stress. During the appointment, Eric didn't look at me or even acknowledge me; he just grunted as I worked on him. I respected his uneasiness.

The following Tuesday afternoon, the day of Eric's next appointment, I spotted an unfamiliar boy walking around the corner of my office into the kids' room. Usually, I don't see new clients at the end of the day, but I thought perhaps this was an emergency. When I asked my receptionist who the child was, she told me it was Eric. I could hardly believe what she was saying.

I ran to the kids' room and looked at Eric. He wasn't wearing his sunglasses or his cap, and he looked straight into my eyes without squinting. Unaware of my shock, he began talking nonstop. When I glanced at his mother, she was smiling. She told me that after receiving the BioSET treatment for sugar sensitivities and beginning the carbohydrate digestive enzyme, Eric had taken off his sunglasses and hat and hadn't worn them since. I was happy, but I tried to be a little conservative. "Let's wait a few more weeks to see if his condition stays improved," I said.

That same day, Joan revealed something to me that she hadn't mentioned earlier: Her husband, Eric's father, had diabetes. As compensation for his own inability to eat sugar, he constantly offered sweets to his son. Eric slowly became ad-

dicted to sugar—so much so that sugary foods often took the place of healthy meals.

Four years after Eric's treatments, Joan sent me a letter, once again thanking me for her son's complete recovery. She also mentioned that Eric—whose severe food sensitivities had prevented him from participating in sports—had become an outstanding soccer player.

Cow's Milk

When young children consume cow's milk, it triggers an autoimmune reaction that directs antibodies to the pancreas.[7] This can interfere with the production of insulin, setting the stage for type 1 diabetes.

"It is a dietary error to cross species to get milk from another animal," writes John R. Christopher, ND, in his book *Herbal Health Care*. "There is a tremendous difference between human babies and baby calves, and a corresponding difference between the milk that is intended to nourish human babies and baby calves."

The difference identified by Dr. Christopher involves not only the amount of protein but also the type of protein in the two types of milk. Cow's milk consists primarily of casein. In fact, it has 20 times more casein than human milk. This makes assimilating cow's milk next to impossible for humans, according to Dr. Christopher.

When the body can't thoroughly break down protein, it could trigger an autoimmune reaction. In infants, symptoms of this reaction can include nasal congestion, bronchial infection, asthma, skin rash, irritability, and fatigue. Taking a protein digestive enzyme before consuming anything that contains cow's milk should prevent or minimize these symptoms.

While we advise patients to steer clear of cow's milk because of the body's response to it, sometimes they can't avoid it. For example, milk casein even turns up in many soy products, including tofu. So taking a protein digestive enzyme is important.

Agent Orange

During the Vietnam War, U.S. troops relied on Agent Orange—an herbicide that contains the chemical dioxin—to strip trees of their leaves so enemy forces couldn't use them for cover. An Air Force study found that veterans who have high blood levels of dioxin are about 47 percent more likely than those who don't to develop type 2 diabetes. Those with the most dioxin in their blood develop the disease the soonest. (Contrary to other research, however, this study did not find a link between Agent Orange and cancer.)[8]

People who have been exposed to Agent Orange should look into detoxification techniques to help clear the chemical from their system. A liver-detoxifying enzyme can do wonders just for this purpose.

PREVENTION IS
THE BEST PROTECTION

Of all that we've discussed in this chapter, the one message that we hope you'll remember is this: *Type 2 diabetes is preventable.* While a family history of this form of diabetes increases your predisposition to it, dietary and lifestyle factors determine whether or not you develop the full-blown disease—or, if you already have it, how well you manage it.

The primary objective of any plan to control diabetes or to reduce your risk of it is to stabilize your blood sugar levels. If you do nothing else, you should follow these two pieces of advice: First, cut back on carbohydrates, which quickly elevate blood sugar; and second, take digestive enzymes, which ensure proper digestion and assimilation of any carbohydrates that you do eat. Just by doing this, you protect against hyperinsulinemia, in which the pancreas continuously churns out insulin in an effort to remove all that excess sugar from the bloodstream. Chronic hyperinsulinemia leads to insulin resistance and eventually to type 2 diabetes. It also contributes to obesity and damages blood vessels, setting the stage for heart disease.

Robert, age 47, had been diagnosed with type 2 diabetes. His doctor prescribed metformin (Glucophage), a medication that helps control blood sugar levels. While Robert remained faithful to his drug regimen, his diet was dreadful, It showed on the scale: He was 55 pounds heavier than he should have been.

Because he was a truck driver, Robert picked up most of his meals from fast-food restaurants. He ate few whole foods such as vegetables and fruits, instead filling up on sugars, breads, and beer every night. Sometimes I wonder how our bodies can function on such garbage.

Robert came to the BioSET Clinic/Institute because the Glucophage was becoming less and less effective. His doctor told him that he might need to go on insulin, which he dreaded. He really wanted help.

An examination revealed that Robert was carbohydrate and fat intolerant and had severe food sensitivities and toxicity. He was also prone to acid reflux. I recommended several enzyme formulas: one to digest carbohydrates (which helps digest fats as well), another to stabilize his blood sugar levels and control his carb cravings, and a third to relieve his gastric distress. I also gave him a probiotic to help cleanse and detoxify his colon.

For almost an hour, Robert and I talked about his eating habits. With some creative thinking, we came up with several ideas for nutritious meals and snacks that he could eat while on the road. For example, I advised him to always order a salad in restaurants and to eat it before taking a single bite of another food. I also said he should cut back on carbohydrates and build his meals around lean protein and vegetables instead. And he should avoid packaged and processed foods, since they tend to be high in trans fats and additives.

As Robert discovered, while eating healthfully takes some effort, it's quite doable. To his credit, he was very willing to follow my prescription. When he came back to see me 2 months later, his health had improved dramatically. His blood sugar remained stable most of the day. He was 14 pounds lighter, and he wasn't as tired as he had been.

Robert continues to work on his diet. Encouraged by the positive results so far, he's determined not only to avoid insulin but also to reduce his dependence on Glucophage.

DR. ELLEN'S PRESCRIPTION

A number of enzyme formulas and nutritional supplements can help balance blood sugar and prevent or manage insulin resistance and type 2 diabetes. For each of the formulas, I've listed all of the ingredients that I would look for, but I know that finding all of them in a single product could be a challenge. You do have a couple of options: You can choose a product that contains just the primary ingredients (in bold), as long as they come with a full-spectrum digestive enzyme blend. Or you can take these ingredients as separate supplements, along with the digestive enzyme formula for optimal absorption.

- Take one or two capsules of a blood sugar–balancing enzyme formula three times a day, 1 hour before or 2 hours after a meal. This formula supports insulin production by the pancreas and assists insulin in moving sugar from the bloodstream into cells. A quality product will contain the following ingredients.

   Digestive enzymes. Look for a product with 600 to 1,000 LU of amylase.

   Gymnema leaf extract (300 to 450 milligrams). This plant, native to the tropical forests of India, has a long history as a treatment for diabetes. *Gymnema sylvestre* appeared on the U.S. market several years ago and has a demonstrated track record of stabilizing blood sugar.

   Vitamin E as d-alpha tocopherol succinate (60 to 80 IU). In cases of type 2 diabetes, vitamin E has been shown to significantly increase the insulin sensitivity of cells.

Vitamin B$_6$ (4 to 8 milligrams). In general, people with diabetes run low in vitamin B$_6$, a deficiency of which can lead to peripheral neuropathy.

Chromium polynicotinate (200 to 300 micrograms). Chromium may positively influence the rate of insulin production. It also promotes insulin responsiveness in muscle and fat cells and maintains healthy blood sugar levels.

Rice bran (100 to 200 milligrams). Rice bran is a natural source of B vitamins, which help maintain healthy nerves and prevent diabetes complications.

Bitter melon extract (200 to 400 milligrams). This herb helps regulate blood sugar levels.

Garlic bulb concentrate (100 to 200 milligrams). Garlic has a long history as an alternative treatment for diabetes. It's effective at helping to lower blood sugar.

Manganese (2 to 4 milligrams). The pancreatic cells that manufacture insulin need manganese to do their job. A deficiency of the mineral can lead to a shortage of insulin.

Fenugreek seed extract (200 to 300 micrograms). Herbalists have used fenugreek seeds as a substitute for oral insulin. The seed extracts appear to lower blood sugar.

Zinc (10 to 20 milligrams). Zinc reduces the risk of type 2 diabetes.

Magnesium (300 to 500 milligrams). Magnesium protects against type 2 diabetes as well as complications in those who already have the disease.

Quercetin (60 to 90 milligrams). Because quercetin helps the body efficiently use blood sugar, it may help prevent diabetes.

Alpha lipoic acid (600 to 1,200 milligrams). A coenzyme in sugar metabolism, alpha lipoic acid also significantly reduces the symptoms of peripheral neuropathy, a common diabetes complication that involves nerve damage.

- Take two capsules of an adrenal enzyme formula twice a day, either 1 hour before or 2 hours after a meal. The adrenal glands play an important role in sugar metabolism. Prolonged stress can exhaust them, which in turn has a negative effect on blood sugar levels. I recommend a product that contains the following ingredients.

    Digestive enzymes: should supply 60,000 to 90,000 HUT of protease.

    Panax ginseng root extract (320 to 500 milligrams): may lower blood sugar levels.

    Bupleurum root extract (200 to 600 milligrams): enhances adrenal function; also known as Chinese thoroughwax.

    Vitamin C from acerola cherry extract (20 to 100 milligrams): helps prevent diabetes complications.

    Pantothenic acid (100 to 200 milligrams): helps the body use carbohydrates, proteins, and fats; also known as vitamin B_5.

    Rice bran (130 to 200 milligrams): a natural source of B vitamins.

    Siberian ginseng root extract (80 to 120 milligrams): helps protect against stress-related illness.

    Riboflavin (25 to 50 milligrams): supports the conversion of carbohydrates, proteins, and fats into fuel for the body; also known as vitamin B_2.

    Niacin (25 to 50 milligrams): helps release energy from carbohydrates; also known as vitamin B_3.

Biotin (100 to 200 milligrams): enables the body to use blood sugar; facilitates the production of various enzymes and the breakdown of carbohydrates, proteins, and fats.

Magnesium (100 to 200 milligrams): helps prevent diabetes complications.

Codonopsis root extract (300 to 600 milligrams): enhances adrenal function; can be a substitute for Panax ginseng.

- Take one capsule of an antioxidant supplement a day, either 1 hour before or 2 hours after a meal. Antioxidants can help prevent the onset of diabetes as well as slow its progression. For a list of recommended ingredients, see page 322.

- If you are carbohydrate intolerant (you can find out by completing the questionnaire on page 53), be sure to take two or three capsules of a carbohydrate digestive enzyme before each meal. It should contain a broad spectrum of enzymes to thoroughly break down carbs into their component sugars and to assimilate the sugars into the bloodstream via the liver. A good carbohydrate digestive enzyme will also promote weight loss—an important benefit for people who need to slim down in order to effectively manage their diabetes. (I'll say more about weight loss a bit later.)

- Take one capsule of an essential fatty acid formula three times a day. Essential fatty acids activate enzymes that in turn stimulate the insulin receptors on cells so the cells are better able to take in sugar. Conjugated linoleic acid, a specific type of essential fatty acid in beef and dairy fats[9], can improve blood sugar transport and insulin sensitivity. Pairing this formula with a pH-balanced, full-spectrum digestive enzyme ensures complete absorption.

- Take 400 to 800 micrograms of folic acid a day. Studies have established a link between a low intake of folic acid and a number of medical conditions, including diabetes, heart disease, stroke, cancer, arthritis, and problems with bone mineral metabolism.

Some people appear to have trouble digesting and absorbing this B vitamin, which increases the chances of a deficiency. This is why pairing the supplement with a full-spectrum digestive enzyme blend is so important.

- If you have insulin resistance or type 2 diabetes, be sure to increase your dietary intake of the following nutrients. They help lower blood sugar levels, diminish sugar cravings, and support weight loss.

  Magnesium[10] *(200 to 400 milligrams).* Good food sources include nuts, legumes, leafy greens, and shellfish.

  Vitamin E[11] *(400 to 800 IU).* Good food sources include nuts and seeds, vegetable oils, and leafy greens.

  Chromium[12] *(100 to 200 micrograms).* Good food sources include potatoes, prunes, peanut butter, nuts, seafood, and brewer's yeast. In general, low-fat foods tend to contain more chromium than high-fat foods.

  Vanadium[13] *(20 to 50 micrograms).* Good food sources include shellfish, mushrooms, and soy products.

  Alpha lipoic acid[14] *(100 to 200 milligrams).* Good food sources include spinach, lean meats, and brewer's yeast.

  Biotin[15] *(250 to 500 milligrams).* Good food sources include soy products, nuts, legumes, cauliflower, and fish.

  Zinc[16] *(15 to 30 milligrams).* Good food sources include lean beef and pork, poultry (especially dark meat), seafood (especially oysters), cheese, beans, nuts, and wheat germ.

To further reduce your risk of type 2 diabetes or slow its progression, be sure to add the following lifestyle strategies to your self-care regimen.

- Maintain a healthy weight. Many people who develop type 2 diabetes later in life can effectively control it just by losing any extra pounds, especially around their midsections. Those who store fat in the abdominal area are more likely to develop diabetes than those who store fat on their hips.[17] As fat collects in the abdominal cells, it prevents insulin from attaching to the hormone receptors on the outer surface of each cell. In response, the pancreas produces even more insulin in an effort to remove sugar from the bloodstream. Over time, this sets the stage for hyperinsulinemia and insulin resistance. (For advice on slimming down, see chapter 7.)

- Eat only minimal amounts of carbohydrates and stick with complex carbs, which enter the bloodstream more slowly than simple carbs. This determines how quickly blood sugar rises, which in turn controls how much and how quickly insulin enters the bloodstream. Curbing your carbohydrate intake is important for balancing blood sugar and preventing insulin resistance.

- Limit your consumption of foods that contain fructose, a natural sugar that's commonly added to soft drinks, breakfast cereals, baked goods, and prepared desserts. Fructose may contribute to insulin resistance as well as diabetes complications.[18]

- Engage in regular aerobic activity for at least 30 minutes 3 days a week. For people with diabetes, the best time to exercise is right after the evening meal. Blood sugar tends to rise higher after dinner than after breakfast.[19] Working out at this time of day can help regulate blood sugar levels. *Note:* If you have diabetes or insulin resistance, be sure to get your doctor's okay before starting a fitness regimen.

CHAPTER 14

Fight
Inflammation

A MONG THE MILLIONS of Americans who cope with frequent or even daily chronic pain, many believe that their only hope for relief lies in using powerful medications that can become addictive or have toxic side effects. There are alternatives.

In fact, enzyme therapy is quite effective in treating many different medical conditions that cause chronic pain. One reason is that enzymes reduce the inflammation that is frequently at the root of such pain.

For example, the joint swelling that's characteristic of rheumatoid arthritis can leave people who have the disease in almost constant distress. If they were to take the enzyme protease between meals, they would probably find that their inflammation and pain diminished significantly. They would need less, or perhaps none, of the conventional medications that can be hard on their bodies. They'd begin to feel better and even look better—and their zest for life would return.

A DEFENSE
MECHANISM GONE BAD

Inflammation plays a central role in the body's immune response. When the immune system detects foreign substances such as viruses, bacteria, fungi, and even foods and chemicals—collectively known as antigens—it initiates a series of events that ultimately leads to the production of antibodies. These antibodies bind to and eliminate the invaders before they do harm.

Sometimes antibodies and antigens join forces to form circulating immune complexes (CICs). The CICs orchestrate their own destruction by alerting other immune cells, called macrophages, to report to the scene and launch an attack.

Once the macrophages have done their job, the immune system calls upon other components to complete the destruction of the CICs. Known as complements, they're mixed bags of proteins and enzymes that wipe out any remaining enemy cells through lysis—literally, by bursting them.

The activation of macrophages and the complement system depends on the size and number of CICs as well as on whether they're floating freely in the bloodstream or have penetrated tissue. The more CICs in the body, the worse the performance of the macrophages, meaning that they can't gobble up the CICs as they normally would. This is what opens the door to inflammation.

Invariably, chronic inflammation involves some sort of enzyme deficiency. An adequate supply of enzymes would discourage the formation of CICs—especially those that contain errant food particles, since enzymes ensure proper digestion. It would also facilitate the normal progression of the immune response.

Without sufficient enzymes to ease the burden on the macrophages, the immune system remains active even though the invading substance no longer is a threat. Eventually, the immune system loses its ability to recognize the body's own cells and mistakes them for foreign substances. It begins attacking perfectly healthy tissues, setting the stage for autoimmune diseases, such as rheumatoid arthritis, ulcerative colitis and Crohn's disease[1] (chronic intestinal inflammation), glomerulonephritis (kidney inflammation), and multiple sclerosis[2] (which involves destruction of the myelin sheath that surrounds and protects nerves).

The question is, Why do we run low on enzymes in the first place? Perhaps it's because the enzymes that would usually help repair and restore tissues must instead step in to help digest foods, which are depleted of their own enzymes.

Why Drugs Don't Really Work

Conventional therapies haven't been very successful in treating autoimmune diseases. The available medications work primarily by blocking or inhibiting the activity of the immune system and suppressing the symptoms of inflammation. Cortisone, a steroid, is the most common of these medications.

Steroids are rapidly catching up with antibiotics as a misused and abused class of pharmaceuticals. They work by mimicking the action of the adrenal glands, the most powerful regulators of immune function and inflammation. They appear to be "miracle cures" because patients with debilitating asthma or arthritis seem to get better as soon as they begin within hours of beginning treatment.

Indeed, steroids can calm the wheezing of asthma and reduce the swelling and pain of arthritis and other conditions, which is why doctors routinely turn to these drugs as a first rather than a last resort. Truly, though, all they do is interfere with the body's normal immune response. Sometimes this "break" allows the body to heal itself, but more often, it causes devastating, permanent damage. We are just beginning to realize how quickly this damage can occur.

Despite what some doctors have said about steroids producing side effects only after many months of use, there is no such thing as a safe dose. Studies have shown that debilitating effects can appear after a single dose, and permanent damage can set in within weeks of starting treatment.

While steroids relieve the symptoms of inflammation, they fail to treat the underlying cause. So as soon as you stop treatment, the symptoms are likely to return. It's a very serious problem because it sets up a cycle of drug dependency.

Enzyme therapy is an effective alternative to steroids and other anti-inflammatory medications. It fights inflammation by supporting the breakdown of CICs and the activation of macrophages to gobble up their components. In this way, enzymes prevent the accumulation of immune complexes—and limiting their number means that they won't inhibit the work of the macrophages, which is what triggers inflammation in the first place.

The process by which enzyme therapy interrupts the chain of events that leads to inflammation was the subject of research by J. Menzel and C. Steffen, professors at the Institute for Immunology of the University of Vienna, in 1985. Steffen administered a concentrated anti-inflammatory enzyme solution to laboratory rabbits with specific levels of CICs. The more concentrated the enzyme solution was, the more CICs it destroyed. The rabbits were completely free of immune complexes within hours.[3]

Sometimes—in the case of injury, for example—inflammation is vital to promote healing, so you wouldn't want to switch off the body's inflammatory response. Even in this circumstance, enzymes help by accelerating the response so the injury heals more quickly. Some scientists theorize that by supporting and enhancing tissue repair, enzyme therapy may be able to cure certain medical conditions for which mainstream medicine has no effective treatments.

In many ways, this chapter may be the most important in terms of illustrating just what enzymes can do. To say that they're safer, faster-acting, and longer-lasting than conventional pharmaceuticals is an understatement. Enzyme therapy should be the first line of defense against any condition in which inflammation plays a role.

FROM DR. ELLEN'S CASE FILES *A very well known South American pianist came to the BioSET Clinic/Institute for an evaluation. Over a 2-year period, this 32-year-old man had developed a severe inflammatory condition that caused a great deal of pain in his joints. He could no longer play the piano, which was his life's passion. He had performed for royalty all over the world, but now he barely could write his name.*

When he first sent an e-mail inquiring about my work, he mentioned that he had been injecting himself with 80 milligrams of the steroid prednisone every day for 2 years. It was the only thing that allowed him to tolerate being alive; nothing else seemed to help. He felt that his life was on hold, and his chances of playing again were diminishing.

By chance, he found a copy of my book The Food Allergy Cure *at his local library. After we exchanged e-mails, he made arrangements to come see me so I could evaluate him for enzyme deficiencies, food sensitivities, and toxicity. I had only 2 weeks to treat him, since that was all the time his visa allowed.*

When I examined him, I noticed that his fingers, hands, and feet were extremely red and swollen. The pain and distress were etched in his face. Further evaluation revealed that he was protein/fat intolerant, with multiple food and environmental sensitivities. His body wasn't able to detoxify adequately. Also, by his own description, he seemed to always be picking up a cold or the flu, most likely because the prednisone had suppressed his immune system. Not surprisingly, he was very depressed.

With only 2 weeks to help him, I needed to do what was most expeditious to relieve his inflammation. Introducing natural therapies when someone has been taking high doses of steroids can be a challenge, but I was determined to do what I could. My father was a pianist, and I remember how distraught he became when anything happened to his fingers or hands. He played until the day before he died, so I understood how important it could be.

When I asked this young man what might have contributed to his high level of toxicity, an interesting and important piece of information came to light. His father owned a big plastics factory, and as a boy, he went to the factory every day after school to spend time with his dad and help out in whatever way he could. He vividly remembered the awful smell of plastic.

With my method of heath care, I can evaluate a patient's level of toxicity and identify the affected organs and systems, but I can't determine the cause. Now I was suspicious; I wondered if the exposure to plastics in the man's youth could be at least partly responsible for his health problems now. Unfortunately, none of his previous health care providers had raised this issue.

I started him on a course of detoxifying enzymes, plus high doses of a protein/fat digestive enzyme, a protease enzyme, and a soft-tissue enzyme for anti-inflammatory support. With this regimen, we were able to slowly reduce his prednisone dosage. After 6 days, the swelling was completely gone, and the movement in his fingers was restored. "I feel like someone oiled them," he said. His pain remained severe, but at last he was getting some relief.

After 10 days of treatment, he returned to the clinic and announced, "Dr. Cutler, I slept straight through the night without waking up in agony." He was improving. Unfortunately, he needed to leave for home the next day. He filled his suitcases with as many bottles of enzyme supplements as he could carry.

Since returning to South America, he has kept in touch. He intends to come back to the clinic as soon as he can get another visa. In the meantime, he continues to improve slowly but surely. While he isn't playing the piano, he is writing music. He mentioned that he hasn't been sick with a cold or the flu since he left the United States. Best of all, he is down to just 20 milligrams of prednisone a day.

COMMON
INFLAMMATORY CONDITIONS

Inflammation in and of itself isn't a bad thing. In fact, it's a normal and essential defense mechanism for fighting disease and healing the body. It becomes problematic only when it persists or recurs. Then it can turn against the organs and systems that it should be protecting.

With this in mind, let's take a closer look at several conditions of which inflammation is a characteristic symptom. In every case, enzyme therapy can bring relief, and perhaps a cure, even when conventional treatments have failed.

Rheumatoid Arthritis

Rheumatoid arthritis (RA) is an autoimmune disease in which the immune system attacks the joints, causing pain, swelling, stiffness, and possibly loss of function. The disease process begins in the synovium, the membrane that surrounds a joint and creates a protective sac containing a lubricant called synovial fluid. Besides cushioning the joints, the synovial fluid supplies nutrients and oxygen to cartilage, the slippery tissue that coats the ends of bones. Cartilage consists primarily of collagen, the body's primary structural protein, which forms a mesh that provides support and flexibility for joints.

In RA, continuous inflammation of the synovium gradually destroys collagen, narrowing the space within the joint and eventually damaging bone. In progressive RA, the destruction of collagen accelerates when fluid and immune cells accumulate in the synovium to produce a pannus, which consists of thickened synovial tissue. The pannus aggravates the joint by attracting more immune cells, thereby perpetuating the inflammatory process. This process not only affects cartilage and bones but also can harm other organs.

Under normal circumstances, inflammation is controlled and self-limiting. In chronic RA, it persists. This is because the body mistakes its own collagen cells for antigens, setting in motion an autoimmune response to eradicate the perceived threat.

Rheumatoid arthritis affects an estimated 2.5 million Americans, more than 60 percent of whom are women. Although the exact cause of the disease isn't known, a growing body of evidence suggests that an infectious agent, such as a virus or bacterium, may trigger RA in people with an inherited predisposition to it. But hundreds of scientific publications have also confirmed a connection between RA and elevated levels of CICs. These immune complexes act as antigens, provoking the release of macrophages and an autoimmune response.

Most mainstream MDs treat RA with immunosuppressive or anti-inflammatory agents. These medications not only have limited success, they also have high risks of side effects. As mentioned earlier, steroids can alleviate symptoms but do so at a price—namely, progressive deterioration in health. Nonsteroidal anti-inflammatory drugs (NSAIDs) such as ibuprofen, which doctors prescribe just as liberally, can provide some relief from pain but do nothing to stop joint deterioration.

In Europe, many physicians are convinced that they can improve RA, or at least slow its progression, with high-dose or long-term enzyme therapy.[4] In their opinion, enzymes support the detection, breakdown, and disposal of CICs that penetrate joint cartilage by way of the synovial fluid. Further, they propose that enzymes can alleviate symptoms such as pain, swelling, stiffness, and loss of grip strength and range of motion. This should be of interest to every patient and physician who deals with RA.

Various clinical trials have compared oral enzyme supplements and NSAIDs in the treatment of rheumatic diseases such as RA. Some of this research was sponsored by MUCOS Pharma, a German pharmaceutical company, and has not been published. The findings suggest that enzyme formulas are effective in treating swelling and inflammation. In many instances, they performed as well as or better than NSAIDs.

Based on their findings, the study authors concluded that enzyme therapy is a plausible treatment for rheumatic diseases, with fewer adverse effects than NSAIDs. After 12 months of taking oral enzyme supplements, study participants showed significant declines in the number of CICs, which meant less inflammation and thus less pain and swelling.[5]

Systemic or proteolytic enzymes appear to be especially effective for inhibiting the joint deterioration that accompanies rheumatic diseases such as RA. These enzymes have analgesic properties in addition to their well-known anti-inflammatory and swelling-reducing activity. This helps explain their therapeutic benefits for rheumatic diseases.

In one study involving patients with periarthritis of the shoulder—that is, inflammation of the tissues surrounding the shoulder joint—systemic enzymes produced significant reductions in pain. Another study, of patients with osteoarthritis of the knee, found that enzyme therapy and NSAIDs produced statistically equivalent improvement in pain.[6]

Rheumatoid arthritis may turn out to be a major proving ground for enzyme therapy.[7] The only potential drawback to this use of enzymes is their delayed action. The research findings point out that patients shouldn't expect treatment to yield dramatic results in a short period of time, especially when a condition has been developing for many years. According to Dr. Klaus-Michael Goebel, professor at the Rheumatological Clinic in Bad Endbach, Germany, a patient may need to take enzymes for weeks or even months before seeing a positive effect. Dr. Goebel further states that enzyme therapy naturally enhances the body's own processes.

For patients with RA, the typical recommendation is for digestive and detoxification enzyme formulas in addition to systemic enzymes. Often, this multipronged approach eliminates many food sensitivities, which contribute to the generation of CICs and the progressive deterioration of synovial tissue. It also restores balance and integrity to the immune response, which helps minimize inflammation while restoring youthful vitality.

DR. ELLEN'S PRESCRIPTION

For rheumatoid arthritis, my enzyme formula of choice is one that contains the following ingredients. I recommend taking one capsule three times a day, either 1 hour before or 2 hours after a meal.

If you can't find all of the ingredients in a single product, you have a couple of options. You can take at least the primary herbs and nutrients (in bold) as single supplements in combination with a full-spectrum digestive enzyme blend. Or you can look for a product that has just these ingredients in a full-spectrum enzyme blend. Either will work just as well.

Digestive enzymes: should include 80,000 to 300,000 HUT of protease and 1,400,000 to 2,800,000 PU of bromelain. (A crude extract of pineapple, bromelain contains compounds with potent anti-inflammatory properties.)

Vitamin C from acerola cherry extract (75 to 220 milligrams): promotes and speeds wound healing, which helps limit the inflammatory process.

Zinc (24 to 42 milligrams): stimulates wound healing.

Quercetin (5 to 10 milligrams): reduces joint inflammation.

White willow bark extract (40 to 80 milligrams): reduces joint inflammation and relieves acute and chronic pain.

Methylsulfonylmethane, or MSM (100 to 350 milligrams): nature's best source of dietary sulfur, clinically proven to enhance joint health by reducing swelling and stiffness.

Boswellia resin extract (240 to 300 milligrams): relieves the pain and stiffness of both rheumatoid arthritis and osteoarthritis via a mechanism similar to that of aspirin.

Turmeric root extract (80 to 160 milligrams): reduces inflammation.

Manganese citrate (15 to 24 milligrams): helps mend ligaments, tendons, and cartilage.

Copper (0.6 to 3 milligrams): strengthens bones and tendons.

Boron citrate (0.8 to 2 milligrams): strengthens bones by preventing calcium loss.

Devil's claw bark extract (300 to 450 milligrams): appears to have anti-inflammatory activity.

Yucca root extract (200 to 270 milligrams): a therapeutic anti-inflammatory that's a common ingredient in herbal pain-relief formulas.

Grapeseed extract (45 to 90 milligrams): often used in treating connective-tissue disorders such as RA; helps reduce inflammation and pain.

Glucosamine sulfate (1,000 to 1,500 milligrams): Relieves joint pain, stiffness, and swelling; may also speed healing.

Chondroitin (800 to 1,200 milligrams): inhibits the breakdown of cartilage and assists in the formation of connective tissue.

FROM DR. ELLEN'S CASE FILES

Lucy arrived at the BioSET Clinic/Institute after her doctor diagnosed her with rheumatoid arthritis. The 25-year-old graduate student had developed severe pain in her hands, fingers, knees, and ankles. The pain was disabling—so much so that she had returned to live with her parents, who assisted with her everyday activities so she could continue her studies.

Some days, Lucy seemed to get along very well. Other days, she couldn't even drive. To aggravate matters, she had been skipping menstrual periods for 3 years, which raised a question about whether she would be able to have children. She was upset, afraid, and frustrated with her condition. She wanted very badly to be normal and healthy—free of the pain that would come on the moment she woke up and linger until she went to bed.

When I first met Lucy, she was taking two analgesics as well as hydroxychloroquine (Plaquenil), a commonly prescribed medication for RA. She had gotten some relief when she began drug therapy, but now it wasn't helping. Her cousin had told her about enzymes, prompting her to seek out my advice.

I talked with Lucy about my research into the relationship between CICs and RA and my use of enzyme therapy to systematically break down the immune complexes as well as improve digestion and detoxification and eliminate food sensitivities. Indeed, a thorough evaluation revealed that Lucy was carbohydrate intolerant, with significant toxicity in her liver, kidneys, and lymphatic system.

I recommended a regimen that included a carbohydrate digestive enzyme, a systemic protease formula, a detoxification formula, and a soft-tissue formula with large amounts of magnesium and bromelain. I also prescribed a probiotic for general colon health. Lucy was to abstain from all the foods to which she was sensitive until I was able to administer BioSET treatments. In the meantime, she continued taking her medication, although I encouraged her to reduce her reliance on analgesics and instead use the protease formula as necessary for pain relief.

I asked Lucy to check back with me in 10 days. Usually, this is enough time to see improvement in symptoms, especially if food sensitivities are a major factor. Sure enough, when Lucy came in for her follow-up visit, she was already noticing a difference. Her pain had diminished by 50 percent, while the range of motion in her fingers and spine had increased. She was walking with greater ease and had even tried a little dancing with her fiancé. Her mood was much better, too.

Lucy's is one of many cases of RA that I have treated, all with excellent outcomes. While the improvement isn't always so dramatic, enzyme therapy has never failed, especially with regard to pain relief.

ULCERATIVE COLITIS AND CROHN'S DISEASE

We first discussed ulcerative colitis and Crohn's disease in chapter 6, but we're revisiting them here because both are forms of inflammatory bowel disease (IBD). Like other inflammatory conditions, colitis and Crohn's can benefit from enzyme therapy.

By one estimate, between one and two million Americans have some form of IBD. So far, medical science has been unable to positively identify a cause. One theory is that the immune system mistakenly targets the bacteria that normally reside in the gut, setting in motion the biochemical processes that lead to inflammation. Some believe that the guilty party is a measles virus that for some reason doesn't leave the body after the initial acute outbreak, instead lying dormant before triggering chronic inflammation in the intestinal tissue.

Various studies have hinted at interesting correlations between certain substances, from toothpaste ingredients to oral contraceptives, and IBD risk. Not surprisingly, dietary factors have come under scrutiny, with some research implicating excessive consumption of sugars, starches, and processed foods. These connections remain to be proven, however.

Conventional treatment for colitis and Crohn's involves long-term drug therapy and sometimes surgical procedures. While these help relieve symptoms, they don't offer a cure. Enzyme therapy can change the course of both conditions by reversing any food sensitivities as well as the immune reactions they cause.

Our collective years of treating hundreds of patients with colitis and/or Crohn's have provided convincing proof that poor digestion and food sensitivities are major contributors to these conditions. When people go on liquid diets for 2 to 3 weeks, their symptoms go into remission, possibly because they've eliminated the foods to which they are sensitive.

We advise all of our patients with colitis or Crohn's—especially those who have difficulty moving their bowels—to pay close attention to their food choices and eating habits. Medical literature singles out fiber-rich foods, which are hard to digest, as well as milk, alcohol, and spicy or fried foods, as potential troublemakers. Yeast may be another culprit, since some research has identified a potential correlation between sensitivity to brewer's and baker's yeast and IBD. One study in England found that patients who avoided foods to which they were sensitive experienced fewer symptom flare-ups than those who ignored the role of diet in their treatment.

DR. ELLEN'S PRESCRIPTION

For a list of supplements and strategies that have produced good results for patients with ulcerative colitis and Crohn's disease, see page 63. Because these are such serious digestive ailments, please be sure to consult your doctor before making any changes in your self-care regimen.

John came to the BioSET Clinic/Institute on the advice of a friend. Then in his early forties, he had been struggling with symptoms of ulcerative colitis—cramping, pain, bleeding with bowel movements, and frequent bouts of explosive diarrhea. He not only got little relief with conventional drug therapy, which included sulfasalazine (Azulfidine) and the steroid prednisolone, he also experienced severe reactions to it. His face was swollen, and he had gained weight.

John's symptoms had become so severe that they were interfering with his job. This caused him great distress since he was a single parent and sole provider for his children.

When I evaluated John, I found that he was severely carbohydrate intolerant. He also tested positive for sensitivities to a number of foods—virtually all of the common culprits, as well as some uncommon ones, such as celery, lettuce, and green beans. He was highly sensitive to grains and yeast, yet incredibly, his doctor hadn't cautioned him to avoid these foods.

I prescribed a carbohydrate digestive enzyme and a protease enzyme, along with a gastric formula and a soft-tissue formula to help heal John's colon. I also recommended a probiotic, which is important for intestinal health. Until he was symptom-free, John was to follow a very strict diet. I would adjust it as he continued to improve, provided he stuck with his enzyme regimen.

John was very appreciative and very compliant. He was determined to be able to work without worrying about symptom flare-ups. When he returned 3 weeks later for his follow-up appointment, I noticed that the swelling in his face had subsided, and he was slimmer than before. I asked how he was doing, and he replied, "I am so much better, Dr. Ellen." He was still experiencing occasional bleeding but had very little cramping. He was much more himself. "I didn't realize how tired and irritable I had become," he told me. "My children have their father back again. But when can I eat grains, breads, and pizza?"

I explained my philosophy about the health effects of grains and carbohydrates. He wasn't too happy about continuing to avoid these foods, but he understood why I recommended it. I hoped that he would follow my advice, because if he resumed eating grains and carbs, they would probably aggravate his symptoms. He might be able to return some of these foods to his diet over time, but only in limited amounts and only with the digestive enzyme.

I did expand John's diet to include yogurt and certain vegetables that had caused problems before but were much more tolerable with the digestive enzyme. After this appointment, we scheduled a follow-up in 2 months. I didn't hear from him for quite a while. Then, 1 week before his appointment, he called me, very distressed. He wasn't doing well at all. Immediately, I asked what he had been eating. When he sighed, I knew he had gone off his diet.

John explained that while on vacation, he had been eating pasta, breads, and pancakes in quantities that I wouldn't care to know—plus lots of ice cream, which is very hard on the gastrointestinal tract. To make matters worse, he had forgotten some of his enzymes. I recommended that he keep his upcoming appointment. In the meantime, he was to be very strict about his diet—no grains, no carbs, and definitely no ice cream!

John took my advice. When I saw him the following week, he was doing very well—a little blood in his stool, but overall, much better. He had learned his lesson. I'm happy to report that he has been well for many years now. He continues to take all supplements but the gastric enzyme formula, although he has cut back to just two or three doses of each per week.

Urinary Tract Infections

Protease enzymes have been very successful in treating inflammatory conditions throughout the body, including urinary tract infections (UTIs), which respond quite well.

In one study, Japanese researchers found that a protease product called Kimotab was able to eliminate pain on urination, a hallmark symptom of UTIs. The researchers believe that Kimotab has anti-inflammatory properties as well as a fibrinolytic, or clot-dissolving, effect. By increasing proteolytic activity in the blood, it inhibits the production of bacteria that cause UTIs. In the study, Kimotab also reduced the number of white blood cells in the urine, an indicator of infection. The researchers concluded that the product improved symptoms in patients with UTIs. It also has a very low incidence of side effects.[8]

DR. ELLEN'S PRESCRIPTION

If you're prone to urinary tract infections, I suggest trying a kidney/bladder enzyme formula similar to the one described here, containing at least the primary ingredients (in bold). The usual dosage is one capsule three times a day, either 1 hour before or 2 hours after a meal.

Digestive enzymes: should contain 80,000 to 225,000 HUT of protease.

Cornsilk extract (120 to 160 milligrams): helps relieve irritation of the urinary tract; also beneficial for cystitis, which involves inflammation of the bladder.

Uva ursi leaf extract (100 to 300 milligrams): makes the bladder a less inviting environment for harmful bacteria and strengthens the body's immune defenses.

Goldenseal root extract (30 to 60 milligrams): fights bacterial infections and thus may be beneficial for UTIs.

D-mannose (300 to 750 milligrams): a naturally occurring simple sugar that appears to be effective in treating UTIs.

White willow bark (30 to 60 milligrams): contains salicin, an aspirin-like compound that relieves pain and inflammation.

Swedish pollen (15 to 30 milligrams): facilitates the complete elimination of urine, which is important for preventing UTIs.

Injury and Trauma

Any injury—whether from a motor vehicle collision, an occupational accident, a sports mishap, a fall, or simple overuse—alerts the body to launch the biochemical processes that promote repair and healing. The onset of inflammation is an indicator of these processes.

Many German studies have examined the effectiveness of anti-inflammatory enzymes as a treatment for injuries.[9] In one of these studies, researchers caused bruises on the arms of volunteers by injecting blood right beneath the skin. Some of the volunteers then took 10 tablets of an anti-inflammatory enzyme blend three times a day, while the rest took placebos (dummy tablets). The researchers tracked how much pain people experienced—including when pressure was applied to the bruises—and how quickly the bruises disappeared.

According to the study results, the enzyme mixture worked quite well. The people who used it experienced less pain at the sites of their bruises, even when the researchers applied pressure. What's more, the bruises healed more quickly. In my own experience, the sooner enzyme therapy begins after an injury, the faster you'll see improvement. It can be quite miraculous.

It's a good idea to keep a bottle of anti-inflammatory enzymes in your medicine chest as first aid for minor injuries. They're great for stimulating repair and healing, reducing pain and swelling while restoring range of motion.

FROM DR. ELLEN'S CASE FILES

Kate rushed her 6-year-old daughter, Alison, to the BioSET Clinic/Institute immediately after she had accidentally slammed a car door on the little girl's finger. Already, the finger appeared quite bruised and swollen. The pain brought Alison to tears.

I immediately reached for my protease enzymes and soft-tissue enzymes. I mixed them in water, then asked Alison to drink the solution. The results were quite astounding: Within 10 minutes, the swelling had subsided, and she was no longer in pain. She even mustered a smile for me.

Shortly after this incident, Kate returned to the clinic with her other daughter, Maggie, who had been stung by a wasp. Thankfully, she hadn't experienced an allergic reaction. But her hand was very red and swollen, and her upper arm was beginning to swell as well. We feared that her symptoms would worsen.

I gave Maggie the same mixture of protease enzymes and soft-tissue enzymes in water. Within minutes, the redness and swelling went away.

Enzymes may have a protective effect as well. Research has shown that taking enzyme supplements prior to activities that pose a risk of injury can reduce healing time by half if an injury occurs.[10] In Europe, where enzyme therapy is already quite popular, surgeons routinely administer enzymes before and after surgery to speed recovery. Also, European athletes rely on enzymes to prevent injury and promote healing.

FROM DR. ELLEN'S CASE FILES *Jonathan, a 36-year-old stockbroker, loved to play basketball. But shooting hoops came to an abrupt end when he suffered a fracture that all but destroyed the inner meniscus of his left knee. He underwent two surgeries to repair the damage, but even after these procedures, he had ongoing stiffness and pain that kept him off the basketball court. This was very upsetting to him because playing basketball was his outlet, an opportunity to destress and unwind.*

When he first came to the BioSET Clinic/Institute, Jonathan was taking glucosamine sulfate and ibuprofen two or three times a day. This regimen made the pain somewhat more tolerable but did little for the stiffness. He hoped that enzyme therapy would allow him to play basketball again, or at least to get some exercise.

I advised Jonathan to take a protease enzyme one to three times a day. The improvement was immediate. His pain disappeared almost completely, and his mobility was much better. Although he didn't return to basketball, he was able to launch a new fitness routine of stationary bicycling and brisk walking at least 4 days a week.

A growing body of evidence indicates that free radicals—the unstable molecules that attack otherwise healthy cells—are major contributors to inflammation and muscle damage after strenuous exercise. The theory is that physical activity steps up the generation of free radicals as a result of a rise in oxygen consumption. Studies suggest that antioxidant enzymes and nutrients can quickly neutralize any free radicals that occur with exercise before they do serious harm.[11]

DR. ELLEN'S PRESCRIPTION

The protease enzyme that's a component of the basic plan (page 32) is important for promoting repair and healing after injury. I also recommend the soft-tissue enzyme formula on page 244. *Note:* Please be sure to seek prompt medical attention for any injury that is serious or potentially life-threatening. In cases like this, emergency medical care is paramount.

ENZYMES TO THE RESCUE

The evidence is clear: Enzyme therapy is far superior to conventional pharmaceuticals for relieving inflammation and the pain, swelling, and stiffness that accompany it—and it's much safer. A cautionary case in point: In its first 3 months on the market, one NSAID caused 10 deaths due to gastrointestinal hemorrhage.[12] Why take something so potentially dangerous when a natural, effective alternative is readily available?

After all, enzymes don't just target the outward symptoms of inflammation. They also intervene in the inflammatory process at multiple levels by:

- Regulating the release of immune mediators, "helper cells" that are the front line of the immune response to invaders

- Breaking down CICs so that macrophages can step in and clean up the debris

- Helping to process the biochemical by-products of inflammation and infection

- Breaking down any protein molecules that have migrated into the bloodstream and penetrated tissues before the proteins can aggravate inflammation

- Improving blood flow by inhibiting the clumping of platelets and reducing clotting

- Facilitating healing not only through better circulation but also through formation of healthy new tissue

- Heading off the errant immune response that can lead to autoimmune disease

For fighting inflammation, enzyme therapy ought to be the first choice—even over pharmaceutical anti-inflammatories. The general public is ready for just such a purely natural approach to pain relief and healing.

DR. ELLEN'S PRESCRIPTION

My standard protocol for treating inflammatory conditions includes the following trio of enzyme formulas. As a reminder, if you can't find products that contain all of the suggested ingredients, you can take at least the primary nutrients and herbs (in bold) as separate supplements with a full-spectrum digestive enzyme blend. Another option is to look for an enzyme blend with at least the primary ingredients. Both options produce virtually the same effects.

- Take two capsules of a soft-tissue enzyme formula two or three times a day, either 1 hour before or 2 hours after a meal. This blend of enzymes, nutrients, and herbs regulates the inflammatory process while supporting tissue repair and healing.

Digestive enzymes. Look for a product made with 80,000 to 600,000 HUT of protease and 1,500,000 to 3,000,000 PU of bromelain.

Malic acid (400 to 800 milligrams). This nutrient can help relieve muscle pain and tenderness.

Magnesium (64 to 128 milligrams). In combination with malic acid, magnesium alleviates the symptoms that commonly occur with soft-tissue injuries. It is critical for transmitting impulses between nerves and muscles.

Ginkgo biloba leaf extract (80 to 160 milligrams). This herb improves blood flow throughout the body by thinning the blood and relaxing smooth muscles. It also has anti-inflammatory and antioxidant properties.

Vitamin C from acerola cherry extract (30 to 100 milligrams). Vitamin C is essential for the synthesis of collagen, a key player in tissue repair and healing.

Grapeseed extract (30 to 60 milligrams). Certain compounds in grapeseed extract have anti-inflammatory properties.

Turmeric root extract (75 to 150 milligrams). Turmeric is a potent anti-inflammatory.

- Take two capsules of a mineral enzyme formula twice a day, either with or between meals. All of these ingredients are vital to tissue repair and healing.

  Digestive enzymes. A quality mineral enzyme formula will contain 12,000 to 60,000 HUT of protease and 150 to 300 FTU of phytase.

  Manganese citrate (3 to 6 milligrams). Manganese is the principal molecule for organizing collagen fibers. It is extremely important for the strength and integrity of spinal disks and ligaments.

Boron citrate (1 to 6 milligrams). Boron reduces loss of calcium and magnesium while elevating levels of estrogen—all properties that make for healthy bones.

Horsetail extract (80 to 120 milligrams). Horsetail is an excellent source of bioavailable silicon, calcium, magnesium, chromium, iron, manganese, and potassium—all necessary for healthy joints and connective tissue.

Oat straw extract (80 to 160 milligrams). Oat straw stems contain silicon and magnesium as well as crude fiber, all of which support and maintain the body's structural systems.

Calcium citrate (6 to 12 milligrams). Calcium is vital for healthy bones. I recommend calcium citrate because the body can use it more easily than other calcium compounds.

Soy isoflavones (6 to 12 milligrams). The soy isoflavones should be standardized to contain 23 percent genistein and 18 percent daidzein.

Chlorella (200 to 400 milligrams). Chlorella are green algae, microscopic freshwater plants that contain an abundance of vitamins, minerals, dietary fiber, nucleic acids, and amino acids. All of these nutrients help nourish bones and connective tissue.

Red clover flower extract (120 to 240 milligrams). This calcium-rich herb supports healthy bones and connective tissue.

• Take one capsule of an antioxidant supplement every day, either 1 hour before or 2 hours after a meal. This supplement helps protect against free radical damage, a factor in inflammation as well as inflammatory conditions. For a list of recommended ingredients, see page 322.

Along with these enzyme formulas, I advise my patients with chronic inflammatory conditions to steer clear of certain foods and ingredients that can aggravate inflammation. The primary offenders are sugar and ice cream, but other potential culprits include the following.

- Grains, such as wheat, oats, barley, and rice
- Starchy vegetables, such as potatoes, carrots, corn, and peas
- Coffee and chocolate
- Artificial sweeteners
- Food colorings and additives

The best diet for fighting inflammation consists primarily of lean meats, poultry, fish, eggs, steamed vegetables, certain fruits, nuts, and oils. You may be able to reintroduce some of the trigger foods after 4 to 6 months, once you're completely symptom-free, as long as you're taking a carbohydrate digestive enzyme. Nevertheless, I strongly recommend eliminating grains altogether for health reasons beyond inflammation.

CHAPTER 15

Defend against Cancer

When Jacalyn's husband called me for the first time, I could hear the concern in his voice. He wanted to know if I could do anything to help his 62-year-old wife, who had been diagnosed with lymphoma—cancer of the lymphatic system, which plays a central role in fighting disease. Jacalyn was receiving chemotherapy, which left her extremely underweight. Her oncologist had advised her to eat more, but she was fearful because of her food sensitivities. She felt that the doctor really didn't understand how debilitating they could be, causing symptoms such as severe fatigue, bloating, cramping, abdominal pain, and rashes. Her typical diet consisted of a few vegetables, amaranth (a grain), and fish.

Jacalyn and her husband lived near Los Angeles, a significant distance from the BioSET Clinic/Institute. Considering her health, I didn't want her to travel if I could recommend something over the phone. I asked if she had taken any enzyme supplements. She said she had, but they weren't helpful. When she mentioned that she had kept the bottle, I asked her to read the label to me. As I suspected, she was taking enzymes from animal sources rather than from plant sources, which is what I recommend. I explained how the types of enzymes differ and why vegetarian enzymes might produce better results.

After our conversation, Jacalyn and her husband decided to make the trip to the clinic after all. Her sister lived close by, so Jacalyn could stay in the area for about a week for follow-up testing.

At her first office visit, I was startled by how thin she was. She even looked malnourished. I performed a complete examination, including an enzyme evaluation and food sensitivity testing. Jacalyn had a number of sensitivities as well as severe carbohydrate, protein, and fat intolerances.

Based on these findings, I recommended both carbohydrate and protein/fat digestive enzymes to improve her digestion and nutrient absorption. Sometimes patients like Jacalyn, who have severely compromised systems, require the extra support of both digestive enzymes. Eventually, one of them becomes their permanent supplement. I also recommended a probiotic and a systemic protease enzyme, which I give to all of my patients, but I use a slightly higher dosage for cancer patients to support their immune systems. I asked Jacalyn to come back in 2 days; I expected that she would see improvement by then and would be able to eat a wider variety and larger quantity of food.

Jacalyn took the enzymes just as I had prescribed. When I tested her 2 days later, some of her "trigger foods" no longer posed a problem. She was eager to try adding them to her meals. Within 10 days, her menu expanded to include 15 new foods, including corn, rice, chicken, lamb, and even cashews. None of them caused symptoms. She gained about 4 pounds in 19 days.

Today, Jacalyn and I touch base about once a month. Her

lymph nodes have returned to normal, and all her tests are perfect. She has gained a little more weight and continues to diversify her diet.

Cancer is a universally feared disease. For a significant number of people, it's a heartbreaking reality, whether it affects them or their loved ones. Although we do not treat cancer in our respective practices, we do work with many patients who are survivors or have a family history of cancer.

The body may harbor cancer cells for many years before they manifest themselves in a way that's detectable through laboratory work and/or physical diagnosis. Having worked with enzyme therapy for so long and witnessed its extraordinary effects in fighting infections and strengthening the immune system, we're convinced that enzyme therapy can play a positive role in cancer prevention and treatment as well as post-treatment recovery and care.

As we've explored the body of research focusing on cancer, we've been greatly impressed by the number of studies involving enzymes. This research data literally could fill an entire book. In this chapter, we'll share the most important of these findings and hopefully open your eyes to yet another revolutionary benefit of enzyme therapy. If you or a loved one has cancer or is at risk for it, the information presented here could change your life.

WHEN CELLS GROW OUT OF CONTROL

The cancer process begins when certain factors—physical, environmental, infectious, and/or genetic—interfere with cell production. Cells become malformed, and when they multiply, they pass on their imperfections to the next generation.

You may be surprised to learn that the presence of cancer cells in the body is quite normal. By one estimate, a healthy person could have between 100 and 10,000 of these cells in his body at any given moment.[1] As long as the immune system can eliminate sufficient numbers of the cells or the body's internal environment can prevent their growth, they won't advance to full-blown cancer.[2]

Typically, most cancer cells are destroyed by the immune system, with enzymes stepping in to remove the debris. But factors such as tobacco smoke, sun exposure, radiation, and even age can disrupt immune function so the body is no longer capable of suppressing cancer cells. When a critical number of them escape destruction, their capabilities change. Some attach to normal cells and make alterations to suit their own metabolic needs.

In theory, because cancer cells look different from normal cells, the immune system should still be able to recognize and destroy them. But somehow they get smarter. Realizing that they're under surveillance, they hide beneath a thick coating of adhesive fibrin. The fibrin conceals the suspicious markings on the cells, including antigens that dot their surfaces.

Cancer cells grow because of the absence or a shortage of enzymes that are capable of stripping away fibrin from individual cells. Adequate enzyme activity exposes the antigens on their surfaces so the immune system can detect the cells and destroy them. Of course, the more cancer cells the body produces, the more enzymes it needs to help fight them.[3] As we grow older, though, enzyme production declines, which may be one reason that cancer risk increases with age.

Even when enzymes are plentiful, cancer cells are a clever and tenacious bunch. Their primary objective is self-preservation. One of the strategies for preventing their own destruction is to deter enzymes from stripping away their fibrin coatings. They do this by releasing blocking factors that act like a big stop sign, thwarting the enzymes and inhibiting the immune system.

To further confuse the immune system, the cancer cells may slough off their antigens. The immune system sends out antibodies to go after these harmless proteins, thinking they're the troublemakers. In the meantime, new antigens form on the cancer cells, which remain unscathed.

As the antibodies attach to the sloughed-off antigens, they form circulating immune complexes (CICs). An excess of these immune complexes also interferes with immune function, especially key immune cells known as macrophages and natural killer cells. With the immune system in disarray, the cancer cells can go on the offensive and multiply.

Eliminating the CICs is important not only to prevent cancer but also to treat the disease once it has established itself. In the absence of CICs, the immune system can resume its mission of seeking out and destroying cancer cells. Among cancer patients, targeting immune complexes has led to improved appetite, increased weight, and enhanced vitality.[4]

Enzyme therapy helps discourage the formation of CICs. It also appears to inhibit the growth of invasive cancer cells and to reduce metastasis (the spread of cancer from its original site to other tissues).[5] As you'll see, this just scratches the surface of how enzymes may support the fight against cancer.

CANCER AND ENZYMES:
A LONG HISTORY

More than a century ago, British embryologist John Beard, MD, began treating cancer patients who had been deemed incurable with a unique protocol involving systemic, or proteolytic, enzymes.[6] His work has been largely forgotten by those who study and use conventional cancer therapies, but it is a centerpiece of complementary and alternative medicine.

In the initial stages of his research, Dr. Beard recognized a similarity between cells called trophoblasts, which are present early in pregnancy, and cancer cells—a similarity that he confirmed through subsequent research. Trophoblasts eat into the uterine lining to prepare it for pregnancy. They switch off about 6 weeks into gestation, once the fetal pancreas begins to function. Otherwise, the cells would undermine the integrity of the uterine lining, harming both the mother and the developing baby.

Because the activation of the pancreas appeared to disrupt the cancerlike action of the trophoblasts, Dr. Beard suspected a connection between some sort of pancreatic insufficiency and cancer. Specifically, he proposed that when the pancreas doesn't produce enough proteolytic enzymes, it can lead to an out-of-control growth process, as is the case with cancer.

To test his theory, Dr. Beard obtained enzymes from the filtered pancreatic juice extract of young pigs and sheep. He used young animals in the belief that they would have the most potent enzymes since they were still in a growth phase. He injected the enzyme fluid into the veins or buttocks of his cancer patients. When he was able to, he also injected it directly into tumors.

Remarkably, the proteolytic enzymes began eradicating cancer cells from the body. Dr. Beard documented how tumor masses disappeared in the presence of the enzymes, how the enzymes inhibited cancer growth, and how numerous patients survived longer than their prognoses had suggested they would.[7]

Through his years of research, Dr. Beard collected enough data to conclude that cancer occurs when the pancreas fails to produce adequate numbers of proteolytic enzymes. By his account, cancer begins when some stimulus—an injury, a medication, or an environmental toxin, for example—causes trophoblasts left over from embryonic development to reproduce. Proteolytic enzymes are responsible for digesting these cells the moment they become active, so when the enzymes run low, the cells can multiply unchecked. The result is cancer—the rapid, uncontrolled growth of cells.

Dr. Beard's research spawned some 40 clinics in London, all using crude proteolytic enzymes to treat cancer. For the most part, though, his work was rejected by his peers. Part of the problem was that no one could consistently replicate his results—a failure that he attributed to the use of commercially available enzymes, which were of variable quality and provided inadequate dosages. At about the same time, Marie Curie was advocating the x-ray as a better cancer therapy because it was so "safe and effective." Gradually, interest in Dr. Beard's ideas faded. He died in 1924, a very disappointed man.

Then, in the early 1940s, Ernst T. Krebs Jr., a graduate student in the anatomy department of the University of California, San Francisco, School of Medicine, began reinterpreting Dr. Beard's writings. In 1946, he published a letter in the *Journal of the American Medical Association* in which he described his theory of cancer and trophoblasts. Based on his data, he concluded that the trophoblast is a malignant cell.

Later, Krebs shifted the focus of his research to the role of vitamins in cancer prevention and treatment. One of his most noteworthy discoveries was vitamin B_{17}, a cyanide-containing glucose that he extracted from apricot pits. B_{17} is also known as amygdalin, or Laetrile. Eventually, Laetrile emerged as a controversial cancer treatment.

The Birth of Systemic Enzyme Therapy

In the 1930s, prior to Krebs's pioneering work, Viennese physician Dr. Ernst Freund collaborated with Dr. Benjamin Kaminer on an article called "The Biochemical Basis of Disposition to Carcinoma." In their research, they had observed that cancer cells in test tubes dissolved when blood from healthy donors was added to the cells. They speculated that something in the blood must combat cancer and that the blood of cancer patients either lacks the substance or contains some sort of "immune-blocking factor."[8]

When Dr. Freund partnered with another colleague, Max Wolf, MD, the two discovered that they could eliminate the immune-blocking factor from the blood by adding very small amounts of chymotrypsin, a digestive enzyme that breaks down protein. In light of these findings, Dr. Wolf revisited Dr. Beard's theory about proteolytic enzymes, which in turn prompted him to investigate the effectiveness of various plant and animal enzymes in treating cancer.

From this research, Dr. Wolf pioneered what he called systemic enzyme therapy. Since Dr. Wolf's death, Karl Ransberger, PhD, a

German molecular biologist, has continued to modify and refine Dr. Wolf's concepts into a well-respected enzyme protocol.[9]

Meanwhile, at the Austrian Cancer Research Institute of the University of Vienna, Heinrich Wrba, MD, and his colleagues have also been studying the role of oral systemic enzymes in disrupting the cancer process.[10] Their findings support the use of enzymes as a complementary therapy in conjunction with conventional cancer treatment. Clinical data substantiate the effectiveness of systemic enzyme therapy for various types of cancer, including leukemia; T-cell lymphoma; melanoma; and cancers of the lung, larynx, pancreas, stomach, colon, breast, cervix, uterus, bladder, testes, and prostate.[11]

Systemic enzymes not only improve key cancer markers, they also enhance the length and quality of life for cancer patients. They appear to disrupt the cancer process by stripping the protective fibrin coating from cancer cells and by activating the immune system. With the fibrin gone, immune system macrophages and natural killer cells can detect the antigens on a cancer cell's surface and target the cell for destruction.[12] They can also help clear out the CICs that inhibit immune function.

According to Dr. Wrba, by the beginning of the 20th century, German physician and scientist Paul Ehrlich, MD, had already established a theory that the development of cancer depends on the outcome of the war between tumor cells and the immune system. "The recognition of tumor cells by the immune system is a very difficult procedure," Dr. Wrba notes. "It should not be forgotten that tumor cells differ only insignificantly from healthy cells. . . . In spite of these difficulties, and according to the knowledge presently available, the healthy immune system is nonetheless able to recognize and to destroy the great majority of tumor cells.[13]

Compelling Reports from the Research Front

Another contemporary of Dr. Beard, Nicolas James Gonzalez, MD, a physician in New York City, has made extraordinary contributions to further our understanding of how systemic enzymes may help manage malignancies and metastatic diseases.[14] In 1993, Dr. Gonzalez presented cases from his own practice to a session of the National Cancer Institute (NCI). After the presentation, the associate director of the NCI suggested that Dr. Gonzalez pursue a pilot study of his treatment program.

Because pancreatic cancer has such an exceptionally aggressive nature and a poor prognosis, it became the focus of Dr. Gonzalez's study. He received funding through the Nestlé Corporation, which awards grants for innovative research in nutritional issues. The NCI reviewed the protocol, and Dr. Gonzalez enrolled the sickest patients.

Dr. Gonzalez's treatment program has three basic components: diet, supplementation (vitamins, minerals, trace elements, and antioxidants), and detoxification. He also prescribes large doses of pancreatic enzymes, the main cancer fighters; his patients take 60 to 70 capsules of pancreatic enzymes throughout the day. He attributes the anticancer effects of his program to the enzymes.[15]

To further investigate the potential of systemic enzyme therapy for cancer management, Dr. Gonzalez spent time with William Kelly, DDS, a dentist in Washington State who had developed an aggressive nutritional protocol to treat a variety of advanced cancers. Dr. Kelly also built on Dr. Beard's work, using large doses of pancreatic enzymes as the cornerstone of his protocol. In case after case, patients with advanced-stage or terminal cancer were alive 5, 10, and even 15 years later. Dr. Gonzales was able to make systematic evaluations of Dr. Kelly's program, then take it into clinical trials.

The average survival time for people with pancreatic cancer is 4 to 5 months after diagnosis. Among the 11 patients in Dr. Gonzalez's pilot study, 5 lived for 2 years, and 4 lived for 3 years. Based on these findings, the NCI decided to fund a large-scale, randomized, placebo-controlled trial that would compare Dr. Gonzalez's treatment protocol directly with chemotherapy. The trial is under way at Columbia University in New York City, with results to be announced in 2009.

HOW ENZYMES SUPPORT
CONVENTIONAL TREATMENT

Not long ago, a woman came to the BioSET Clinic/Institute to find out whether enzyme therapy might help improve her energy and stamina. She had been diagnosed with leukemia 2 years earlier; after beginning chemotherapy, she noticed declines in both her energy level and her resistance to colds and flu. When she asked her internist about it, the doctor recommended a B vitamin and a multivitamin (which the woman was already taking regularly). The doctor proceeded to say that strengthening the immune system has nothing to do with treating cancer or preventing it.

On the contrary, a healthy immune system is paramount to fighting cancer. It can also help reduce the risk of developing the disease in the first place.

With help from enzymes, the immune system is more effective in detecting and destroying tumor cells, as measured by the number of immune cells in the blood and lymph fluid and in the region of the tumor.[16] What's more, injecting enzymes directly into tumors completely disintegrates them. A growing number of European enzymologists are advocating this procedure as an alternative to surgery, which can weaken the immune system. Some administer enzyme enemas as well. According to these clinicians, cancer patients who use enzymes regain their weight and appetite, no longer suffer from depression, and feel considerably more alive—both physically and psychologically.[17]

When cancer patients require chemotherapy and/or radiation, taking enzymes in combination with these conventional treatments may fortify immune function while reducing side effects.[18] Enzymes also have analgesic properties.[19] Once Dr. Ellen's patient began enzyme therapy, she sailed through her remaining treatments with very few missed workdays. As a bonus, she developed fewer colds, and she felt more energetic during the day.

Clinical data prove that systemic enzymes can mitigate the harsh side effects of radiation and chemotherapy.[20] Here's a sampling of the research to date.

- One study evaluated the efficacy of enzymes in preventing side effects among patients who received radiation for head and/or neck cancer. With the addition of enzyme therapy, patients were better able to tolerate treatment; their side effects were less severe and didn't occur as soon after treatments.[21]

- In another study involving patients who received radiation for head and/or neck cancer, oral enzyme supplements showed potent anti-inflammatory and anti-swelling properties. They also reduced the side effects of treatment while increasing life expectancy among the patients.[22]

- When researchers gave oral enzyme therapy to women with locally advanced cervical cancer, the enzymes significantly reduced the side effects of radiation. These include thickening of the skin, swelling beneath the skin, deterioration of the lymph nodes, and reactions in the mucous membranes of the vagina.[23]

- In a German study, patients with abdominal cancer who combined enzyme therapy with radiation had shorter bouts of side effects than those who didn't take enzymes.[24]

Among oncologists, the prevailing wisdom seems to support aggressive rejuvenation of the immune system after chemotherapy or radiation. Yet they seldom dispense advice explaining just how to rebuild immune function, which means the patients must fend for themselves. This matter is too important to leave to chance, since cancer cells may linger even after treatment is complete—which is why cancer recurrence is so common. If the cancer spreads, or metastasizes, it can become even more serious. Most cancer deaths occur not because of the primary tumor but because of metastasis.

Besides weakening the immune system, chemotherapy and radiation can induce free radical damage, another risk factor for cancer recurrence. Minimizing free radicals begins with a diet of organic raw foods and juices, supplementation with antioxidant nutrients and enzymes, and limited exposure to environmental toxins. Systemic enzymes can further limit the reproduction and growth of cancer cells. Many European health care practitioners recommend taking systemic enzymes to prevent metastasis.[25]

The very latest research suggests that inflammation may cause or aggravate the metastatic process. Many cancers arise at sites of chronic inflammation, irritation, and infection. A substantial body of evidence supports the theory that a chronic inflammatory condition can predispose a person to cancer, as demonstrated by the association between inflammatory bowel disease and increased colon cancer risk.

Inflammation also contributes to tumor progression. The environment inside a tumor is important to the development of cancer (a process known as carcinogenesis) as well as to the survival and metastasis of the tumor. Inflammatory cells largely determine this environment.

Such insights are fostering new approaches to fighting cancer that target inflammation.[26] For example, since metastasis is more likely in the presence of inflammatory conditions, researchers are investigating whether anti-inflammatory medications may help reduce cancer risk. Likewise, a wholesome diet and proper digestion may help combat inflammation by encouraging production of cytokines, small proteins that regulate the inflammatory process.[27]

Of course, enzymes can play an important role in alleviating inflammation. They not only promote optimal digestion and clear up food sensitivities, which contribute to the inflammatory response, they also restore the body's innate healing power and rejuvenate cells and tissues. As we learn more about the connection between inflammation and cancer, enzymes are certain to figure prominently in how we address both conditions.

TARGETED IMPROVEMENTS
IN CANCER CARE

Some of the most compelling research involving enzyme therapy concentrates on specific types of cancer. While the findings require further study, they hold infinite promise for the patients who battle these cancers.

Colon cancer. Colon cancer has the dubious distinctions of being the third most common cancer in the United States and the second leading cause of cancer deaths. For 2003, experts projected that approximately 131,600 Americans would develop colon cancer, and more than 50,000 would die from it.

Another 80 to 90 million people—approximately 25 percent of the U.S. population—are at risk for the disease because of age or other factors.

When researchers have used systemic enzymes to treat colon cancer, they've recorded significant reductions in disease-related symptoms. The adverse effects of chemotherapy and radiation appeared to decline as well.[28]

Among patients with Dukes D colon cancer, which involves metastasis of the cancer to organs such as the liver, researchers noticed a trend toward longer survival time among patients who took oral systemic enzymes. This is significant in light of the fact that only 5 percent of people with this type of cancer survive for 5 years after diagnosis.[29] Adjunctive enzyme therapy also appeared to minimize metastasis and improve quality of life.

Melanoma. When researchers administered systemic enzymes to mice with melanoma, the enzymes inhibited the growth of primary tumors and reduced the number of recurrent tumors. Perhaps most noteworthy, the rate of metastasis declined in the area of the primary tumor as well as in other areas.[30] Since this research involved laboratory animals, human trials will be necessary to further evaluate and confirm the findings.

Lymphedema. Although it isn't a type of cancer, lymphedema (exaggerated swelling) often occurs in the arms of women who have had mastectomies and radiation for breast cancer. This swelling can have considerable impact on a woman's life, both physically and psychologically. Researchers report that they have been able to prevent lymphedema by administering enzymes, beginning immediately after surgery or radiation.[31]

FROM DR. ELLEN'S CASE FILES *Eleanor, age 54, originally came to the BioSET Clinic/Institute after experiencing some structural problems in her neck. She sought my help again after being diagnosed with breast cancer. Her oncologist had recommended an aggressive treatment protocol that included mastectomy, chemotherapy, and radiation. Eleanor did very well with all of the treatments. Unfortunately, she developed lymphedema, which caused more debility than the treatment side effects.*

When Eleanor returned to the clinic for follow-up about her neck, she asked if I could do anything to relieve the lymphedema. While I didn't have much experience with the condition, I was certain that Eleanor might benefit from enzymes because of their excellent anti-inflammatory properties. After evaluating her for food sensitivities and nutrient deficiencies, I recommended a carbohydrate digestive enzyme, along with six to eight capsules a day of a systemic protease enzyme. This is more than I usually prescribe, but Eleanor's swelling was severe, and she was desperate for relief.

I assumed Eleanor would see results in approximately 10 to 14 days. To her pleased surprise, her swelling decreased by about 25 percent within the first 48 hours and continued to diminish every day. It was all but gone in about 10 days—a relatively short time.

I now recommend a systemic protease enzyme to all of my cancer patients, and I increase the dosage for those with breast cancer to offset the occurrence of lymphedema.

ENZYMES WITH ANTICANCER BENEFITS

Throughout this chapter, we've explored myriad ways in which systemic enzyme therapy can slow, stop, and perhaps even reverse the cancer process. Before we discuss specific enzyme recommendations, let's take a closer look at key enzymes and their cancer-fighting potential.

Papain, trypsin, and chymotrypsin. Many of the clinical trials involving systemic enzymes have used a preparation that combines papain, trypsin, and chymotrypsin. According to a Swiss medical review, this preparation can minimize the adverse effects of chemotherapy and radiation. Some evidence suggests that it may also prolong survival with some types of tumors. Its benefits seem to derive in part from its ability to limit the number of immune mediators, specialized immune cells that are integral to the inflammatory process.[32]

Bromelain. Studies of bromelain, a pineapple extract, suggest that the enzyme has anti-inflammatory properties. Results from preclinical and pharmacological research validate the use of oral bromelain as a complementary cancer therapy. In trials involving laboratory animals, the enzyme has demonstrated an ability to prevent metastasis and appears to inhibit the growth of tumor cells. Trials involving humans are forthcoming.[33]

Mushroom enzymes. In Japan, physicians counsel patients not only on conventional therapies—surgery, chemotherapy, and radiation—but also on nutritional therapy. For them, as in most Asian cultures, the use of mushrooms such as shiitake, reishi, maitake, and enoki to enhance immune function is standard practice. Mushrooms contain a number of enzymes that may slow the growth of invasive tumors.[34]

DR. ELLEN'S PRESCRIPTION

While systemic enzymes have shown their value as complements to conventional cancer therapies, I generally recommend them only after a patient has completed treatment. I have absolute confidence in their safety, but at the same time, I don't want to risk undermining the treatment process. I do encourage my patients with cancer to take a full-spectrum digestive enzyme blend, a protease enzyme, and a probiotic—perhaps in slightly larger doses than in the basic plan. Together, these supplements help minimize the side effects of chemotherapy and radiation while enhancing immune function.

For people who have completed treatment and are ready for aftercare, as well as for those who want to avoid cancer in the first place, I recommend the following enzyme supplements. Ideally, you'll be able to find formulas that contain all of the listed ingredients. If you can't, you have a couple of options. You can take at least the primary ingredients (in bold) as separate supplements, in combination with a full-spectrum digestive enzyme blend. Or you can choose a product that supplies the primary ingredients in a full-spectrum digestive enzyme blend. Both options are effective.

- Take one capsule of a protease enzyme three to five times a day on an empty stomach. Protease not only fortifies the immune system but also interrupts the formation and growth of tumors. (*Note:* This is a higher dosage than I recommend in my basic plan. It is safe, and it can only help immune function.)

- Take one capsule of an immune health enzyme formula three to five times a day on an empty stomach. After about 4 months, take a break for a month or two before resuming supplementation. Look for a product with these ingredients.

   Digestive enzymes. Check the product label for 80,000 to 225,000 HUT of protease.

   Astragalus root extract (320 to 525 milligrams). Astragalus not only enhances disease resistance but also may have antiviral and antibiotic properties. It's safe to use in combination with conventional medications since it won't interfere with their action.

   Reishi mushroom extract (120 to 240 milligrams). Studies have shown that reishi mushroom extracts enhance the effectiveness of chemotherapy drugs, allowing for lower dosages while protecting healthy cells from damage. Reishi mushrooms also fortify the immune system.

   Shiitake mushroom extract (120 to 240 milligrams). Shiitake mushrooms contain lentinan, a potent tumor fighter. In Japan, physicians use lentinan to treat an array of cancers while reducing the side effects of chemotherapy. It also appears to reduce the risk of cancer recurrence and extend the life expectancies of cancer patients.

Cat's claw herb extract (120 to 240 milligrams). Cat's claw helps stimulate immune function in cancer patients, whose disease resistance may decline with chemotherapy and/or radiation.

Burdock root (80 to 160 milligrams). Burdock is well known for inhibiting tumor growth and destroying bacterial and fungal cultures. Japanese researchers have identified in burdock a new type of desmutagen, a substance that's uniquely capable of reducing cell mutation.

Echinacea angustifolia *root extract (120 to 240 milligrams) and* E. purpurea *root extract (120 to 240 milligrams).* A popular immune stimulant, echinacea limits the severity and duration of infections.

Goldenseal root extract (25 to 50 milligrams). Like echinacea, goldenseal is an immune stimulant.

Vitamin C from acerola cherry extract (100 to 200 milligrams). Vitamin C enhances the immune system.

Beta-carotene (10 to 15 milligrams). A potent immune booster and antioxidant, beta-carotene may reverse certain precancerous conditions.

Zinc (10 to 15 milligrams). Zinc enhances the immune system.

Coenzyme Q_{10} (10 to 20 milligrams). This coenzyme has properties that may help prevent cancer.

Quercetin (30 to 50 milligrams). Quercetin is effective for fighting viral infections.

- Take one capsule of an antioxidant supplement once a day, either 1 hour before or 2 hours after a meal. Antioxidants neutralize the free radicals that otherwise could damage cells in ways that lead to cancer. A good-quality formula will contain the ingredients listed on page 322.

CHAPTER 16

Slow the
Aging Process

Just as I was beginning to write this chapter, I had a serendipitous encounter in a local bookstore, where I stopped to browse before going to dinner with a friend. As I scanned the alternative medicine shelves, a fellow customer struck up a conversation with me. He said that I reminded him of someone he knew. He had recently relocated to the area from Costa Rica and was studying public health at the University of California, Berkeley. He mentioned that he was writing a paper on the rate of breast cancer in Marin County, which is where I live.

When the man asked me what I did, I told him about enzyme therapy. He was all ears. We found my book, The Food Allergy Cure, and I signed a copy as we talked about cancer and enzymes. Since I had just finished writing about cancer for this book, I was very eager to share what I had learned from my research.

Then, a woman who had overheard our conversation

267

asked if I was Dr. Cutler. When I told her I was, she reached up and removed her wig. She had ovarian cancer, she explained, and was undergoing chemotherapy. Because of the treatment, she wasn't eating very well, and she felt tired all the time. She wanted to find something that would allow her to continue her treatment while restoring her appetite and energy and improving her immune function. If she felt better, she reasoned, she could do more to fight the disease.

I told the woman a little about how enzyme supplements have helped cancer patients recover after chemotherapy and radiation. She was so eager to try a regimen of digestive and systemic enzymes that she asked for the address of my Web site so she could go online and place an order. Her oncologists had not been able to help alleviate the side effects of chemotherapy, and although she felt secure in their care, she wasn't thriving. She was seeking advice that would bolster her chances of survival and longevity. That was her word: longevity.

Longevity means something very different to each of us. For some, it's striving to prevent age-related decline; for others, it's maintaining a youthful appearance; and for still others, such as this woman, it's sticking around for another day and being able to enjoy life as she did not too long ago. No matter how we define it, whether we achieve it depends on a variety of factors—some we can't control, such as our genetic predisposition to disease, and some that we can, such as our lifestyle choices.

Taking enzyme supplements promotes longevity by repairing the damage left behind by a lifetime of less-than-healthy habits and behaviors. In this way, it also offsets genetic risk. While our genetic makeups help determine the quantity and quality of our years, our lifestyles dictate just how much influence genetics ultimately has.

Of course, for enzymes to carry out their respective assignments, we must commit ourselves to wellness and balance in each aspect of our lives. We can't continue to exhaust our brains and bodies and depend on enzymes to compensate for our actions. As we begin making healthier choices, enzymes reward us by facilitating optimal function of the organs and systems that make us as vibrant and vital as we are meant to be.

Enzyme therapy is not a drug or a quick fix. It is a natural means of gradually restoring our inherent youthfulness and preventing the diseases that shorten our life spans. We have the ability to achieve anything we desire—and if we desire to live to a ripe old age, free of debilitating illness, why not set out to achieve it? Taking enzymes is the all-important first step in this quest.

LIVE LONGER, AGE LESS

Of course, how long we live depends in large part on how well we age. Like it or not, all of us get older. We need to remember, though, that chronological age—the number of years that we've been on this Earth—only remotely correlates to biological age, which is driven by key physiological markers. Sometimes outward appearance reveals biological age, but as we all know, appearance can be deceiving. So many patients get compliments on how young they look after they begin taking enzymes. They feel youthful, too. No wonder: Enzyme therapy restores and preserves their natural energy and radiance. And it shows.

In general, we associate aging with a random and gradual loss of function leading to a greater risk of health problems such as heart disease, cancer, diabetes, memory loss, osteoarthritis, and osteo-porosis. With them comes a higher incidence of mortality. But we need to remember that they are not inevitable. Throughout our life-times, we make choices that influence the aging process for better or for worse. In this way, we help determine whether we develop age-related illness.

We must never accept that we are "just getting older" or that we must "learn to live with" a particular health problem. We have plenty of options, beginning with enzyme therapy—especially since the aging process correlates to a decline in enzyme production. According to Edward Howell, MD, author of *Enzyme Nutrition*, the body produces fewer enzymes over time, and the available enzymes don't perform their jobs as well. As each year passes, the body requires more supplemental enzyme support to avoid age-related illness.

Enzyme deficiency is just one of many factors that can accelerate aging. Others include poor digestion and nutrient absorption; physical inactivity; excessive stress; and repeated exposure to toxins, radiation, and sunlight. Collectively, these factors take a toll on the body's various organs and systems, impairing their function and setting the stage for premature aging.

Sometimes premature aging proceeds without any symptoms until the sudden onset of a catastrophic health event, such as a heart attack or stroke. Other times, it manifests itself as atrophy, or a gradual wasting away of tissue—the muscle weakness that occurs from lack of exercise, for example, or the mucous membrane deterioration that's a by-product of diminished hormone levels.

More often than not, however, a body that's getting old before its time sends out signals to alert its owner that it's in crisis. The most common of these signals is pain, which can occur with any number of underlying imbalances, including inflammation, joint instability, insufficient blood supply, or pressure within an organ or the surrounding tissue.

By taking steps to stop or prevent premature aging, the vast majority of us could live longer and stay healthier than we ever might imagine. Consider that the human body, free of age-related illness, could last for 120 years. Unfortunately, conventional medicine concentrates on relieving symptoms with medications and surgical interventions instead of reversing the aging process, a potentially more effective long-term strategy.

We can "turn back the clock," without resorting to drastic or dubious measures. Enzyme therapy delivers on the promise of optimal health and longevity. With it, we become ageless—energetic, resilient, and radiating life.

AVOID THE YOUTH ROBBERS

The beauty of enzymes is that they fight aging on multiple fronts. With this in mind, let's take a closer look at how certain lifestyle factors accelerate the aging process and how enzymes can intervene.

Food Sensitivities

A leading cause of premature aging is food sensitivities brought about primarily by a decline in digestive function, which impedes the thorough breakdown of foods and absorption of nutrients. Eating is essential to our survival, but if we can't digest what we eat, we don't get the nutrients we need. This weakens our defenses against pathogens and pollutants that would wreak havoc on our bodies and accelerate aging.

To aggravate matters, poor digestion allows food particles to find their way into the bloodstream, where they set in motion an immune response. Over time, the immune system turns against the body, causing chronic inflammation and other debilitating changes that seriously undermine health and longevity.

By supporting proper digestion, enzyme therapy helps restore and maintain healthy immune function. In this way, it protects us from the chronic inflammation and illness that not only accelerate aging but also keep us from living to a ripe old age.

(FROM DR. ELLEN'S CASE FILES) *Carrie's story began in 1999, when the stress of a personal tragedy set the stage for severe fatigue and depression as well as multiple chemical and environmental sensitivities. By the time she called the BioSET Clinic/Institute to schedule a consultation, she was no longer working. In fact, she could barely leave her home.*

Carrie's symptoms were formidable. Besides digestive distress, such as constipation, bowel urgency, and occasional loss of bowel control, she described persistent muscle cramps and twitching, numbness in her arms and legs, headaches, skin rashes, food cravings, and poor sleep. Flare-ups of her allergies caused red, itchy eyes; sneezing; and difficulty breathing. She also showed signs of cognitive impairment, with slowed thinking and spaciness, and an inability to regulate her body temperature (she often felt cold).

Carrie had already been diagnosed with Hashimoto's thyroiditis, an autoimmune disease that results in low levels of thyroid hormone. Before calling the clinic, she had tried an array of therapies—an elimination diet, homeopathy, acupuncture, and chiropractic, along with an assortment of nutritional and herbal supplements. None of them was effective, which left her even more discouraged and desperate. Just as she was about to give up, a friend of hers who was a medical doctor advised her to contact me. Her friend felt hopeful that I could help.

Because Carrie lives in Arizona, I suggested that she make arrangements to stay near my office so I could monitor her treatment. She came for 2 weeks initially, then for 1 month later in the year.

Prior to her initial office visit, no one had screened Carrie for sensitivities of any kind. That first day, we spent more than 3 hours together, during which I evaluated her for food and environmental sensitivities as well as for enzyme deficiency and toxicity. Carrie turned out to be sensitive to just about everything she ate, but especially to vegetables, fruits, nuts, and oils. According to the enzyme tests, she couldn't tolerate carbohydrates, proteins, or fats. Yet while her body was starving for nutrients, she was overweight. What's more, her kidneys, liver, and colon showed signs of toxicity, which helped explain her fatigue, skin problems, and constipation.

Based on Carrie's test results, I recommended five enzyme formulas—two for digestion, plus one each for detoxification, adrenal support, and thyroid support—along with a probiotic. We also set up a schedule for BioSET treatments to help clear up her food and environmental sensitivities.

In order to appreciate Carrie's progress, imagine being barely able to get out of bed and eat, then just a year later driving, shopping, cooking, and even taking college courses. That was Carrie's experience. She still had occasional moments of irritability as well as an occasional rash, but her symptoms were quite mild.

Today, Carrie is living proof of the power of enzyme therapy. She has lost 40 pounds, and she looks at least 15 years younger. Seldom does a day go by without someone remarking on her fabulous appearance. I am so pleased with her progress—as is she!

Dietary Fat

A growing body of research suggests that eating too much saturated fat contributes to the aging process by promoting inflammation, which in turn generates free radicals. As you may remember, free radicals are renegade molecules that steal electrons from other molecules to stabilize themselves. In the process, they damage cells and, more precisely, the DNA inside them. This damage, known as oxidative stress, can set the stage for age-related illness.

One of the pitfalls of the low-carbohydrate craze is that few of the popular diets set any kind of limit on total fat, let alone saturated fat. The most common dietary sources of saturated fat—which is also strongly associated with high cholesterol—are animal products such as red meat and dairy foods. Certain tropical oils, such as palm and coconut, contain an abundance of this unhealthy fat as well.

Limiting consumption of saturated fat and animal protein and taking enzymes to ensure proper digestion help guard against the inflammation that leads to free radical production and oxidative stress.

Stress

More than 50 years of research have shown how physical and emotional stress can accelerate aging. If you think about it for a moment, you probably know someone who seemed to age overnight while dealing with a stressful situation. The human body is well equipped to cope with stress, but it can tolerate only so much. Eventually, it shows the effects; we not only feel older, we look older.

Persistent, unrelenting stress can set the stage for a host of health problems, including diabetes, high blood pressure, and ulcers. The health effects are more pronounced in the elderly, who have lower tolerance for stress and are less able to recover from it. Among the elderly, stress can trigger poor immune function, senility, and exhaustion. Digestion—which declines with age anyway—suffers considerably, leading to symptoms such as heartburn and indigestion.

The human body reacts to stressors in virtually the same way today as it did thousands of years ago when our prehistoric ancestors encountered some sort of threat. Blood pressure rises, muscles tense, breathing becomes shallow and rapid, hunger and sexual desire fade, and digestion shuts down. These changes, collectively known as the fight-or-flight response, prepare us to either confront the perceived threat or flee from it—although we're more likely to be speaking before a large group, taking an important test, or running late for an appointment than facing down a saber-toothed tiger.

Coincidentally, the very hormones that set the stress response in motion—adrenaline and cortisol—are the same ones that drive the aging process. In order to slow or reverse aging, we need to somehow inhibit the release of these hormones. Cortisol can be especially problematic, as too much of it suppresses immune function.

The job of producing adrenaline and cortisol falls to the adrenal glands. In cases of extreme or chronic stress, the adrenals must work overtime to keep up with demand for the hormones. Eventually, they begin to malfunction, leaving the body more vulnerable to the effects of stress.

The good news is that we can repair and protect the adrenal glands so they don't wear out. The most important strategies are managing our reactions to life events to avoid repeatedly triggering the stress response and strengthening our bodies to withstand the physical and psychological demands of stress. This is where enzyme therapy can help. Because enzymes ensure that your body properly breaks down food and absorbs nutrients, it gets the nutrition it needs to stay healthy. Enzymes also minimize production of CICs, helping to maintain immune function even as stressors attempt to wear down our resistance.

The body is remarkable in its ability to repair and rejuvenate its own tissues and organs. When it's nutritionally fortified and in balance, it remains resilient no matter what life has in store. It withstands stress rather than becoming overwhelmed. This is important because stress is an unavoidable fact of life. Even if we were to move into a cave far from civilization, stress would find us—whether triggered by fear, boredom, or something else.

If you travel as much as both of us do, which is quite a bit, you probably have hit a snag at an airport. No one can do anything about a thunderstorm that delays takeoff for 3 hours or mechanical problems that cause us to miss a connecting flight, yet passengers become extremely upset when something like this occurs. As the stress response kicks in, their bodies age just a little more.

The uniquely personal way in which each of us perceives and filters life events determines how we react or don't react to them. Whether we're stuck in an airport, tied up in a traffic jam, facing a deadline, or cleaning up a bottle of spilled milk, we can either give in to the stressor or rise above it. Once it gets the best of us, we no longer have control over it.

To be resistant to stress, we must develop the wisdom and strength to step back from day-to-day stressors so we witness them from the perspective of an objective bystander. In this way, we can regulate the body's stress response so it doesn't switch on for even the most minor events. This not only supports health and longevity, it also can be quite liberating.

Toxicity

We've already discussed how a high intake of saturated fat can elevate production of free radicals. Exposure to toxins has the same effect. Chemicals, pollutants, radiation, and other toxic substances generate the renegade molecules that wreak havoc on the body by contributing to aging and age-related illness.

Free radicals not only cause cellular damage, they also play a role in cross-linkages. These undesirable bonds form between amino acids, which make up the protein chains in collagen, or connective tissue. The most visible result of cross-linkages is the loss of elasticity in the skin, which causes fine lines and wrinkles.

An easy test of elasticity is to raise the skin on the back of one hand between two fingers of the other hand, then release it. If the skin flattens out immediately, it's free of cross-linkages.

In healthy skin, some of the protein chains join together in spiral structures that lie parallel to each other. The more free radical attacks these chains are subject to, the more cross-linkages their amino acids form. Insufficient enzyme activity can lead to more rigid connective tissue, which affects not only your skin but also your muscles, nerves, and blood vessels.

Research has shown that systemic, or proteolytic, enzymes not only break down cross-linkages but also prevent them in the first place. When taken over a long period, these enzymes help maintain the elasticity and function of connective tissue throughout the body, slowing the aging process inside and out.[1]

Antioxidant enzymes are important for neutralizing and detoxifying free radicals. The body manufactures its own supply of these enzymes, but because of stress or toxin overload, we may need extra in supplement form. Remember to always take nutritional supplements in combination with enzymes; otherwise, the body may not be able to absorb the nutrients, which can increase free radical production and aggravate toxicity.

Free radicals are the body's enemies and are certainly major factors in poor health and premature aging. By choosing nutritious foods and taking the appropriate enzymes, you ensure a healthy internal environment that's less vulnerable to toxins.

THE SECRETS
OF LASTING YOUTH

Just as science continues to turn up information about what promotes aging, it's also revealing exciting new details about how we can slow and even reverse the process. Some of the most compelling evidence to date pertains to a trio of anti-aging measures: calorie restriction, nutritional supplementation, and physical activity. Let's look at each in turn.

Calorie Restriction

Richard Weindruch, PhD, professor in the department of medicine at the University of Wisconsin–Madison, is a pioneer in the study of calorie restriction and the aging process. His research has shown that reducing calorie intake by 20 to 30 percent can measurably extend life span in laboratory animals. While his diet reduces calories, it doesn't sacrifice vitamins and minerals, which remain at nutritionally sound levels.[2]

Other researchers have confirmed the connection between eating less—especially meats and fats—and living longer. When Roy Walford, MD, an immunologist and gerontologist at the University of California, Los Angeles, put mice (ages 30 to 33 in human years) on a low-calorie diet, they survived 29 percent longer than normal. They remained in excellent health all of their lives, with just a fraction of the heart disease and tumors that occurred in mice on full diets.

Dr. Walford also experimented with total fasting and other alternatives to a low-calorie diet. He determined that limiting calorie intake every other day was highly effective in increasing the life span of mice. This strategy works, he surmised, by reversing the immune dysfunction that occurs with overeating, though the mechanism isn't really well understood.[3]

Based on his research, Dr. Walford recommended that humans reduce their daily calorie intake by 49 percent. By eating this way, he theorized, we could live to age 120 or even longer. He also recommended eliminating sugar and fat to make room for nutrient-dense whole foods.[4]

Taking digestive enzymes with meals usually helps with the transition to a low-calorie diet. The stomach isn't all that big; when empty, it can hold about 2 cups, or ½ liter, of solids or liquids. But it can stretch to accommodate a lot more—for example, a full meal and a beverage. See if you can fit your lunch into 2 cups or ½ liter.

How much food do you need to fill your stomach? The answer lies in the size of your fist. Less than this, and you're not eating enough; more than this, and you're eating too much.

Nutritional Supplementation

The absorption and utilization of nutrients is vital to the prevention of age-related illness. As we get older, the combination of nutrient deficiency and enzyme deficiency can be devastating to our health. Overwhelming evidence suggests, however, that even among the elderly, intervention with nutritional supplements can improve immune function and disease resistance.[5]

In the United States, a year's supply of supplements costs less than three doctor visits and much less than 1 day of hospitalization.[6] It can reduce the frequency and duration of infection while increasing stamina and vitality.

At the end of the chapter, you'll find a number of enzyme formulas that contain key anti-aging nutrients. You can take these nutrients in combination or as separate supplements. Either way, they offer valuable nutritional insurance for optimal health and maximum longevity.

Physical Activity

Like calorie restriction and nutritional supplementation, regular physical activity helps fight aging. Studies have shown that exercise increases blood flow, which improves delivery of nutrients and oxygen to cells while speeding the removal of toxins and waste products from them.[7] It also strengthens the cardiovascular system, which promotes heart health.

For maximum anti-aging benefit, we recommend at least 30 to 45 minutes of aerobic activity—such as brisk walking, jogging, cycling, or swimming—at least 3 days a week. A longer workout of moderate intensity is much more effective than a short workout of high intensity. Walking is an excellent aerobic exercise because it promotes overall fitness with low risk of injury.

Just as important for lifelong good health is strength training with free weights and/or weight machines. It helps counteract the muscle loss and sluggish metabolism that come with age. A number of fitness books offer short but effective strength-training routines. Another option is to work with a personal trainer for at least a few weeks to learn specific exercises as well as proper lifting technique. Most experts suggest lifting 2 or 3 days a week, perhaps alternating strength-training sessions with aerobic workouts.

Incidentally, enzyme supplementation is an essential adjunct to exercise. By supporting proper digestion, it ensures the bioavailability of nutrients to cells. This means the cells can function at 100 percent of their capacity so you feel stronger and more energetic during your workouts.

On the Horizon

As enzyme therapy continues to grow in popularity, research will not only confirm its known anti-aging benefits but also identify more ways in which it protects against age-related illness. We're convinced that enzymes will become an accepted alternative for preventing and treating all manner of health problems, from inflammatory bowel disease and thyroid disorders to autoimmune conditions and cancer.

For example, because enzymes dissolve blood clots, they can reduce the risk of heart attack and stroke—and with it, the incidence of heart disease in the United States, where it ranks as the number one cause of death. Indeed, enzymes could improve the cardiovascular health of populations worldwide, in which heart disease is also on the rise.

Perhaps one of the most intriguing findings in anti-aging research involves the identification of a potent anti-aging enzyme that's present in living cells. The enzyme, called surtuins, regulates the aging process in virtually all living organisms—including bacteria, plants, and people. Experts expect that the discovery of surtuins could speed the development of drugs to prevent age-related illness and extend the human life span.

Like other enzymes, surtuins support essential biochemical reactions inside cells. In people, they help rejuvenate cells by beefing up the repair process and stimulating production of protective antioxidants. Surtuins also enhance the survival of cells during times of stress. They even delay cell death.[8]

One compound that appears to serve as a booster to surtuins is resveratrol. Researchers believe that resveratrol is responsible for the ability of red wine to lower the risk of heart disease. It's an exciting area of study that's certain to reveal more about why we age—and how we may be able to regulate the process.

AGE-RELATED
HEALTH CONCERNS

Enzyme therapy can be quite effective in managing and fighting an array of health concerns that become more prevalent with age. We've discussed a number of these—including heart disease, cancer, digestive distress, and even wrinkles—in previous chapters. Menopausal problems and sexual dysfunction improve with enzymes as well.

Menopausal Problems

While the decline in estrogen that occurs at menopause certainly plays a role in menopausal discomforts, poor digestion and food sensitivities can seriously aggravate the problem. For female patients who are menopausal, Dr. Ellen routinely recommends taking a carbohydrate digestive enzyme and following the carbohydrate-intolerance diet (see page 295). This is often enough to alleviate symptoms or at least minimize their frequency and severity.

Both of us have seen firsthand how enzyme therapy can slow and stop the premature graying that can accompany menopause. Enzymes restore nutritional completeness and balance; your hair—and your general appearance—will reflect this.

FROM DR. ELLEN'S CASE FILES *At age 44, Rachel noticed the first signs of perimenopause—insomnia, hot flashes, and severe mood swings. Her memory wasn't as sharp as it had been, and even though she adhered to a strict organic vegetarian diet and a regular exercise program, she was gaining 2 to 3 pounds every 6 months. Her hair was thinning and turning gray. In her mind, she looked and felt older than her years.*

When Rachel consulted me, I assured her that many of her symptoms would subside with enzyme therapy. The gray hair would be a challenge, though. In my years of practice, I had seen a few cases in which graying slowed down, but I didn't want to raise her hopes.

At my suggestion, Rachel reduced her calorie intake, especially from carbohydrates. Since she was vegetarian, this limited her food choices, but we worked through it. (I am also vegetarian, and I eat very few carbs and no grains.) She rebuilt her diet around organic vegetables as well as high-quality protein sources, such as nuts and soy and other beans. She also began taking a mineral enzyme formula that supplied extra calcium, magnesium, and trace minerals.

When Rachel returned for a follow-up visit 2 weeks later, she was already seeing results. Her hair had stopped falling out right away, and her hot flashes diminished in about 6 days. Usually this takes about 10 days, so she was a little ahead of schedule.

To Rachel's disappointment, though, her hair was continuing to turn gray. I didn't say anything when she raised the issue; I just listened while she talked. I advised her to stick with her regimen for another 3 months, then return for a complete examination.

When we met again, I couldn't believe my eyes. Rachel's hair was almost completely red. I assumed she had colored it and didn't mention it.

As her examination confirmed, Rachel was doing beautifully. Her hot flashes had stopped, she was sleeping much better, and she had lost 6 pounds. She felt like a new woman.

Before she left my office, Rachel turned to me and said, "Dr. Ellen, I can't believe you didn't notice my hair."

"Of course I did," I replied. "I assumed you had colored it."

She proceeded to tell me how her hair had stopped graying after 5 weeks of following her regimen. After 3 months, it had returned to its natural color. This was a monumental breakthrough; I will never forget it.

Sexual Dysfunction

Sexual dysfunction is so prevalent among older men that even many doctors consider it an inevitable consequence of aging. A study of this phenomenon found that overall, sexual dysfunction is strongly associated with poor health.[9] Some decline in sexual performance is normal, but contrary to popular belief, it is treatable.

Among men, the most common sexual effects of aging are diminished desire and slower arousal. It takes more stimulation over a longer period to produce an erection, which tends to not last as long as before. It may also take more time to reach orgasm, with more occasions when orgasm doesn't occur.

Studies have shown that erectile dysfunction—also known as impotence—affects approximately half of all men over age 50, with the prevalence increasing as men get older. Most cases of erectile dysfunction involve a problem with circulation.

During an erection, a muscle in the penis relaxes, allowing blood to flow into the organ. Researchers—among them Louis Ignarro, MD, professor of pharmacology in the department of molecular and medical pharmacology at the University of California, Los Angeles, School of Medicine[10]—have identified a chemical called nitric oxide that triggers the erectile process and may become deficient with age. Dr. Ignarro is studying the genes that regulate production of nitric oxide to see whether ultimately, an effective treatment may send more of this chemical into the penis.

Erectile dysfunction can be an early warning sign of vascular disease, diabetes, or prostate cancer. It can also be a side effect of certain medications. For example, drugs that act on the autonomic nervous system—such as antihypertensives, tranquilizers, and antidepressants—may interfere with sexual function. This is why seeing a doctor for an accurate diagnosis is so important.

For women, the story is similar. As they get older, they may experience a decline in sexual interest, greater discomfort during intercourse (especially after menopause), and diminished ability to achieve orgasm. These changes seem driven in large part by the hormonal changes that occur with age—although interestingly, sexual activity in both women and men begins to decline in the late thirties and early forties, well before the onset of significant hormonal shifts. This is when other factors associated with aging may come into play. For example, medical conditions such as cardiovascular disease, diabetes, and thyroid disorders may contribute to sexual dysfunction in women. So, too, can depression, which becomes more common with age. The use of medications and alcohol may also dampen sexual desire and arousal.

The onset of menopause—whether natural or surgical—brings with it dramatic drops in levels of circulating estrogen and progesterone. The shortage of estrogen results in vaginal dryness and diminished genital sensation, both of which may impair sexual function. As they get older, women also experience declines in testosterone, the "male hormone" that's important for maintaining libido.

Dr. Ellen has successfully treated sexual dysfunction in both women and men by combining systemic enzymes with herbal extracts that have positive track records for enhancing sexual performance and desire. Throughout the book, we've described the positive effects of enzymes on circulation. Good circulation is the key to healthy sexuality.

The heart is responsible for continuously pumping between 4 and 6 liters of blood throughout the body via an intricate network of arteries, veins, and capillaries. Healthy sexual function depends on the increased flow and accumulation of blood in the genital area. Enhancing this process is precisely what enzymes, in combination with certain herbs, can do. They may not work for everyone, but they can help—naturally and safely.

Of course, sex is more than a physical act. At its most meaningful and satisfying, it is a whole-body experience that grows from compassion, intimacy, and boundless love. According to Dean Ornish, MD, author of *Love and Survival: The Scientific Basis for the Healing Power of Intimacy*, "An open heart can lead to the most joyful and ecstatic sex." His research into intimacy and its effects on health has shown that "anything that promotes feelings of love and intimacy is healing."

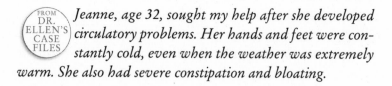 *Jeanne, age 32, sought my help after she developed circulatory problems. Her hands and feet were constantly cold, even when the weather was extremely warm. She also had severe constipation and bloating.*

While Jeanne was perplexed by her symptoms, she wasn't all that concerned about them. After all, she wasn't a smoker, she ate fairly healthfully, and she worked out regularly. But her husband complained about her cold feet at night when they went to bed. He believed that something could be done and that she should look into it.

At first, Jeanne made an appointment with a vascular surgeon, but a thorough evaluation turned up nothing. When her symptoms persisted, she decided to consult me. She thought that food sensitivities might be contributing to her poor circulation as well as her constipation. She also mentioned that her libido wasn't as strong as it had been. She wondered whether all of these symptoms could stem from the same underlying problem.

A thorough digestive evaluation and food sensitivity testing revealed that Jeanne had trouble digesting proteins and fats. For this reason, I suspected that she might be deficient in some amino acids (which make up proteins) and fatty acids. I recommended a protein/fat digestive enzyme and a circulatory enzyme, along with a probiotic, a colon health formula, and an adrenal support formula. We agreed that she would follow this regimen for 3 months, at which time she'd come in for follow-up.

During those 3 months, there seemed to be a dramatic increase in the number of men calling my office for circulatory enzymes. My receptionist wondered what was behind the rush. When I began asking these men where they had heard about the enzymes, they rather sheepishly mentioned Jeanne's husband. How interesting.

When Jeanne came in for her appointment, I asked how she was doing. Her hands were much warmer, she reported, and her feet were finally catching up. She was far less constipated and no longer needed laxatives. What pleased her most, though, was the change in her libido, which had increased substantially. She was very grateful.

Then Jeanne mentioned that her husband had begun taking the circulatory enzyme after noticing how well it worked for her. He was so happy with the results that he told all his tennis buddies! I smiled as I realized why we had been getting all the new requests for these enzymes.

YOUNG FOR LIFE

We don't need to age. We may grow older in a chronological sense, but we can slow the biological process so we stay youthful. With enzyme therapy, we can repair the damage that accelerates aging and build our resistance to age-related illness. Enzymes are the natural solution to life-long good health and vitality. They allow us to live to a ripe *young* age.

Free of the disease and debility that we tend to associate with getting older, we are able to truly live in the present, where each moment becomes special and purposeful. We discover and experience who we truly are and the reasons we were put on this Earth. We become ageless.

DR. ELLEN'S PRESCRIPTION

If the promise of radiant health and long life appeals to you, you may want to consider taking one or more of the enzyme formulas that appear here. Collectively, they support the structures and processes that are most vulnerable to damage with age.

For each formula, I've listed what I consider the ideal ingredients and their respective dosages. You can choose a product with just the primary ingredients (in bold) as long as it also contains a pH-balanced, full-spectrum enzyme blend. Or you can take these ingredients as individual supplements with a full-spectrum digestive enzyme blend for optimal nutrient absorption.

- Take one capsule of an antioxidant supplement once a day, either 1 hour before or 2 hours after a meal. Antioxidants help neutralize free radicals as well as repair the damage caused by them. I recommend a product with the ingredients listed on page 322.

- Take one capsule of a cardiovascular enzyme formula twice a day, 1 hour before or 2 hours after a meal. Typically, I prescribe this formula to patients with high blood pressure, high cholesterol, or circulatory problems. It supports the heart and cardiovascular system to ensure steady blood flow throughout the body. Check product labels for the following ingredients.

  Digestive enzymes. I recommend 30,000 to 100,000 HUT of protease; 200 to 1,500 LU of lipase, cellulase, and bromelain; and 1,500 to 2,000 FTU of natokinese. (*Note:* Be sure to consult your doctor before taking natokinese in any form if you're already on a blood thinner such as warfarin, or Coumadin.)

  Hawthorn leaf and flower extract (200 to 500 milligrams). Hawthorn improves blood flow and has diuretic properties, which are beneficial for managing blood pressure.

  Garlic bulb concentrate (60 to 300 milligrams). Garlic has a lengthy history of use for therapeutic purposes. The latest research focuses on the herb's ability to reduce heart disease risk by inhibiting hardening of the arteries and reducing the "stickiness" of blood platelets so they're less likely to clump.

  Vitamin E as d-alpha tocopherol succinate (50 to 100 IU). Research has shown that vitamin E helps prevent heart attack and stroke by reducing the harmful effects of unhealthy LDL cholesterol and preventing blood clots. It may also inhibit the inflammatory process that appears to contribute to heart disease.

  Coenzyme Q_{10} (25 to 50 milligrams). The primary function of CoQ_{10} is to serve as a catalyst in the breakdown of food for use as energy. It's especially abundant in the energy-intensive cells of the heart, which beats 100,000-plus times each day. As an antioxidant, it also helps neutralize free radicals.

Grapeseed extract (20 to 40 milligrams). Grapeseed protects against blood vessel disorders.

Alpha linolenic acid (30 to 50 milligrams). This is a source of heart-healthy omega-3 fatty acids.

Vitamin B_6 (6 to 12 milligrams); vitamin B_{12} (175 to 250 micrograms); and folic acid (25 to 50 micrograms). This trio of B vitamins protects against heart disease.

Potassium (50 to 100 milligrams). Potassium helps lower blood pressure.

Acetyl-L-carnitine (50 to 100 milligrams). Because it strengthens the heart, L-carnitine is beneficial in cases of congestive heart failure. It may also improve recovery after a heart attack.

• Take two capsules of a mental focus enzyme formula once a day, either 1 hour before or 2 hours after a meal. I recommend this formula because the ingredients not only maintain optimal blood flow to the brain but also support the production of neurotransmitters.

Digestive enzymes. For optimal cognitive function, the ideal product will supply 16,000 to 50,000 HUT of protease.

Ginkgo biloba leaf extract (200 to 360 milligrams). Ginkgo contains a number of compounds, including bioflavonoids and terpenoids, that sharpen memory and concentration.

Gotu kola herb extract (50 to 300 milligrams). Gotu kola prevents mental fatigue while enhancing memory and concentration. It also supports healthy circulation.

Panax ginseng root extract (150 to 240 milligrams). This form of ginseng has a longstanding reputation for enhancing energy and concentration.

Water hyssop herb extract (80 to 100 milligrams). Water hyssop improves mental sharpness.

Schizandra fruit extract (100 to 150 milligrams). Like water hyssop, schizandra enhances mental acuity.

Phosphatidylserine (300 to 500 milligrams). An amino acid, phosphatidylserine may support mental function.

Acetyl-L-carnitine (1,500 to 2,000 milligrams). This amino acid may boost production of compounds that improve memory.

Vitamin B$_{12}$ (3 to 6 micrograms). This B vitamin may play a role in memory.

- For perimenopausal and menopausal complaints, take one or two capsules of a women's enzyme formula two or three times a day. The ingredients in this formula promote hormone balance, which in turn can alleviate hot flashes, mood swings, vaginal dryness, and diminished libido.

  Digestive enzymes. Look for 32,000 to 60,000 HUT of protease.

  Black cohosh root extract with triterpene glycosides (400 to 800 milligrams). Black cohosh is especially effective for relieving hot flashes, among other menopausal discomforts. It also reduces menstrual and muscle pain.

  Deglycyrrhizinated licorice root extract (200 to 400 milligrams). Licorice is beneficial for an array of menopausal and menstrual problems.

  Soy isoflavone extract with genistein and daidzein (10 to 15 milligrams). Soy may reduce the frequency and severity of hot flashes, along with other discomforts.

Vitamin E as d-alpha tocopherol succinate (40 to 90 IU). Vitamin E may alleviate some perimenopausal complaints.

St. John's wort extract (80 to 160 milligrams). A popular and effective herbal remedy for depression, St. John's wort also provides relief from premenstrual symptoms.

Chaste tree berry extract (150 to 225 milligrams). This herb can ease menopausal hot flashes.

- For male sexual dysfunction, take two or three capsules of a men's enzyme formula once or twice a day. This formula helps restore and maintain optimal levels of male sex hormones, including testosterone. It also improves blood flow and excitatory nerve impulses to the genitals, promoting natural sex drive with sufficient stamina.

  Digestive enzymes. Choose a product with 28,000 to 54,000 HUT of protease.

  Panax ginseng root extract (160 to 320 milligrams). This species of ginseng may correct erectile dysfunction and infertility. It's also a natural energy booster.

  Damiana leaf extract (160 to 320 milligrams). Beyond its long history of use as an aphrodisiac, damiana is excellent for strengthening the nervous and endocrine systems.

  Ginkgo biloba leaf extract (120 to 240 milligrams). Ginkgo may restore erections in men with erectile dysfunction.

  Vitamin E as d-alpha tocopherol succinate (80 to 160 IU). Because it supports heart health, vitamin E may be helpful for erectile dysfunction, which often involves poor circulation.

  Zinc citrate (28 to 54 milligrams). Zinc enhances male fertility.

Yohimbe bark extract (140 to 320 milligrams). This herb has shown great promise as a treatment for erectile dysfunction. Since it can raise blood pressure, consult your physician before trying it if you have hypertension.

Muira puama extract (375 to 750 milligrams). The bark and roots of the muira puama tree, native to Brazil, are a popular folk remedy for sexual dysfunction.

Pygeum bark extract (45 to 100 milligrams). Herbalists often prescribe pygeum as a treatment for prostate enlargement.

- Take two capsules of a sexual enhancement formula twice a day. All of the ingredients in this formula improve sexual health and function for both men and women.

  Digestive enzymes: should include 28,000 to 54,000 HUT of protease.

  Ginkgo biloba leaf extract (120 to 240 milligrams): helps restore erections in men with erectile dysfunction.

  Damiana leaf extract (160 to 320 milligrams): enhances sexual function.

  Vitamin E as d-alpha tocopherol succinate (80 to 160 IU): improves circulation.

  Vitamin C from acerola cherry extract (1,000 to 2,000 milligrams): supports the structure of blood vessels and improves blood flow to the genitals.

  Hawthorn leaf and flower extract (300 to 400 milligrams): improves circulation.

  Yohimbe bark extract (140 to 280 milligrams): beneficial for erectile dysfunction.

Resources

Carbohydrate-Intolerance Diet

People who are carbohydrate intolerant may experience symptoms such as fatigue, depression, low blood sugar, bloating, chronic constipation, asthma, premenstrual syndrome, and severe allergies. They tend to crave sugar and/or carbohydrates.

A carbohydrate-intolerance diet should consist of the following:

- Liberal quantities of vegetables (raw or cooked without fat or salt), mineral water, and select herbal teas

- Moderate quantities of healthy fats, plant proteins, and animal proteins

- Minimal amounts of sugars, fruits, dairy products, and sweet vegetables, such as carrots and corn

- Limited intake of salty foods, such as soy sauce

- Limited consumption of alcohol

- Avoidance of most grains, with the exception of quinoa, buckwheat, and wild rice

- Avoidance of all artificial sweeteners and caffeinated beverages

PROTEINS (3 TO 5 SERVINGS PER DAY, UNLESS OTHERWISE NOTED)

4 ounces beef (3 or fewer servings per week)
2 ounces low-fat cottage cheese
1 egg
2 egg whites
4 ounces fish or shellfish
4 ounces lamb
2 ounces part-skim mozzarella cheese
4 ounces poultry
2 ounces part-skim ricotta cheese
4 ounces soy protein powder
1 ounce spirulina or green protein substitute
3 ounces tofu
4 ounces veal
1 cup low-fat or fat-free yogurt

VEGETABLES

Unlimited

Alfalfa sprouts
Bell peppers
Bok choy
Cabbage
Celery
Cucumbers

Endive
Escarole
Green or yellow beans
Jicama
Kale
Lettuce (all types)

Okra

Onions

Radishes

Spinach

Tomatoes

Yellow squash

Zucchini

3 or 4 Servings per Week

1 small artichoke

4 ounces carrots

4 ounces corn

4 ounces potatoes

4 ounces pumpkin

4 ounces sweet peas

4 ounces sweet potatoes

4 ounces yams

FRUITS

2 Servings per Day

1 apple

2 medium apricots

1 cup berries

½ cantaloupe

10 cherries

10 grapes

¼ honeydew

1 nectarine

1 peach

1 pear

½ cup fresh pineapple

2 plums

2 prunes

2 small tangerines

1 cup cubed watermelon

3 or 4 Servings per Week

½ banana

½ cup cranberries

1½ dates

1½ dried figs

8 ounces fruit juice

½ mango

1 cup cubed papaya

½ cup raisins

FATS

2 Servings per Day

7 almonds or ½ teaspoon almond butter

½ tablespoon avocado

⅓ teaspoon canola oil

⅓ teaspoon olive oil

1 teaspoon olive oil and vinegar dressing

3 olives

⅓ teaspoon peanut oil

6 peanuts

½ tablespoon tahini

FATS

3 or 4 Servings per Week

2 teaspoons bacon bits

½ teaspoon Brazil nuts

⅓ teaspoon butter

½ tablespoon cream

1 teaspoon cream cheese

⅓ teaspoon lard

⅓ teaspoon margarine

1 teaspoon mayonnaise

½ tablespoon peanut butter

½ teaspoon sesame oil

½ tablespoon low-fat sour cream

⅓ teaspoon soybean oil

½ teaspoon walnuts

LEGUMES AND GRAINS (2 SERVINGS PER DAY)

⅓ cup cooked beans

½ cup cooked buckwheat

1 corn tortilla (6-inch)

⅓ cup cooked lentils

2 cups popped popcorn

½ cup cooked quinoa

½ cup cooked spelt

½ ounce tortilla chips

½ cup cooked wild rice

RECIPES FOR CARBOHYDRATE INTOLERANCE

Fruit Slushy

4   ounces soy protein powder
1   fruit of choice
6   ounces water
½   cup ice

In a blender, combine the soy powder, fruit, water, and ice. Blend well.

Makes 1 to 2 servings

Tabbouleh with Buckwheat

1   cup buckwheat
1½   cups boiling water
¼   cup fresh lemon juice
2   teaspoons olive oil
2   cloves garlic, crushed
    Ground black pepper to taste
4   scallions, finely chopped
1   cup packed parsley, finely chopped
10–15   fresh mint leaves, finely chopped
2   medium tomatoes, chopped
1   medium green bell pepper, seeded and chopped

In a large bowl, combine the buckwheat and boiling water. Cover and let stand for at least 20 to 30 minutes, or until the buckwheat is tender. Add the lemon juice, olive oil, garlic, and black pepper and mix well. Cover tightly and refrigerate.

About 30 minutes before serving, stir in the scallions, parsley, mint, tomatoes, and bell pepper and mix well. Refrigerate until ready to serve.

Makes 6 servings

Skillet Eggplant and Tofu Pasta

⅔ teaspoon olive oil

2 cups chopped peeled eggplant

¼ cup chopped onion

¼ cup chopped red bell pepper

¼ cup quartered mushrooms

3 ounces tofu, chopped

1 small clove garlic, minced

1 cup canned crushed tomatoes

2 teaspoons fresh basil, chopped

⅛ teaspoon fresh oregano

⅛ teaspoon ground black pepper

1 cup cooked buckwheat pasta

3 ounces shredded part-skim mozzarella cheese

Heat the oil in a 9- or 10-inch nonstick skillet over medium-high heat. Add the eggplant and cook, stirring occasionally, for about 5 minutes, or until slightly softened.

Add the onion, bell pepper, mushrooms, tofu, garlic, tomatoes, basil, oregano, and black pepper. Increase the heat to high, cover, and cook, stirring occasionally, for about 5 minutes, or until the vegetables are crisp-tender.

Add the pasta and stir to combine. Simmer for 5 minutes longer. Serve sprinkled with the mozzarella.

Makes 2 servings

No-Sugar-Added Tofu Smoothie

3 ounces silken tofu

1 cup berries, any type

6 ounces water

½ cup ice

In a blender, combine the tofu, berries, water, and ice. Blend well.

Makes 1 to 2 servings

Stuffed Zucchini

4	medium zucchini (about 7 inches long)
2	teaspoons olive oil
1½	cups chopped onions
8	ounces mushrooms, finely chopped
6	cloves garlic, minced
1½	cups cooked wild rice
25	almonds, finely chopped or ground
3	tablespoons lemon juice
	Ground black pepper to taste
	Ground red pepper to taste
	Small handfuls of freshly chopped herbs, such as parsley, basil, thyme, dill, chives, and/or marjoram (optional)

Cut each zucchini lengthwise down the middle. Use a spoon to scoop out the insides, leaving ¼-inch-thick shells. Set the shells aside and finely chop the insides.

Heat the oil in a medium skillet. Add the onions and sauté over medium heat for 5 to 8 minutes, or until soft. Add the zucchini and mushrooms and sauté for 8 to 10 minutes. Add the garlic during the last few minutes of cooking.

Preheat the oven to 350°F.

In a large bowl, combine the rice and almonds. Stir in the zucchini mixture and lemon juice and mix well. Add the black pepper, red pepper, and fresh herbs (if using). Fill the zucchini shells, place on a baking sheet, and bake for 30 to 40 minutes, or until heated through.

Makes 4 servings

CARBOHYDRATE INTOLERANCE
7-DAY MEAL PLAN

Monday

Breakfast

> 4 ounces soy protein powder mixed with ½ cup cooked quinoa

Lunch

> 1 corn tortilla spread with 1 tablespoon mayonnaise and filled with kale, spinach, and 4 ounces turkey breast

Snack

> 10 grapes
> ½ cup low-fat yogurt

Dinner

> 2 cups grilled zucchini, squash, and tomatoes with ⅓ teaspoon canola oil, topped with 2 ounces melted part-skim mozzarella cheese

Snack

> 1 Fruit Slushy (page 299) made with a peach

Tuesday

Breakfast

> ½ buckwheat waffle
> 2 egg whites prepared with cooking spray

Lunch

4 ounces grilled salmon
½ cup cooked quinoa or buckwheat pasta
1 cup grilled bell peppers, tomatoes, and onions
  with ⅓ teaspoon olive oil

Snack

1 pear
1 ounce part-skim mozzarella cheese

Dinner

4 ounces grilled or broiled lean beef
1 serving Tabbouleh with Buckwheat (page 299)
1 cup grilled mushrooms with ⅓ teaspoon olive oil

Snack

¼ honeydew melon
2 egg whites poached or prepared with cooking spray

Wednesday

Breakfast

½ corn tortilla filled with tomato slices and
  2 ounces part-skim mozzarella cheese

Lunch

Spinach salad topped with 4 ounces grilled skinless chicken
  breast, ½ mango, and ⅓ teaspoon peanut oil

Dinner

4 ounces grilled or broiled lamb
½ cup cooked quinoa pasta
Tossed salad with 1 teaspoon olive oil and vinegar dressing

Snack

> ½ cup cubed cantaloupe
> 2 ounces low-fat cottage cheese

Thursday

Breakfast

> 2 ounces low-fat cottage cheese
> 1 corn tortilla

Lunch

> 1 serving Skillet Eggplant and Tofu Pasta (page 300)

Snack

> 2 apricots
> ½ cup low-fat yogurt

Dinner

> 4 ounces grilled skinless chicken breast
> 1 small baked sweet potato with ⅓ teaspoon butter
>   and a dash of cinnamon
> 1 cup cooked cauliflower with ⅓ teaspoon butter

Snack

> 2 plums
> ½ cup low-fat yogurt

Friday

Breakfast

> 1 No-Sugar-Added Tofu Smoothie (page 300)

Lunch

> 4 ounces grilled skinless chicken breast with spinach, bok choy, and ½ teaspoon walnuts

Snack

> 7 almonds

Dinner

> 4 ounces grilled tuna
> 1 serving Stuffed Zucchini (page 301)

Snack

> 1 cup berries
> 2 ounces low-fat cottage cheese

Saturday

Breakfast

> 1 cup low-fat yogurt
> ½ cup raisins and 7 almonds

Lunch

> 4 ounces grilled fish
> 4 ounces cooked peas
> 1 cup grilled mushrooms and onions with ⅓ teaspoon olive oil

Snack

> 1 apple
> 1 ounce part-skim mozzarella cheese

Dinner

> 4 ounces grilled or broiled veal
> 1 cup grilled okra, bell peppers, and onions with ⅓ teaspoon canola oil
> ½ cup cooked wild rice

Snack

> 6 peanuts

Sunday

Breakfast

> 1 egg plus 2 egg whites prepared with cooking spray
> ½ banana

Lunch

> 4 ounces very lean grilled or broiled ground beef with lettuce, tomato, onion, and mustard
> ½ cup buckwheat

Snack

> 1 Fruit Slushy (page 299) made with a nectarine

Dinner

> 4 ounces grilled skinless chicken breast with 3 olives
> 1 sliced cucumber with 1 cup low-fat yogurt and 1 teaspoon dried dill

Snack

> ½ cup fresh pineapple
> ½ cup low-fat yogurt

Protein/Fat
Intolerance Diet

People who are protein or fat intolerant may feel sluggish after eating animal protein. They are prone to symptoms such as anxiety, hypoglycemia (low blood sugar), fluid retention, and constipation. They may also be deficient in essential fatty acids. A protein/fat-intolerance diet should consist of the following:

- Liberal quantities of vegetables (raw or cooked without fat or salt), fruits, vegetable juices, fruit juices, mineral water, and select herbal teas

- Moderate quantities of starchy vegetables, such as potatoes, yams, and winter squash

- Minimal amounts of proteins, including legumes and low-fat dairy products

- Limited consumption of olives and avocados

- Limited intake of salty foods, such as soy sauce

- Limited consumption of alcohol

- Avoidance of most grains, with the exception of buckwheat, quinoa, and wild rice

- Avoidance of animal fats, tropical oils, hydrogenated vegetable oils, fried foods, whole-milk dairy products, coconut, and macadamia nuts

- Avoidance of nuts and nut butters, cream cheese, sour cream, bacon, artificial sweeteners, and caffeinated beverages

PROTEINS (1 OR 2 SERVINGS PER DAY, UNLESS OTHERWISE NOTED)

3 ounces lean beef (3 or fewer servings per week)
2 ounces low-fat or fat-free cottage cheese
2 eggs (3 or fewer servings per week)
3 ounces fish or shellfish
3 ounces lean lamb (3 or fewer servings per week)
2 ounces nonfat dry milk
2 ounces part-skim mozzarella cheese
3 ounces poultry
2 ounces part-skim ricotta cheese
⅔ cup cooked soybeans
4 ounces soy protein powder
1 ounce spirulina or green protein substitute
3 ounces tofu
1 cup low-fat or fat-free yogurt

VEGETABLES

Unlimited

Alfalfa sprouts	Bok choy
Artichokes	Broccoli
Beets	Cabbage

Cauliflower
Cucumbers
Endive
Escarole
Green or yellow beans
Jicama
Kale
Leeks
Lettuce (all types)

Mushrooms
Onions
Pumpkin
Radishes
Spinach
Swiss chard
Turnips
Water chestnuts

3 or 4 Servings per Week

4 ounces bell peppers
4 ounces carrots
4 ounces corn
4 ounces okra
4 ounces parsley
4 ounces potatoes
4 ounces rutabagas

4 ounces squash
4 ounces sweet peas
4 ounces sweet potatoes
4 ounces tomatoes
4 ounces watercress
4 ounces yams

LEGUMES AND GRAINS
(3 OR 4 SERVINGS PER DAY)

⅓ cup cooked beans
½ cup cooked buckwheat
½ cup cooked buckwheat
  noodles

1 corn tortilla (6-inch)
⅓ cup cooked lentils
½ cup cooked quinoa
⅓ cup cooked wild rice

FRUITS (3 SERVINGS PER DAY)

1 small apple
4 medium apricots
¾ cup berries
⅓ cantaloupe

12 cherries
2½ dates
1½ dried figs
½ grapefruit

FRUITS (CONT.)

10 grapes

¼ honeydew

½ mango

1 orange

1 cup cubed papaya

1 peach

1 small pear

¾ cup fresh pineapple

2 plums

2 medium prunes

1¼ cups strawberries

2 small tangerines

FATS

2 Servings per Day

½ tablespoon avocado

⅓ teaspoon canola oil

¼ teaspoon olive oil

1 teaspoon olive oil and
vinegar dressing

3 olives

¼ teaspoon peanut oil

½ tablespoon tahini

FATS

3 to 4 Servings per Week

⅓ teaspoon butter

½ tablespoon cream

⅓ teaspoon lard

⅓ teaspoon margarine

1 teaspoon low-fat mayon-
naise

½ teaspoon sesame oil

⅓ teaspoon soybean oil

RECIPES FOR PROTEIN/FAT INTOLERANCE

Chilled Pasta Salad

8   ounces buckwheat noodles
1   tablespoon olive oil
2   cloves garlic, minced
½   cup chopped broccoli
½   cup chopped cauliflower
½   cup chopped mushrooms
½   cup chopped squash
    Ground black pepper to taste
6   ounces part-skim ricotta cheese

Cook the noodles according to the package directions. Drain and set aside to cool in a large bowl.

Heat the oil in a large skillet. Add the garlic and sauté until opaque. Add the broccoli, cauliflower, mushrooms, squash, and pepper and sauté until tender.

Add the vegetables to the pasta and stir to combine. Crumble in the ricotta and mix well. Let cool before serving.

Makes 4 servings

Asian Salad

½   cup chopped cabbage
½   cup chopped bok choy
¼   cup chopped alfalfa or other sprouts
½   cup chopped mushrooms
¼   cup chopped water chestnuts
2   teaspoons olive oil and vinegar dressing
    Ground black pepper to taste

In a large bowl, toss the cabbage, bok choy, sprouts, mushrooms, and water chestnuts with the dressing. Mix well and add the pepper.

Makes 2 servings

Cauliflower Seldess

1½	cups quinoa
2½	cups water
1	tablespoon olive oil
2	cups chopped onions
1	pound mushrooms, sliced
	Ground black pepper to taste
1	teaspoon dried basil
1	large head cauliflower, cut into 1-inch pieces
3	cloves garlic, minced
2	tablespoons lemon juice
6	ounces shredded part-skim mozzarella cheese
	Dash of paprika

In a medium saucepan, bring the quinoa and water to a boil. Reduce the heat, cover, and simmer for 15 to 20 minutes, or until tender. Drain, transfer to a large bowl, and fluff with a fork.

Preheat the oven to 350°F. Coat a 9 × 13-inch baking pan with cooking spray.

Heat the oil in a large skillet. Add the onions, mushrooms, pepper, and basil and sauté for about 5 minutes, or until the onion softens. Add the cauliflower and garlic and sauté for about 10 minutes longer, or until the cauliflower is tender. Add the lemon juice.

Stir the vegetables and mozzarella into the quinoa. Mix well and spread in the baking pan. Dust with the paprika and bake for 30 minutes.

Makes 4 servings

Perfect Protein Salad

¾   cup dry soybeans, soaked
1½   cups cooked wild rice
     Ground black pepper to taste
¼   cup dill weed, minced
2   teaspoons low-fat mayonnaise
2   small cloves garlic, minced
½   cup packed parsley, finely chopped
1   cup low-fat cottage cheese
3   scallions, finely chopped
1   medium carrot, finely chopped
1   small cucumber, peeled, seeded, and finely chopped
     Finely chopped onion or celery, fresh alfalfa sprouts, and/or
     sliced radishes (optional)

Place the soybeans in a medium saucepan with enough water to cover and bring to a boil. Reduce the heat and simmer, partially covered, until tender but still crunchy, about 1¼ hours. Rinse and drain well in a colander.

In a medium bowl, combine the soybeans, rice, pepper, dill, mayonnaise, garlic, parsley, cottage cheese, scallions, carrot, cucumber, and other vegetables (if using). Mix well.

Makes 6 servings

Wild Rice and Bean Casserole

4   cups cooked navy beans, drained and liquid reserved
2   cups cooked wild rice
¾   teaspoon dried thyme
½   teaspoon dried sage
1   teaspoon ground black pepper
6   cloves garlic, minced
1   tablespoon olive oil
1   cup chopped peeled eggplant
1   cup chopped mushrooms
½   teaspoon dried rosemary
6   ounces shredded part-skim mozzarella cheese

Add enough water to the bean liquid to make 1 cup. Set aside.

In a large bowl, combine the beans, rice, thyme, sage, pepper, and half of the garlic. Set aside.

Preheat the oven to 400°F. Coat an 11 × 7-inch baking dish with cooking spray.

Heat the oil in a nonstick skillet. Add the eggplant, mushrooms, rosemary, and the remaining garlic. Mix well and cook for 5 minutes. Add the bean liquid and simmer uncovered for 10 minutes, or until all the liquid has evaporated.

Layer half of the bean mixture in the bottom of the baking dish and top with half of the mozzarella. Add the mushroom mixture and cover with the remaining beans and cheese. Bake uncovered for 25 minutes.

Makes 8 servings

PROTEIN/FAT INTOLERANCE
7-DAY MEAL PLAN

Monday

Breakfast

1 cup cooked buckwheat mixed with 4 ounces soy protein
powder

Lunch

Tossed salad with cucumbers, beets, mushrooms,
and balsamic vinegar
1 small sweet potato baked with butter-flavored spray
and cinnamon
1 small apple

Snack

6 peanuts

Dinner

4 ounces grilled skinless chicken breast topped with
lettuce, onion, alfalfa or other sprouts, and 1½ teaspoons
avocado

Snack

1 pear

Tuesday

Breakfast

3 ounces low-fat cottage cheese
⅓ cantaloupe

Lunch

> 1 serving Chilled Pasta Salad (page 311)
> ¼ honeydew

Snack

> 12 cherries

Dinner

> 3 ounces grilled tofu prepared with cooking spray and seasonings
> ⅔ cup cooked wild rice
> 1 serving Asian Salad (page 311)

Snack

> 10 grapes

Wednesday

Breakfast

> 1 cup fat-free yogurt
> ½ cup raisins

Lunch

> 1 teaspoon peanut butter with 1 apple
> 2½ medium dates
> 1 cup sliced raw carrots

Snack

> 1 cup cubed papaya

Dinner

> 4 ounces grilled tuna
> ⅔ cup cooked lentils with 3 olives
> 1 cup chopped grilled eggplant with 1 teaspoon olive oil

Snack

¾ cup fresh pineapple

Thursday

Breakfast

2 eggs prepared with cooking spray
½ slice quinoa bread (no wheat)

Lunch

⅓ cup cooked red beans over ⅓ cup cooked wild rice
Salad made with kale, lettuce, and alfalfa or other sprouts
  and topped with ⅓ teaspoon peanut oil and 1 sliced orange

Snack

1½ dried figs

Dinner

4 ounces shrimp boiled or grilled with ⅓ teaspoon canola oil
½ cup cooked buckwheat noodles
1 serving Cauliflower Seldess (page 312)

Snack

1 peach

Friday

Breakfast

½ cup cooked quinoa mixed with 4 ounces soy protein powder

Lunch

Peanut butter and banana sandwich made with 2 slices quinoa
  bread, ½ banana, and ½ teaspoon peanut butter

Snack

  1½ cups strawberries

Dinner

  1 serving Perfect Protein Salad (page 313)

Snack

  ½ grapefruit

Saturday

Breakfast

  1 slice quinoa bread with 2 ounces melted part-skim mozzarella
  cheese

Lunch

  ½ slice quinoa bread, toasted
  Tossed salad topped with ½ mango, balsamic vinegar,
    and ⅓ teaspoon olive oil

Snack

  2 plums

Dinner

  4 ounces grilled salmon
  ⅔ cup cooked black beans with onion
  Tossed salad topped with cucumbers and 1 teaspoon olive oil
    and vinegar dressing

Snack

  1 orange

Sunday

Breakfast

2 eggs prepared with cooking spray
½ cup cooked buckwheat

Lunch

½ cup cooked wild rice mixed with ¾ cup berries

Snack

⅓ cantaloupe

Dinner

1 serving Wild Rice and Bean Casserole (page 314)

Snack

2 small tangerines

Choosing an
Antioxidant Formula

Throughout this book, we've discussed how damage by unstable molecules known as free radicals can set the stage for disease and accelerate the aging process. The antioxidants in the following formula can repair and prevent this sort of damage.

The ideal product will contain all of the nutrients and herbs, plus protease (as a digestive enzyme) and at least one of the "additional ingredients." As a general dosage guideline, take one capsule of this formula once a day, either 1 hour before or 2 hours after a meal. For specific health concerns, follow the recommendations in the appropriate chapters in part 3. The full-spectrum digestive enzyme blend in the basic plan (page 32) will ensure optimum antioxidant absorption.

DIGESTIVE ENZYME

- Protease: 15,000 to 50,000 HUT

NUTRIENTS

- Vitamin A as beta-carotene: 7,500 to 15,000 IU
- Vitamin C from acerola cherry extract: 45 to 100 milligrams
- Vitamin E as d-alpha tocopherol succinate: 90 to 200 IU
- Copper citrate: 0.75 to 1.5 milligrams
- Manganese citrate: 3 to 6 milligrams
- Selenium citrate: 30 to 90 micrograms
- Zinc citrate: 9 to 18 milligrams
- Alpha lipoic acid: 2 to 12 milligrams
- Quercetin: 15 to 40 milligrams

HERBS

- Bilberry fruit extract: 3 to 10 milligrams
- Grapeseed extract (standardized to contain 95 percent anthocyanidins): 6 to 12 milligrams
- Green tea leaf extract (standardized to contain 40 percent catechins): 15 to 40 milligrams
- Lutein: 15 to 30 milligrams

ADDITIONAL INGREDIENTS

- Citrus bioflavonoids: 15 to 30 milligrams
- Coenzyme Q_{10}: 50 to 150 milligrams

- Concentrated cruciferous vegetable blend (containing broccoli, cabbage, brussels sprouts, cauliflower, kale, and watercress): 18 to 36 milligrams

- Hesperidin: 15 to 30 milligrams

- L-methionine: 1,000 to 1,500 milligrams

- Lycopene: 15 to 30 milligrams

- Milk thistle leaf extract (standardized to contain 24 percent ginkgolides): 3 to 6 milligrams

- N-acetylcysteine: 400 to 600 milligrams

- Rutin: 15 to 30 milligrams

- Turmeric root extract (standardized to contain 95 percent curcumin): 20 to 40 milligrams

What to Look For in a Multivitamin

S EVERAL OF THE CONDITION-SPECIFIC chapters in part 3 include a recommendation for a daily multivitamin/mineral formula. Look for a product that contains all of the following vitamins and minerals, plus at least one of the ingredients listed under "Additional Nutrients." Remember to take it with a full-spectrum digestive enzyme blend to ensure optimal absorption.

VITAMINS

Biotin (100 to 300 micrograms). Biotin supports fatty acid production, cell growth, and nutrient metabolism. It's also important for healthy skin and hair.

Choline (25 to 200 milligrams). Choline facilitates the transmission of nerve impulses from the brain to the nervous system and contributes to hormone production and liver health.

Folic acid (400 to 800 micrograms). This B vitamin is essential for energy production and helps to lower levels of homocysteine, a key marker for cardiovascular problems. Moms-to-be need folic acid to regulate fetal nerve cell formation and ensure normal fetal development.

Inositol (25 to 200 milligrams). A key nutrient for hair growth, inositol also helps protect against atherosclerosis by lowering cholesterol.

Niacin/niacinamide (50 to 300 milligrams). This B vitamin, also known as vitamin B_3, is necessary for healthy circulation and normal nervous system function.

Pantothenic acid (50 to 200 milligrams). Another B vitamin, pantothenic acid helps convert carbohydrates, proteins, and fats into energy.

Para-aminobenzoic acid (25 to 50 milligrams). This little-known antioxidant helps the body assimilate pantothenic acid. It also protects against sunburn and skin cancer.

Riboflavin (25 to 50 milligrams). Riboflavin, or vitamin B_2, supports carbohydrate metabolism, cell respiration, and red blood cell formation.

Thiamin (25 to 75 milligrams). Sometimes referred to as vitamin B_1, thiamin assists in carbohydrate metabolism and enhances circulation.

Vitamin A as beta-carotene (10,000 to 25,000 IU). Vitamin A enhances immune function and helps heal skin disorders and wounds. It also maintains eye health.

Vitamin B_6 (25 to 75 milligrams). This B vitamin is vital to the formation of DNA, RNA, and other genetic material. It supports the absorption of proteins and fats, too.

Vitamin B_{12} (50 to 200 micrograms). Vitamin B_{12} helps the body utilize iron, which is important for preventing anemia. It also ensures proper digestion and nutrient absorption.

Vitamin C from acerola cherry extract (100 to 1,000 milligrams). Perhaps best known as an immune enhancer, vitamin C also speeds wound healing.

Vitamin D (100 to 400 IU). Vitamin D promotes strong bones and teeth by helping the body absorb calcium.

Vitamin E as d-alpha tocopherol succinate (100 to 400 IU). This antioxidant helps protect against heart disease and cataracts.

MINERALS

Boron (1 to 3 milligrams). Boron is important for building strong bones, teeth, and nails.

Calcium (250 to 1,300 milligrams). An essential mineral for healthy bones and teeth, calcium also plays a role in muscle contraction and nerve impulses. It protects against blood clots and high blood pressure, too.

Chromium (100 to 200 micrograms). Chromium is essential for breaking down carbohydrates, proteins, and fats. It may also help stabilize blood sugar.

Iodine (50 to 150 micrograms). Iodine is essential for a healthy thyroid and helps the body utilize fats.

Magnesium (125 to 600 milligrams). Doctors routinely recommend magnesium to stabilize irregular heartbeats. This mineral is also known to relieve headache, asthma, and fibromyalgia symptoms.

Manganese (2 to 15 milligrams). Manganese may play a role in treating heart arrhythmias, osteoporosis, and back pain.

Potassium (50 to 99 milligrams). This mineral may help lower high blood pressure.

Selenium (100 to 200 micrograms). Selenium works with vitamin E to protect against heart disease and cancer. On its own, it may enhance thyroid function and reduce the frequency and severity of cold sores and shingles.

Zinc (1 to 2 milligrams). Zinc helps fight colds and flu, treat skin disorders, and maintain healthy hair. It also may be beneficial for an underactive thyroid.

ADDITIONAL NUTRIENTS

Antioxidant blend containing grapeseed extract, turmeric root extract, green tea leaf extract, bilberry fruit extract, ginkgo biloba leaf extract, hawthorn extract, milk thistle seed extract, lutein, lycopene, alpha lipoic acid, and coenzyme Q₁₀ (100 to 300 milligrams). Antioxidants are important for repairing and preventing free radical damage to cells.

Citrus bioflavonoid blend containing hesperidin, rutin, and quercetin (100 to 300 milligrams). Citrus flavonoids are potent antioxidants that appear to reduce the risk of heart disease and protect against age-related vision problems, such as cataracts and macular degeneration. They can also minimize hay fever and asthma symptoms and fight viral infections.

Essential fatty acid blend containing safflower, flax, and black currant seed (100 to 300 milligrams). Essential fatty acids help lower cholesterol and triglycerides. They also are important for producing new cells, repairing existing cells, and transmitting nerve impulses.

Iron (10 to 20 milligrams). Iron is essential for the production of hemoglobin and myoglobin and for the oxygenation of red blood cells. Note that men and postmenopausal women seldom need supplemental iron.

Molybdenum (50 to 150 micrograms). This mineral helps the body metabolize nitrogen, which in turn supports the production of uric acid. It also promotes healthy cell function.

Silica (1 to 10 milligrams). By contributing to the formation of collagen, silica helps ensure healthy bones, skin, hair, and nails. It also protects against heart problems by maintaining pliable arteries.

Vanadium (50 to 100 micrograms). This mineral is essential to healthy bones and teeth. It also may prevent high cholesterol.

Vitamin K (60 to 120 micrograms). Vitamin K helps protect against osteoporosis by supporting bone formation.

Acupressure
Balancing Technique

D R. ELLEN DEVELOPED THE FOLLOWING technique to help patients release negative thoughts that may impede the healing process. It is especially useful for overweight, chronic pain, depression, and anxiety. Use it when you feel an overwhelming desire to overeat or give in to food cravings.

To begin, sit quietly and breathe deeply. Then use your thumbs, fingers, or knuckles to stimulate the following points in sequence, applying light pressure in a clockwise circular motion. Repeat three times at each point. If you feel any discomfort, ease up on your touch. Proceed in order from one point to the next.

LI 4, right: Near the webbing between the thumb and index finger on the back of the right hand.

LI 11, right: In the depression between the right elbow and the end of the elbow crease.

TW 10, right: In the depression just above the right elbow on the back of the right arm.

BL 10, right: At the back of the head, about 1 inch to the right of the spine, in the center of the large muscle just below the bony ridge at the base of the skull.

GV 20: If you imagine a line that runs from the tip of one ear over the head to the tip of the other ear, this point is on top of the head, exactly at the midpoint of the line.

BL 10, left: At the back of the head, about 1 inch to the left of the spine, in the center of the large muscle just below the bony ridge at the base of the skull.

TW 10, left: In the depression just above the left elbow on the back of the left arm.

LI 11, left: In the depression between the left elbow and the end of the elbow crease.

LI 4, left: Near the webbing between the thumb and index finger on the back of the left hand.

BL 40, left: In the middle of the large crease directly behind the left knee.

ST 36, left: About 2 to 3 inches (three or four finger-widths) directly below the lower edge of the left kneecap and directly in line with the little toe.

SP 6, left: On the inside of the left leg, about 2 inches above the anklebone, in the soft tissue just behind the tibia (the larger of the two bones in the lower leg).

LIV 3, left: In the depression between the first and second tarsal bones (the big toe and second toe) of the left foot.

SP3, left: In the arch of the left foot, closest to the big toe.

SP3, right: In the arch of the right foot, closest to the big toe.

LIV 3, right: In the depression between the first and second tarsal bones (the big toe and second toe) of the right foot.

SP 6, right: On the inside of the right leg, about 2 inches above the anklebone, in the soft tissue just behind the tibia (the larger of the two bones in the lower leg).

ST 36, right: About 2 to 3 inches (three or four finger-widths) directly below the lower edge of the right kneecap and directly in line with the little toe.

BL 40, right: In the middle of the large crease directly behind the right knee.

The entire sequence should take about 15 minutes. If you happen to fall asleep while you're doing it, don't worry; use the time for meditation and balance.

Notes

CHAPTER 1

1. J. Beard, "The Action of 'Trypsin' upon Living Cells of the Jensen Sarcoma," *Brit Med J* 1 (1906): 140–41.
2. Aftab J. Ahmed and Edmund A. Byrke, "Difference between Systemic Enzymes and Digestive Enzymes"; "Role of Ribose in Stimulating Natural Energy Production"; "Importance of methyl-sulfonyl-methane." AN: 26043-3, ISSN: 0274-6743, *Alt HealthWatch*. Provides information on the importance of systemic enzyme on the body's healthy physiological functions.
3. Ellen W. Cutler, "Detoxification," in *The Food Allergy Cure* (New York: Three Rivers Press, 2001), 181–207.
4. "Prescription Drug Expenditures in the Year 2000: Upward Trend Continue," A research report by The National Institute for Health Care Management, *McDougall Newsletter* 1, no. 1: 2.
5. J. Kuby, *Immunology*, 3rd ed. (New York: W. H. Freeman and Company, 1997), 79.

CHAPTER 3

1. M. U. Schneider et al., "Pancreatic Enzyme Replacement Therapy: Comparative Effects of Conventional and Enteric-Coated Microspheric Pancreatic and Acid-Stable Fungal Enzyme Preparation on Steattorhea in Chronic

Pancreatitis," *Hepatogastroenterology* 32 (1985): 97–102. See also W. D. Heizer, C. R. Cleaveland, and F. L. Iber, "Gastric Inactivation of Pancreatic Supplements," *Bull Johns Hopkins Hosp* 116 (1965): 261–70.
2. D. V. Graham, "Enzyme Replacement Therapy of Exocrine Pancreatic Insufficiency in Man," *N Engl J Med* 296 (1977): 1314-17.

CHAPTER 6

1. William F. Ganong, *Review of Medical Physiology,* 8th ed. (Los Altos, CA: Lange Medical Publications, 1977), 550.

CHAPTER 7

1. Robert Michael Kaplan, "Losing Weight Wisely," *Alive: Canadian Journal of Health & Nutrition,* March 1992, no. 117: 16.
2. Heidi M. Connolly et al., "Valvular Heart Disease Associated with Fenfluramine-Phentermine," *CNN.com,* July 8, 1997, www.cnn.com/HEALTH/9707/08/fenphen.report/.
3. Ellen W. Cutler, "Detoxification," in *The Food Allergy Cure* (New York: Three Rivers Press, 2001), 181–207.
4. V. C. Strasberger, "Children and TV Advertising: Nowhere to Run, Nowhere to Hide," *Behav Pediatr* 22, no. 3 (June 2001): 185–87.
5. L. Cordain, J. B. Miller, S. B. Eaton, et al., "Macronutrient Estimations in Hunter-Gatherer Diets." *American Journal of Clinical Nutrition* 72, no. 6 (December 2000): 1589–92.
6. L. Cordain, B. A. Watkins, G. L. Florant, et al., "Fatty Acid Analysis of Wild Ruminate Tissues: Evolutionary Implications for Reducing Diet-Related Chronic Disease," *Eur J Clin Nutr* 56 (2002): 181–91.
7. "Carb Blockers for Weight Loss?" *Prevention,* October 2002, 68.
8. Jeffrey S. Zavik, "Common Mistakes Overweight Sufferers Make When They Try to Lose Weight And . . . How You Can Avoid Them" *Better Health USA*; Immuno Laboratories, Inc., "Strangest Secret about Weight Loss . . . Plus Medical References on Why You May Be Binging, Craving, Eating Compulsively and More," *Better Health USA,* www.betterhealth usa.com/public/151.cfm.

CHAPTER 8

1. Roberta Wilson, "Plant Enzymes Can Make Your Skin Healthier," *Let's Live,* April 1993, 61–64.
2. T. R. Klaenhammer, "Probiotic Bacteria: Today and Tomorrow," *J Nutr* 130 (2000): 415S–16S.
3. C. Edlund and C. E. Nord, "Effect on the Human Normal Microflora of Oral Antibiotics for Treatment of Urinary Tract Infections," *J Antimircrob Chemother* 46, Suppl. 1 (2000): 41–48. See also A. Sullivan, C. Edlund, and

C. E. Nord, "Effect of Antimicrobial Agents on the Ecological Balance of Human Microflora," *Lancet Infect Dis* 1, no. 2 (2001): 01–14.

4. R. D. Wagner, C. Pierson, T. Warner, et al., "Biotherapeutic Effects of Probiotic Bacteria on Candidiasis in Immunodeficient Mice," *Infec Immun* 65, no. 10 (1997) 4165–72. See also B. R. Goldin, L. Swensen, L. Dwyer, et al., "Effect of Diet and Lactobacillus acidophilus Supplements NCFM Functionality as a Probiotic," *J Dairy Sci* 84, no. 2: 319–31. B. R. Goldin and S. L. Gorbach, "Alterations of the Intestinal Microflora by Diet, Oral Antibiotics and Lactobacillus: Decreased Production of Five Amines from Aromatic Nitro Compounds, Azo Dyes, and Glucorides," *J Natl Cancer Inst* 73 (1984): 689–95. P. R. Marteau, M. de Vrese, C. J. Cellier, et al., "Protection from Gastrointestinal Diseases with the Use of Probiotics," *Am J Clin Nutr* 73, no. 2 (2001): 430S–36S.

5. M. Bekaroglu, Y. Aslan, Y. Gedik, et al., "Relationships between Serum Free Fatty Acids and Zinc, and Attention Deficit Hyperactivity Disorder: A Research Note," *J Child Psychol Psychiatry* 37, no. 2 (1996): 225–27.

6. L. Cordain, "The Nutritional Characteristics of a Contemporary Diet Based upon Paleolithic Food Groups," *J Am Neutraceut Assoc* 5 (2002): 15–24.

7. Ryszard Zaba and Robert A. Schwartz, "Acne Fulminans," *eMedicine.com*, last updated June 19, 2003, www.emedicine.com/derm/topic757.htm.

8. B. Dreno, D. Moyse, M. Alirezai, et al., "Multicenter Randomized Comparative Double-Blind Controlled Clinical Trial of the Safety and Efficacy of Zinc Gluconate versus Minocycline Hydrochloride in the Treatment of Inflammatory Acne Vulgaris," *Dermatology* 203, no. 2 (2001): 135–40. See also M. Amer, M. R. Bahgat, Z. Tosson, et al., "Serum Zinc in Acne Vulgaris," *Int J Dermatol* 21, no. 8 (1982): 481–84; B. Dreno, "Low Doses of Zinc Gluconate for Inflammatory Acne," *Acta Derm Venereol* 70, no. 4 (1990): 304–8; K. Weisman, S. Wadskov, and J. Sondergaard, "Oral Zinc Sulphate Therapy for Acne Vulgaris," *Acta Derm Venereol* 69, no. 6 (1989): 541–43; R. J. Cochran, S. B. Tucker, and S. A. Flannigan, "Topical Zinc Therapy for Acne Vulgaris," *Acta Derm Venereol* 66, no. 4 (1986): 305–10; T. J. David, et al., "Low Serum Zinc in Children with Atopic Eczema," *Acta Derm Venereol* 60, no 4 (1980): 337–40; K. C. Verma, A. S. Saini, and S. K Dhamija, "Oral Zinc Sulphate Therapy in Acne Vulgaris," *Acta Derm Venereol* 57, no. 4 (1977): 357–60.

9. BioSET Allergy Desensitization home treatment is outlined in *The Food Allergy Cure* by Ellen W. Cutler (New York: Three Rivers Press, 2001), 169–80.

10. *Better Nutrition* 65, no. 4 (April 2003): 63, www.gmabrands.com/news/docs/NewsRelease.cfm?DocID=1124.

11. Jeffrey Light, "Skin Care Enzymes for Beauty," *Total Health* 20, no. 4 (August/September 1998): 44.

CHAPTER 9

1. S. Rigden, E. Barrager, and J. S. Bland, "Evaluation of the Effect of Modified Entero-Hepatic Resuscitation Program in Chronic Fatigue Syndrome Patients," *J Adv Med* 11 (1998): 247–62.
2. I. M. Cox, M. J. Campbell, and D. Dowson, "Red Blood Cell Magnesium and Chronic Fatigue Syndrome," *Lancet* (1991): 337–757.

CHAPTER 10

1. G. P. Tilz and H. Becker, "Antigen Antibody Complexes—Physiology and Pathology," *General Medicine (Allgemeinmedizin)* 19, no.4 (1990): 138–39.
2. Syd Baumel, *Dealing with Depression Naturally* (New Canaan, CT: Keats Publishing, 1995). See also Priscilla Slagle, *The Way Up from Down*, (New York: St. Martin's Paperbacks, 1992).
3. Allen Darman, "The Turning Point," *Alive: Canadian Journal of Health & Nutrition,* May 2001, no. 223: 48.
4. Methylphenidate is a medication prescribed for individuals (usually children) who have an abnormally high level of activity or attention-deficit hyperactivity disorder (ADHD). According to the National Institute of Mental Health, about 3 to 5 percent of the general population has the disorder, which is characterized by agitated behavior and an inability to focus on tasks. Methylphenidate also is occasionally prescribed for treating narcolepsy. Methylphenidate is a central nervous system (CNS) stimulant. It has effects similar to but more potent than caffeine and is less potent than amphetamines. It has a notably calming effect on hyperactive children and a "focusing" effect on those with ADHD.

CHAPTER 11

1. R. Fiasse et al., "Circulating Immune Complexes and Disease Activity in Crohn's Disease," *Gut* 19 (1978): 611–17.
2. A. J. Barrett and P. M. Starkey, "The Interaction of Alpha-2m with Proteinases," *Biochem J* 133 (1973): 709. See also A. J. Barrett, *Proteinases in Mammalian Cells and Tissues* (New York: Elsevier/North Holland Biomedical Press, 1977), 209–48.
3. M. T. Debanne, R. Bell, and J. Dolovich, "Uptake of Proteinase-Alpha-Macroglobulin Complexes by Macrophages, *Biochim Biophys Acta* 411 (1975): 295.
4. R. S. Targan, F. M. Kagnoff, M. D. Brogan, and F. Shanahan, "Immunological Mechanisms in Intestinal Disease," *Ann Int Med* 106 (1987): 854–70.
5. Stephen Holt, *Natural Ways to Digestive Health* (M. Evans and Co., 2000).
6. L. Ketikangas-Jarvinene, K. Raikkonen, A. Hautanenen, and H. Adlercreutz, "Vital Exhaustion, Anger Expression, and Pituitary and Adrenocorticol Hormones: Implications for the Insulin Resistance Syndrome,"

Atherscler Thrombo Vasc Biol 16, no. 2 (1996): 275–80. See also D. S. Kelly and A. Bendick, "Essential Nutrients and Immunologic Functions." *Am J Clin Nutr* 63, no. 6 (June 1996): 994–96.

7. E. Schlosser, *Fast Food Nation* (New York: Houghton Mifflin, 2001).

8. N. Cousins, *Anatomy of an Illness* (New York: Bantam, 1991).

CHAPTER 12

1. "Reflux Disease and Heartburn" Source: A.D.A.M. Inc., Well-Connected series, March 31, 2003, www.healthandstage.com/PHome/gm=6! gid6=8501;jsessionid=08DDAC9E48C106E8143B6391053A8A01.

2. Angioplasty is a revascularization procedure during which a coronary artery is opened to increase blood flow to the heart muscle. This procedure is also called percutaneous transluminal angioplasty, or PCTA. Angioplasty uses a catheter to reach the coronary artery, so the procedure is less invasive and has a shorter recovery time than bypass surgery.

3. Homocysteine "is an amino acid (a building block of protein) that is produced in the human body. Homocysteine may irritate blood vessels, leading to blockages in the arteries (called atherosclerosis). High homocysteine levels in the blood can also cause cholesterol to change to something called oxidized low-density lipoprotein, which is more damaging to the arteries. In addition, high homocysteine levels can make blood clot more easily than it should, increasing the risk of blood vessel blockages. A blockage might cause you to have a stroke or a problem with blood flow. Up to 20 percent of people with heart disease have high homocysteine levels.

4. M. Wolf, "Der Einfluss von Proteasen auf Venenentzundungen," in M. Wolf and K. Ransberger, *Enzymthempie* (Vienna: 1971).

5. H. Denck, "Wirksamkeit von Enzymen bei Gefasserkrankungen," in Medizinische Enzyme-Forschungsgesellschaft e.V., (ed), *Systemische Enzymtherapie,* 2nd Symposium, Dusseldorf, 1987. See also E. Ernst and A. Matrei, "Orale Tharapie Mit Proteolytischen Enzymen Modifiziert diet Blutrheologie," *Kin Wschr* 65 (1987): 994.

6. Rohit Medhekar, *Proteases: Function and Applications,* www.naturaldot com.com/categoria.asp?area=naturalhealth&subarea=&categoria=Enzymes &numpagina=1.

CHAPTER 13

1. G. S. Kelly, "Insulin Resistance: Lifestyle and Nutritional Interventions," *Altern Med Rev* 5, no. 2 (2000): 109–32. See also K. D. Kulkarni, "Glycemic Control through Modulation of Carbohydrate Metabolism," *Diabetes Spectrum* 12, no. 1 (1999): 7–11. B. Levi and M. J. Werman, "Long-Term Fructose Consumption Accelerates Glycation and Several Age-Related Variables in Male Rats," *J Nutr* 128 (1998):1442–49. D. E. Estrada, H. S. Ewart, T.

Tsakiridis, A. Volchuk, T. Ramlal, H. Tritschler, and A. Klip, "Stimulation of Glucose Uptake by the Natural Coenzyme Alpha-Lipoic Acid/Thioctic Acid: Participation of Elements of the Insulin Signaling pathway," *Diabetes* 45, no. 12 (1996): 1798–1804. T. C. Wascher, W. F. Graier, P. Dittrich, et al., "Effects of Low-Dose L-Arginine on Insulin-Mediated Vasodilation and Insulin Sensitivity," *Eur J Clin Invest* 27 (1997): 690–95. E. J. Mayer-Davis, R. D'Agostino, A. J. Karter, et al., "Intensity and Amount of Physical Activity in Relation to Insulin Sensitivity," *JAMA* 279, no. 9 (1998): 669–74. R. M. Bergenstal, "Management of Type 2 Diabetes Mellitus," *Postgrad Med* 105, no. 1 (1999): 121–36. J. S. Flier, "Big Deal about a Little Insulin," *Nature Med* 5, no. 6 (1999): 614–15.

2. M. A. Testa and D. C. Simonson, "Health Economic Benefits and Quality of Life during Improved Glycemic Control in Patients with Type 2 Diabetes Mellitus," *JAMA* 280, no. 17 (1998): 1490–96.

3. K. D. Kulkarni, "Glycemic Control through Modulation of Carbohydrate Metabolism," *Diabetes Spectrum* 12, no. 1 (1999): 7–11.

4. Testa and Simonson, 1490–96.

5. G. S. Kelly, "Insulin Resistance: Lifestyle and Nutritional Interventions," *Altern Med Rev* 5, no. 2 (2000): 109–32.

6. Bergenstal, 121–36.

7. J. Paronen, M. Knip, E. Savilahti, et al., "Effect of Cow's Milk Exposure and Maternal Type 1 Diabetes on Cellular and Humoral Immunization to Dietary Insulin in Infants at Genetic Risk for Type 1 Diabetes: Finnish Trial to Reduce IDDM in the Genetically at Risk Study Group," *Diabetes* 49 (2000): 1657–65.

8. Committee to Review the Evidence Regarding the Link Between Exposure to Agent Orange and Diabetes, Division of Health Promotion and Disease Prevention, *Veterans and Agent Orange: Herbicide/Dioxin Exposure and Type 2 Diabetes* (Washington, DC: Institute of Medicine National Academy Press).

9. B. S. Bector, V. Sharma, and T. Rai, "Effect of Starter Culture and Temperature of Clarification on the Total Conjugated Linoleic Acid of Deshi Ghee," *J Food Sci Technol–Mysore* 40, no. 1 (2003): 74–75. See also L. Granlund, L. K. Juvet, J. I. Pedersen, and H. I. Nebb, "*Trans*10, *cis*12-Conjugated Linoleic Acid Prevents Triacylglycerol Accumulation in Adipocytes by Acting as a PPAR Gamma Modulator," *J Lipid Res* 44, no. 8 (2003): 1441–52. E. J. Kim, I. J. Kang, H. J. Cho, et al., "Conjugated Linoleic Acid Downregulates Insulin-Like Growth Factor-I Receptor Levels in HT-29 Human Colon Cancer Cells," *J Nutr* 133, no. 8 (2003): 2675–81. J. Kraft, M. Collomb, P. Mockel, et al., "Differences in CLA Isomer Distribution of Cow's Milk Lipids," *Lipids* 38, no. 6 (2003): 657–64. A. Miller, E. McGrath, C. Stanton, and R. Devery, "Vaccenic Acid (t11-18:1) Is Converted to c9,

t11-CLA in MCF-7 and SW480 Cancer Cells," *Lipids* 38, no. 6 (2003): 623–32. D. Oikawa, T. Nakanishi, Y. Nakamura, et al., "Dietary CLA and DHA Modify Skin Properties in Mice," *Lipids* 38, no. 6 (2003): 609–14. H. Oku, S. Wongtangtintharn, H. Iwasaki, and T. Toda, "Conjugated Linoleic Acid (CLA) Inhibits Fatty Acid Synthetase Activity in Vitro," *Biosci Biotechnol Biochem* 67, no. 7 (2003): 1584–86. H. W. Soita, J. A. Meier, M. Fehr M, et al., "Effects of Flaxseed Supplementation on Milk Production, Milk Fatty Acid Composition and Nutrient Utilization by Lactating Dairy Cows," *Archiv Anim Nutr* 57, no 2 (2003): 107–16. N. D. Su, X. W. Liu, M. R. Kim, et al., "Protective Action of CLA against Oxidative Inactivation of Paraoxonase 1, an Antioxidant Enzyme," *Lipids* 38, no. 6 (2003): 615–22.

10. G. Paolisso, S. Sgambaro, G. Pizza, et al., "Improved Insulin Response and Action by Chronic Magnesium Administration in Aged NIDDM Subjects," *Diabetes Care* 12 (1989): 265–69.

11. G. Paolisso, A. D'Amore, D. Giugliano, et al., "Pharmacologic Doses of Vitamin E Improve Insulin Action in Healthy Subjects and Non-Insulin-Dependent Diabetic Patients," *Am J Clin Nutr* 57 (1993): 650–56.

12. M. D. Althuis, N. E. Jordan, E. A. Ludington, and J. T. Wittes, "Glucose and Insulin Responses to Dietary Chromium Supplements: A Meta-Analysis," *Am J Clin Nutr* 76 (2002): 148–55.

13. G. Boden, X. Chen, J. Ruiz, et al. "Effects of Vanadyl Sulfate on Carbohydrate and Lipid Metabolism in Patients with Non-Insulin-Dependent Diabetes Mellitus," *Metabolism* 45 (1996): 1130–35.

14. K. Yaworsky, R. Somwar, T. Ramlal, et al., "Engagement of the Insulin-Sensitive Pathway in the Stimulation of Glucose Transport by Alpha-Lipoic Acid in 3T3-L1 Adipocytes," *Diabetologia* 43 (2000): 294–303.

15. H. Shang, K. Osada, M. Maebashi, et al., "A High Biotin Diet Improves the Impaired Glucose Tolerance of Long-Term Spontaneously Hyperglycemic Rats with Non-Insulin-Dependent Diabetes Mellitus," *J Nutr Sci Vitaminol* 42 (1996): 517–26.

16. D. C. Haynes, M. E. Gershwin, M. S. Golub, et al., "Studies of Marginal Zinc Deprivation in Rhesus Monkeys: VI. Influence on the Immunohematology of Infants in the First Year," *Am J Clin Nutr* 42 (1985): 252–62.

17. Delma J. Nieves, Miriam Cnop, Barbara Retzlaff, et al., "The Atherogenic Lipoprotein Profile Associated with Obesity and Insulin Resistance Is Largely Attributable to Intra-Abdominal Fat," *Diabetes* 52 (2003): 172–79.

18. B. Levi and M. J. Werman, "Long-Term Fructose Consumption Accelerates Glycation and Several Age-Related Variables in Male Rats," *J Nutr* 128 (1998): 1442–49.

19. R. White and C. Sherman, "Exercise in Diabetes Management," *Phys Sportsmed* 4, no. 27 (April 1999), www.physsportsmed.com/issues/1999/04_99/white.htm.

CHAPTER 14

1. R. Fiasse, A. Z. Lurhuma, C. L. Cambiaso, et al., "Circulating Immune Complexes and Disease Activity in Crohn's Disease," *Gut* 19 (1978): 611–17.
2. M. K. Dasgupta, K. G. Warren, K. V. Johny, and J. B. Dossetor, "Circulating Immune Complexes in Multiple Sclerosis: Relation with Disease Activity," *Neurology* 32 (September 1982): 1000–1004.
3. D. Steffen and J. Menzel, "Enzyme Consumption from Immune Complexes," *Journal for Rheumatology (Z Rhematol)* 42 (1989): 249–55. See also C. Steffen and J. Menzel, "In Vivo Destruction of Immune Complexes in the Kidneys after the Administration of Oral Enzymes," *Vienna Clinical Weekly (Wien Klin Wochenschr)* 99, no. 15 (1987): 525–31. C. Steffen and J. Menzel, "Basic Investigation of Enzymatic Treatment of Immune Complex Disease," *Vienna Clinical Weekly (Wien Klin Wochenschr)* 97, no. 8 (1985): 376–85.
4. G. Klein, G. Pollmann, and W. Kullich, "Clinical Experience with Enzyme Therapy in Patients with Rheumatoid Arthritis in Comparison with Gold," *General Medicine (Allgemeinmedizin)* 19, no. 4 (1990): 144–47. See also G. Klein, H. Schwann, and W. Kullich, "Enzyme Therapy in Chronic Polyarthritis," *Nature-und Ganzheitsmedizin* 1 (1988): 112–16.
5. Felix Iten Leipner and Reinhard Saller, Department of Natural Medicine, University Hospital, Zurich, Switzerland, "Therapy with Proteolytic Enzymes in Rheumatic Disorders," *BioDrugs* 15, no 12 (2001): 779–89. See also W. Borth, A. Dunky, and K. Keesick, "Alpha 2-Macroglobulin-Proteinase Complexes as Correlated with Alpha 1-Proteinase-Inhibitor-Elastase Complexes in Synovial Fluids of Rheumatoid Arthritis Patients," *Arthritis Rheum* 29 (1986): 319–25. V. I. Majurov, A. M. Lila, N. N. Klimko, et al., "The Efficacy of Systemic Enzyme Therapy in the Treatment of Rheumatoid Arthritis," *Int J Immunother* 13 (1997): 85–92.
6. G. Klein and W. Kullich, "Reducing Pain by Oral Enzyme Therapy in Rheumatic Diseases," *Wien Med Wochenschr* 149 (1999): 577–80.
7. K. Nouza, "Outlooks of Systemic Enzyme Therapy in Rheumatoid Arthritis and Other Immunopatholgical Diseases," *Acta Univ Carol (Med) (Praha)* 40 (1994): 101–4.
8. Mori Shintaro, Ojima Yoshiyasu, Hirose Tamaki, et al., "The Clinical Effect of Proteolytic Enzyme Containing Bromelain and Trypsin on Urinary Tract Infection Evaluated by Double Blind Method," *Acta Obstet Gynec Jap* 19, no. 3 (1972): 147–53.
9. W. F. Hiss, "Enzymes in Sports Medicine and Traumatology," *Journal for Natural Therapy Methods (Zeitschrift fur Naturheilmethoden)* 2 (1979): 1.
10. S. Worschhauser, "Conservative Therapy in Sports Injuries. Enzyme Preparations for Treatment and Prophylaxis," *General Medicine (Allgemeinmedizin)* 19, no. 4 (1990): 173.

11. J. C. Dekkers, L. J. van Doornen, and H. C. Kemper. "The Role of Antioxidant Vitamins and Enzymes in the Prevention of Exercise-Induced Muscle Damage," *Sports Med* 21, no. 3 (March 1996): 213–38.
12. The Associated Press, "Report: Celebrex Linked to 10 Deaths," April 20, 1999. See also D. R. Lichtenstein and M. M. Wolfe, "COX-2-Selective NSAIDs," *JAMA* 284, no. 10 (2000): 1297–99.
Rodenburg RJ, Ganga A, van Lent PL, van de Putte LB, Venrooij WJ. The anti-inflammatory drug sulfasalazine inhibits tumor necrosis factor a expression in macrophages by inducing apoptosis. *Arthritis Rheum* 43 (2000): 1941–50.

CHAPTER 15

1. National Cancer Institute, Cancer Facts, www.cdc.gov/cancer/natlcancer data.htm#all.
2. Heinrich Wrba and Otto Pecher, *Enzyme—Wirkstoffe der Zukunft Mit der Enzymtherapie das immunsystem starken* (Vienna: Verlag Orac, 1993).
3. R. K. Oldham, *Principles of Cancer Biotherapy* (New York: Raven Press, 1991). See also M. Wolf and K. Ransberger, *Enzymes Therapy,* (Vienna: Maudrich-Verlad, 1970), 156–66, 193–94.
4. H. K. Kim, C. C. Kim, and C. J. Kin, "The Alteration in Cellular Immunity Following the Enzyme Therapy: The Influence of Wobe-Mugos on the Destructibility of Natural Killer Cell Mediated Cytotoxicity," 7th Korean Cancer Research Society at Seoul National University.
5. F. X. Hasselberger, *Uses of Enzymes and Immobilized Enzymes* (Chicago: Nelson-Hall, 1978), 143–47. See also E. V. Kameke, "Die Entzundung and Ihre Kausaltherapie Tait Hydrolytischen Enzymen and Rutin," Forum des Praktischen and Allgmeinarzies, Heft 9, 1981. See also E. V. Kameke, "Protolytische Enzyme und Thymusextrakt-eine Sinnvolle Waffe Genen Krebs," *Krebsgeschehen* 1 (1982): 1.
6. John Beard, *The Enzyme Treatment of Cancer and Its Scientific Basis* (London: Chatto & Windus, 1911).
7. Ibid.
8. Max Wolf and Karl Ransberger, *Enzyme Therapy* (Los Angeles: Regent House, 1972), 156–66, 193–94.
9. K. Ransberger, "Schutze dich vor Krebs," Informationsschrift der Mucos Emulsiongsgesellschaft GmbH, Geretsried, Germany, 1980.
10. H. Wrba, "Systemic Enzyme Therapy: Newest Status and Progress," *Therapie Woche* 37, no. 7 (1987).
11. H. Wegener, "Indikation zur subkutanen Mastektomie und Weideraufbauplastik: Voraussetzungen, Bedingungen, nachbehandlung," Referet anlaa1.d. Syrup. D. Deutschen Krebekongresses, Sept. 12–14, 1980, Munich, Germany. See also O. Rokitansky, "Die Operative Behadlung des mamma-Carcinoms ait adjuvanter Enzymtherapie," *Dr Med* 1/2:16, 1989a.

O. Rokitansky, "Praoperative Tumortherapie zur Verbessrung der hellungsergebrisse beim mammakarzinom," *Krebsgeschehan* 5:198Ob.

O. Rokitansky, "15 Hagre perative Behandlung des Mammakarzinoms tait adjuvanter Enzymtherapie," *Erahrungsheilkunde* 3 (1983):115.

Stoger, R, "Geziette interne Nachbehandung nach Brustoperationen, *Wien Med Wochenschr* 126, no. 10 (1976): 121.

G. Zimmerman, O. Boeckl, and K. Karrer, "Zur Beurteilung der Prognose des Brustdrusenkarzinoms," *Krebsarzt* 23, no. 4 (1968): 16.

W. Scheef, and W. Konig, "Gutartige Veranderungen der weiblichen Brust— proteolytische Enzyme und Vitamin E als wirksames Behandungsprinzp," *Therapiewoche* 35 (1985): 5909.

I. C. Wolf-Zimper, "Erfogestatstik der Therapie mit WOBE-Mugos," Bericht an die MUCOS-Pharma GmbH, Geretsried, Germany, 1964.

12. Wrba and Pecher, *Enzyme—Wirkstoffe der Zukunft Mit der Enzymtherapie das immunsystem starken.*

13. Heinrich Wrba and Otto Pecher, *Enzymes: A Drug of the Future* (Vienna: Verlag Orac Ecomed Verlagsgesellschaft AG & Co., 1993).

14. J. Beard, "The Action of Trypsin upon the Living Cells of Jensens' Mouse Tumor," *Brit Med J* 4 (1906), 140–41.

15. N. J. Gonzalez and L. L. Isaacs, "Evaluation of Pancreatic Proteolytic Enzyme Treatment of Adneocarcinoma of the Pancreas, With Nutrition and Detoxification Support," *Nutrition & Cancer* 33, no. 2 (1999): 117.

16. O. Rokitansky, in H. Wrba, "Systemic Enzyme Therapy: Newest Status and Progress," *Therapie Woche* 37, no. 7 (1987). See also K. J. Johnson and A. W. Peter, "Newer Concepts in the Pathogenesis of Immune Complex Induced Tissue Injury," *Lab Invest* 3 (1982): 218.

17. R. Dulbecco, "Progress in Cancer Research," proceedings of the 4th International conference on progress in cancer research, San Remo, Italy.

18. F. Beaufort, "Reduction of Side Effects of Radiation Therapy with Hydrolytic Enzymes," *Therapeutikon* 10 (1990): 577–80.

19. W. Glenk and S. Neu, *Enzyme Die Bausteine des Lebens Wie sie wirken, helfen and hellen* (Munich: Willhelm Heyne Verlag, 1990), 118.

20. Beaufort, *Therapeutikon* 577–80.

21. M. S. Gujral, P. M. Patnaik, R. Kaul, et al., "Efficacy of Hydrolytic Enzymes in Preventing Radiation Therapy-Induced Side Effects in Patients with Head and Neck Cancers," *Cancer Chemother Pharmacol* 47 (July 2001): S23–S28.

22. R. Kaul, B. K. Mishra, P. Sutradar, et al., "The Role of Wobe-Mugos in Reducing Acute Sequele of Radiation in Head and Neck Cancers—A Clinical Phase III Randomized Trial," *Indian J Cancer* 36, no. 2–4 (June–December 1999): 141–48.

23. P. S. Dale, C. P. Tamhankar, D. George, and G. V. Daftary. "Co-medication

with Hydrolytic Enzymes in Radiation Therapy of Uterine Cervix: Evidence of the Reduction of Acute Side Effects," *Cancer Chemother Pharmacol* 47 (July 2001): S29–S34.

24. "Reduzierung von Strahlennebenwirkungen durch hydrolytische Enzyme Therpeutikon," *Zeitchrift fur die gesamte Medizine* 4, no. 10 (1990): 577–80.

25. G. Stojanow, "Metastasis Overview: Metastasis Prophylaxis and Tumor Treatment with Enzymes from the Standpoint of the Gynecologist," *Austrian Journal for Research and Treatment of Cancer* 5 (1970): 25.

26. L. M. Coussens and Z. Werb, "Inflammation and Cancer," *Nature* 420 (2002): 860–67.

27. K. J. Helzlsouer, O. Selmin, H. Y. Huang, et al., "Association between Glutathione S-Transferase M1, P1, and T1 Genetic Polymorphisms and Development of Breast Cancer," *J Natl Cancer Inst* 90, no. 7 (1998): 512–18. See also D. S. Michaud, D. Spiegelman, S. K. Clinton, et al., "Fruit and Vegetable Intake and Incidence of Bladder Cancer in a male Prospective Cohort," *J Natl Cancer Inst* 91, no. 7 (1990): 605–13.

28. M. P. Napier, S. K. Sharma, C. J. Springer, et al., "Antibody-Directed Enzyme Prodrug Therapy: Efficacy and Mechanism of Action in Colorectal Carcinoma," *Clin Cancer Res* 6 (2000): 765–72.

29. T. Popiela, J. Kulig, J. Hanisch, and P. R. Bock, "Influence of a Complementary Treatment with Oral Enzymes on Patients with Colorectal Cancers—An Epidemiological Retrolective Cohort Study," *Cancer Chemother Pharmacol* 47 (July 2001) : S55–S63.

30. M. Wald, T. Olejar, V. Sebkova, et al., "Mixture of Trypsin, Chymotrypsin, and Papain Reduces Formation of Metastases and Extends Survival Time of C57B16 Mice with Syngeneic Melanoma B$_1$6," *Cancer Chemother Pharmoacol* 47 (July 2001): S16–S22.

31. W. Scheef and M. Pischnamazadeh, "Proteolytic Enzymes as a Simple and Safe Method for the Prevention of Lymphedema after Mastectomy," *Med World (Med Welt)* 35 (1984): 1032–33.

32. J. Leipner and R. Saller, "Systemic Enzyme Therapy in Oncology: Effect and Mode of Action," *Drugs* 59, no. 4 (2000): 769–80.

33. H. R. Maurer, "Bromelain: Biochemistry, Pharmacology, and Medical Use," *Cell Mol Life Sci* 58, no. 9 (2001): 1234–45.

34. Professor Armin Karmali-Biotechnology Section, Instituto Superior de Engenharia de Lisboa. Rua Conselheiro Emidio Navarro; The Role of Mushroom Nutrition as a Delivery Agent for Enzyme Therapy in Cancer Care, www.aneid.pt/mrl/mrl_rd_role_mush.htm.

CHAPTER 16

1. N. C. Price and L. Stevens, *Fundamentals of Enzymology,* 2nd ed. (London: Oxford Unversity Press, 1989).

2. Richard Weindruch, "Caloric Intake, Oxidative Stress, and Aging" (Seminar at Iowa State University, March 8, 2000).
3. Dr. Walford & Caloric Restriction, www.walford.com.
4. M. M. G. Wilson and J. E. Morley, "Invited Review: Aging and Energy Balance," *J Appl Physiol* 95, no. 4 (2003): 1728–36. See also R. Wan, S. Camandola, and M. P. Mattson, "Intermittent Food Deprivation Improves Cardiovascular and Neuroendocrine Responses to Stress in Rats," *J Nutr* 133, no 6 (2003): 1921–29.
5. R. K. Chandra, "Effect of Vitamin and Trace-Element Supplementation on Immune Responses and Infection in Elderly Subjects," *Lancet* 340 (1992): 1124–27. See also W. R. Beisel, R. Edelman, K. Nauss, and R. M. Suskind, "Single-Nutrient Effects on Immunologic Functions. Report of a workshop sponsored by the Department of Food and Nutrition and its nutrition advisory group of the American Medical Association," *JAMA* 245, no. 1 (1981): 53–58.
6. R. K. Chandra, "Graying of the Immune System. Can Nutrient Supplements Improve Immunity in the Elderly?" *JAMA.* 277, no. 17 (1997): 1398–99.
7. J. Anderson and J. Stine, "Detoxing from Toxins," in T. Nichols and N. Faas, eds. *Optimal Digestion* (New York: Harper Collins, 1999).
8. Rick Weiss, "Enzymes Found to Delay Aging Process. Discovery Could Lead to Drugs to Extend Life Span," *Washington Post,* August 25, 2003.
9. T. Mulligan, S. M. Retchin, V. M. Chinchilli, and C. B. Bettinger, "The Role of Aging and Chronic Disease in Sexual dysfunction," *J Am Geriatr Soc* 36, no. 6 (1988): 520–24.
10. UCLA Healthcare, *Patient Learning Series,* "Male Impotence," www.healthcare.ucla.edu/ . . . cle-display?article_id=303 − 37K.

References

Aamodt, S. 2000. "Gut Reaction." *Nature Med* 6:130.

Ahmed, A. 2000. "Metabolic Networks, Homeostasis, Pathogenesis, and Therapeutic Strategies," in press, *J Theor Biol.*

Ahmed, R. and D. Gray. 1996. "Immunological Memory and Protective Immunity: Understanding Their Relation." *Science* 272:54–56.

Alberts, B., B. Dennis, J. Lewis, M. Raft, K. Roberts, and J. D. Watson. 1989. *Molecular Biology of the Cell.* 2nd ed. New York: Garland Publishing, Inc.

Alper, S. L. 2002. "Genetic Diseases of Acid-Base Transporters." *Annu Rev Physiol* 64:899–923.

Aoki, T., H. Miyakoshi, Y. Usuda, and R. B. Herberman. 1993. "Low NK Syndrome and Its Relationship to Chronic Fatigue Syndrome." *Clin Immunol Immunopathol* 69:253–65.

Areces, L. B., M. B. Bonino, M. A. Parry, E. R. Fraile, H. M. Fernandez, and O. Cascone. 1992. "Purification and Characterization of a Milk Clotting Protease from Mucor bacilliformis." *Appl Biochem Biotechnol* 37 (3): 283–94.

Arem, Ridha. 1999. *The Thyroid Solution.* New York: Ballantine Books.

Atman, Daryl, and Lawrence Chiaramonte. 1996. "Public Perception of Food Allergy." *J Allergy Clin Immunol,* June: 1247–51.

Banhazi, T., C. Cargill, G. Marr, A. Kefford, K. Moore, S. Koch, H. Payne, and R. Nicholls. 2000. Relating Airborne Pollution to Management and Housing Factors. Project No. 1202. Final report to the Pig Research and Development Corporation, Canberra, Australia.

Baschetti R, A.C. Chester, N. F. Devitt, and A. L. Komaroff. 1998. "Chronic Fatigue Syndrome." *JAMA.* 279 (6): 431–33.

Bataille, R., D. Chappard, C. Marcelli, P. Dessauw, P. Baldet, J. Sany, and C. Alexander. 1991. "Recruitment of New Osteoblasts and Osteoclasts Is the Earliest Critical Event in the Pathogenesis of Human Multiple Myeloma." *J Clin Invest* 88:62–69.

Bataille, R., and J. L. Harousseau. 1997. "Multiple Myeloma." *N Engl J Med* 336:1657–61.

Bates, D. W., W. Schmitt, D. Buchwald, N. C. Ware, J. Lee, E. Thoyer, et al. 1993. "Prevalence of Fatigue and Chronic Fatigue Syndrome in a Primary Care Practice." *Arch Intern Med* 153:2759–65.

Batkin, S., S. J. Taussig, J. and Szekerczes. 1988. "Modulation of Pulmonary Metastasis (Lewis lung carcinoma) by Bromelain, and Extract of the Pineapple Stem (Ananas comosus)." *Cancer Invest* 6 (2): 241–42.

Beard, J. 1906. "The Action of Trypsin upon the Living Cells of Jensen's Mouse Tumor." *Br Med J* 4:140–41.

Beckman, J. S., and J. P. Crow. 1993. "Pathological Implications of Nitric Oxide, Superoxide, and Peroxynitite Formation." *Biochem Soc Trans* 21:330–34.

Benjamini, Eli, Richard Coico, and Geoffrey Sunshine. 2000. *Immunology: A Short Course.* 4th ed. New York: Wiley-Liss.

Berg, W. 1998. *Emissions from Animal Husbandry and Their Assessment,* 289–95. Proceedings of the 13th CIGR International Congress on Agricultural Engineering, Rabat, Morocco, February 2–6.

Berge, K. G., and P. L. Canner. 1991. "Coronary Drug Project: Experience with Niacin." Coronary Drug Project Research Group. *Eur J Clin Pharmacol* 40 (Suppl. no. 1): S49–S51.

Bhat, M. 2000. "Cellulases and Related Enzymes in Biotechnology." *Biotech Adv* 18:355–83. This review paper discusses present and possible future trends; xylanases were first suggested for pulp bleaching by VTT-Biotechnology in Finland. Röhm Enzyme is the leader in the field; see www.roehmenzyme.com.

Bienenstock, J. 1984. "The Mucosal Immunologic Network." *Ann Allergy* 53:535.

Bland, Jeffrey. 1983. *Digestive Enzymes: 20 Million Americans Suffer from Digestive Disorders. Are You One of Them?* New Canaan, CT: Keats Publishing.

Bloch, K. J., D. B. Bloch, M. Steams, and W. A. Walker. 1979. "Intestinal Uptake of Macromolecules. VI. Uptake of Protein Antigen in vivo in Normal Rats and in Rats Infected with Nippostrongylus brasiliensis or Subjected to Mild Systemic Anaphylaxis." *Gastroenterology* 77 (5): 1039–44.

Bondy, C., B. D. Cowley Jr., S. L. Lightman, and P. F. Kador. 1990. "Feedback Inhibition of Aldose Reductase Gene Expression in Rat Renal Medulla. Galactitol Accumulation Reduces Enzyme mRNA Levels and Depletes Cellular Inositol Content." *J Clin Invest* 86 (4): 1103–8.

Borish, L., K. Schmaling, J. D. DiClementi, et al. 1998. "Chronic Fatigue Syndrome: Identification of Distinct Subgroups on the Basis of Allergy and Psychological Variables." *J Allergy Clin Immunol* 102:222–30.

Breviario, F., P. Proserpio, F. Bertocchi, M. G. Lampugnani, A. Mantovani, and E. Dejana. 1990. "Interleukin-1 Stimulates Prostacyclin Production by Cultured Human Endothelial Cells by Increasing Arachidonic Acid Mobilization and Conversion." *Arteriosclerosis* 10 (1): 129–34.

Brostroff J., G. K. Scadding, D. Male, and I. M. Roitt. 1991. *Clinical Immunology.* London: Gower Medical Publishing.

Buchwald, D., R. Herrell, S. Ashton, M. Belcourt, K. Schmaling, P. Sullivan, M. Neale, and J. Goldberg. 2001. "A Twin Study of Chronic Fatigue." *Psychosom Med* 63:936–43.

Buchwald, D., P. Umali, J. Umali, P. Kith, T. Pearlman, and A. L. Komaroff. 1995. "Chronic Fatigue and the Chronic Fatigue Syndrome: Prevalence in a Pacific Northwest Health Care System." *Ann Intern Med* 123:81–88.

Caligaris-Cappio, E., M. Gregoretti, P. Ghia, and L. Bergui. 1992. "In Vitro Growth of Human Multiple Myeloma: Implications for Biology and Therapy." *Hematol Oncol Clin North Am* 6:257–65.

Caligiuri, M., C. Murry, D. Buchwald, et al. 1987. "Phenotypic and Functional Deficiency of Natural Killer Cells in Patients with Chronic Fatigue Syndrome." *J Immunol* 139:3306–13.

Campbell, J. T. 1907. "Trypsin Treatment of a Case of Malignant Disease." *JAMA* 48:225–26.

Campbell, Nell A. 1993. *Biology.* 3d ed. Redwood City, CA: The Benjamin/Cummings Publishing Co.

Carmel, R. 1997. "Cobalamin, the Stomach, and Aging." *Am J Clin Nutr* 66:750–59.

Chao, C. C., E. N. Janoff, S. X. Hu, et al. 1991. "Altered Cytokine Release in Peripheral Blood Mononuclear Cell Cultures from Patients with the Chronic Fatigue Syndrome." *Cytokine* 3:292–98.

Chauhan, D., S. Kharbanda, A. Ogata, M. Urashima, G. Teoh, M. Robertson, D. Kufe, and K. Anderson. 1997. "Interleukin-6 Inhibits Fas-Induced Apoptosis and SAP Kinase Activation in Multiple Myeloma Cells." *Blood* 89:227–31.

Cheson, B. "Treatment Strategies for Multiple Myeloma," ASCO Education Book (Spring 1997): 115.

Chopra, Deepak. 1993. *Ageless Body, Timeless Mind: The Quantum Alternative to Growing Old.* 2d pbk. ed. New York: Three Rivers Press.

Chotani, G., T. Dodge, A. Hsu, M. Kumar, R. LaDuca, D. Trimbur, W. Weyler, and K. Sandford. 2000. "The Commercial Production of Chemicals Using Pathway Engineering." *Biochim Biophys Acta* 1543:434–55. This review article discusses the latest trends in using engineered organisms in chemical production.

Cichoke, Anthony J., 1995. "Absorption of Enzymes." *Townsend Letter for Doctors and Patients,* October: 24–26.

————. 1999. *The Complete Book of Enzyme Therapy.* Garden City Park, NY: Avery Publishing.

————. 1994. *Enzymes and Enzyme Therapy: How to Jump Start Your Way to Lifelong Good Health.* Los Angeles: Keats Publishing.

————. 1994. "Enzyme Treatment of Circulatory Disorders." *Townsend Letter for Doctors and Patients,* December: 1322.

Cichoke, Anthony J., and L. Marty. 1981. "The Use of Proteolytic Enzymes with Soft Tissue Athletic Injuries." *American Chiropractor,* September/October: 32–33.

Clark, D. G., and K. Wyatt. 1996. *Colostrum: Life's First Food. The Ultimate Anti-Aging Weight Loss, and Immune Supplement.* Salt Lake City: CNR Publications.

Cleaver, J. E., D. L. Mitchell, L. Feeney, and V. Afzal. 1996. "Chromatid Exchanges May Be Induced by Damage in Sites of Transcriptional Activity." *Mutagenesis* 11 (2): 183–87.

Coico, Richard, Geoffrey Sunshine, and Eli Benjamini. 2003. *Immunology: A Short Course.* 5th ed.. New York: John Wiley & Sons.

Cooke, John P., and Judith Zimmer. 2002. *The Cardiovascular Cure: How to Strengthen Your Self-Defense Against Heart Attack and Stroke.* New York: Broadway.

Cordain, L., S. B. Eaton, J. B. Miller, et al. 2002. "The Paradoxical Nature of Huntergather Diets: Meat-Based, yet Non-Atherogenic." *Eur J Clin Nutr* 56 (Suppl. no. 1): 542–52.

Cornell, R., W. A. Walker, and K. J. Isselbacher. 1971. "Small Intestinal Absorption of Horseradish Peroxidase." *Lab Invest* 25 (1): 42–48.

Cowell, D.A., and H. M. ApSimon. 1998. "Cost-Effective Strategies for the Abatement of Ammonia Emissions from European Agriculture." *Atmospheric Environment* 32 (3): 573–80.

Cutler, Ellen W. 2001. *The Food Allergy Cure.* New York: Three Rivers Press.

————. 1998. *Winning the War Against Asthma and Allergies.* Albany, NY: Delmar Publishers.

————. 1998. *Winning the War Against Immune Disorders and Allergies.* Albany, NY: Delmar Publishers.

Demitrak, M. A. 1997. "Neuroendocrine Correlates of Chronic Fatigue Syndrome: A Brief Review." *J Psychiatr Res* 31:69–82.

Demitrak, M. A., J. K. Dale, S. E. Straus, et al. 1991. "Evidence for Impaired Activation of the Hypothalamic-Pituitary-Adrenal Axis in Patients with Chronic Fatigue Syndrome." *J Clin Endocrinol Metab* 173:1223–34.

Diplock, A. T., J. L. Charleux, G. Crozier-Willi, et al. 1998. "Functional Food Science and Defence against Reactive Oxidative Species." *Br J Nutr* 80 (Suppl. no. 1): S77–S112.

Doran, P. M. 1999. *Bioprocess Engineering Principles.* New York: Academic Press. This textbook describes engineering aspects of bioprocesses.

Dyckner, T., and P. O. Wester. 1983. "Effect of Magnesium on Blood Pressure." *Br Med J* 286 (January): 1847–49.

Dyer, Wayne. 2001. *There's a Spiritual Solution to Every Problem.* Carlsbad, CA: Hay House.

Eby, N., S. Grufferman, M. Huang, et al. 1988. "Natural Killer Cell Activity in the Chronic Fatigue–Immune Dysfunction Syndrome." In *Natural Killer Cells and Host Defense,* eds. E. W. Ades and C. Lopez, 141–45. Basel, Switzerland: Karger.

Ehlers, C. L., and D. J. Kupfer. 1987. "Hypothalamic Peptide Modulation of Sleep EEG in Depression: A Further Application of the S-Process Hypothesis." *Biol Psychiatry* 22:513–17.

Erikson, Roger H., and Young S. Kim. 1990. "Digestion and Absorption of Dietary Protein." *Annu Rev Med* 41:133–39.

Evangard, B., R. S. Schacterle, and A. L. Komaroff. 1999. "Chronic Fatigue Syndrome: New Insights and Old Ignorance." *J Intern Med* 246:455–69.

Evans, W., J. Thompson, and I. H. Rosenberg. 1992. *Biomarkers: The 10 Keys to Prolonging Vitality.* New York: Simon and Schuster.

Fearon, D. T., and R. M. Locksley. 1996. "The Instructive Role of Innate Immunity in the Acquired Immune Response." *Science* 272:50–53.

Filella, X., J. Blade, A. Guillermo, R. Molina, C. Rozman, and A. Ballesta. 1996. "Cytokines (IL-6, TNF-alpha, IL-1-alpha) and Soluble Interleukin-2 Receptor as Serum Tumor Markers in Multiple Myeloma." *Cancer Detect Prev* 20:52–59.

Flickinger, M. C., and S. W. Drew, eds. 1999. *Encyclopedia of Bioprocess Technology: Fermentation, Biocatalysis, and Bioseparation.* 5 vols. New York: John Wiley. A good resource book on all aspects of modern bioprocess technologies.

Freeman, R., and A. Komaroff. 1997. "Does the Chronic Fatigue Syndrome Involve the Autonomic Nervous System? *Am J Med* 102:357–64.

Fukuda, K., S. E. Straus, I. Hickie, M. C. Sharpe, J. G. Dobbins, A. Komaroff, et al. 1994. "The Chronic Fatigue Syndrome: A Comprehensive Approach to Its Definition and Study." *Ann Intern Med* 121:953–60.

Galas, D. J., 1990. "Transposable Genetic Elements: Agents of Complex Change. Mutation and the Environment, Part A." *Prog Clin Biol Res* 340A (1990): 135–44.

Galley, H. F., et al. 1997. "Combination Oral Antioxidant Supplementation Reduces Blood Pressure." *Clin Sci* 92:361–65.

Gardner, M. L. G. 1988. "Gastrointestinal Absorption of Intact Proteins." *Annu Rev Nutr* 8:329–50.

Gaubatz, J. W., and B. H. Tan. 1994. "Aging Affects the Levels of DNA Damage in Postmitotic Cells." *Ann NY Acad Sci* 719 (May 31): 97–107.

Geller, A. N. 1972. "Proteolytic Enzymes in the Treatment of Some Nonspecific Disorders of the Motor-Supporting Apparatus." *Vestn Khir Im I I Grek* 107 (1): 58–61. Russian. No abstract available.

Gerard, G. 1974. "Therapeutique Anti-Cancreuses et Bremelaines." *Agressologie* 3:261–74.

Gionchetti, P., F. Rizzello, A. Venturi, and M. Campieri. 2000. "Probiotics in Infective Diarrhea and Inflammatory Bowel Disease." *J Gastroenterol Hepatol* 15 (5): 479–93.

Glenk, Wilhelm, and Sven Neu. 1990. *Enzyme.* Munich: Wilhelm Heyne Verlag.

Goeth, R. A. 1907. "Pancreatic Treatment of Cancer, with Report of a Cure." *JAMA* 48:1030.

Goldberg, Burton, and the editors of *Alternative Medicine Digest.* 1998. *Alternative Medicine Guide to Heart Disease.* Tiburon, CA: Future Medicine Publishing.

Gordon, T., et al. 1977. "High-Density Lipoprotein as a Protective Factor Against CHD." *American Journal of Medicine* 62:707–14; Williams, P., et al. 1979. *Lancet* 1:72–75.

Grendell, J. H., and S. S. Rothman. 1981. "Digestive End Products Mobilize Secretory Proteins from Subcellular Stores in the Pancreas." *Am J Physiol* 241 (1): G67–73.

Griedbel, P. J., and W. R. Hein. 1996. "Expanding the Role of Peyer's Patches in B-Cell Ontogeny." *Immunol Today* 17 (1): 30–39.

Grusky, F. L., 1955. "Gastrointestinal Absorption of Unaltered Protein in Normal Infants." *Pediatrics* 16:763.

Guarner, F., and J. R. Malagelada. 2003. "Gut Flora in Health and Disease." *Lancet* 360:512–19.

Gullo, L. 1993. "Indication for Pancreatic Enzyme Treatment in Non-Pancreatic Digestive Diseases." *Digestion* 54 (Suppl. no. 2): 43–47.

Haas, Elson M. 2003. *Staying Healthy with the Seasons.* Berkeley, CA: Celestial Arts.

Haas, Elson M., and Cameron Stauth. 2000. *The False Fat Diet.* New York: Ballantine.

Hager, E. D. 1996. *Complementary Oncology.* Grafelfing, Germany: Forum Medizin.

Hallek, M., E. Bergsagel, and K. Anderson. 1998. "Multiple Myeloma: Increasing Evidence for a Multistep Transformation Process," *Blood* 91:3–21.

Halsey, Eugenia. 1996. "Researchers Pinpoint Link between Smoking and Heart Disease." *CNN Interactive Food and Health,* May 3, 1996. www.cnn.com/HEALTH/9605/03/nfm/smoking.blood.test/.

Harmatz, P. R., K. J. Bloch, M. Brown, W. A. Walker, and R. E. Kleinman. 1989. "Intestinal Adaptation during Lactation in the Mouse. I. Enhanced intestinal uptake of dietary protein antigen." *Immunology* 67 (1): 92–95.

Hartung, J., and V. R. Phillips. 1994. "Control of Gaseous Emissions from Livestock Buildings and Manure Stores." *Journal of Agricultural Engineering Research* 57:173-189.

Hattersley, J. G. 1992. "Heart Attacks and Strokes." *Townsend Letter for Doctors and Patients,* February/March: 104.

Hawkins, David R. 2002. *Power vs. Force.* Carlsbad, CA: Hay House.

Hayflick, L. 2000. "The Future of Ageing." *Nature* 408:267–69.

Hebuterne, X. 2003. "Gut Changes Attributed to Ageing: Effects on Intestinal Microflora." *Curr Opin Clin Nutr Metab Care* 6:49–54.

Heinecke, R. M., L. van der Waal, and M. Yokoyama. 1974. "Effect of Bromelain (Ananase) on Human Platelet Aggregation." *Experientia* 28:844.

Hemmings, W. A., and E. W. Williams. 1978. "Transport of Large Breakdown Products of Dietary Protein through the Gut Wall." *Gut* 19:715

Hertog, M. G., et al. 1997. "Antioxidant Flavonoids and Coronary Heart Disease Risk." *Lancet* 349:699.

Hieber, F. 1967. "Therapy of Degenerative Bone and Joint Diseases with the Aid of Proteolytic Enzymes." *Med Welt* 35 (September 2): 2058–60. German. No abstract available.

Hitchcox, Lee. 1996. *Long Life Now: Strategies for Staying Alive.* Berkeley, CA: Celestial Arts.

Holmes, G. P., J. E. Kaplan, N. M. Gantz, A. L. Komaroff, L. B. Schonberger, S. E. Straus, et al. 1988. "Chronic Fatigue Syndrome: A Working Case Definition." *Ann Intern Med* 108:387–89.

Hörnig, G., W. Berg, and M. Türk. 1997. "Harmful Gas and Odor Emissions under Use of Feed and Slurry Additives," 78–85. Proceedings of the Fifth International Symposium on Livestock Environment, Bloomington, MN, May 29–31.

Horrobin, D. F. 2000. "Essential Fatty Acid Metabolism and Its Modification in Atopic Eczema." *Am J Clin Nutr* 71: 367S–72S.

Howell, Edward. 1985. *Enzyme Nutrition: The Food Enzyme Concept.* Wayne, NJ: Avery Publishing Group.

———. 1980. *Enzymes for Health and Longevity.* Woodstock Valley, CT: Omangod Press.

Hunt, J. N., and A. Oginski. 1962. "The Regulation of Gastric Emptying of Various Meals." *J Physiol* 163:34.

Hurwitz, B. E., K. A. Brownely, M. A. Fletcher, and N. G. Klimas. 2000. "Chronic Fatigue Syndrome: Evidence Supporting the Hypothesis of a Behaviorally Activated Neuromodulator of Fatigue." *Journal of Chronic Fatigue Syndrome* 6 (2): 45–63.

Lapp, Charles W. 2003. International AACFS Conference on Chronic Fatigue Syndrome, Fibromyalgia and Related Illnesses. Summary of the AACFS Sixth International Conference on Chronic Fatigue Syndrome, Fibromyalgia, and Related Illnesses, Chantilly, VA.

Jacobson, L. D., et al. 1999. "Literature Review for Air Quality and Odor." Topic IIIH of Generic Environmental Impact Statement prepared for the Minnesota Environmental Quality Board, June 22.

Jacobson, L. D., B. Hetchler, K. A. Janni, and L. J. Johnston. 1998. "Odor and Gas Reduction from Sprinkling Soybean Oil in a Pig Nursery." ASAE Paper No. 98-4125. St. Joseph, MI: ASAE.

Jakobsson, I., T. Lindberg, L. Lothe, I. Axelsson, and B. Benediktsson. 1986. "Human Alpha-Lactalbumin as a Marker of Macromolecular Absorption." *Gut* 27 (9): 1029–34.

Jepson, M. A., N. L. Simmons, T. C. Savidge, P. S. James, and B. H. Hirst. 1993. "Selective Binding and Transcytosis of Latex Microspheres by Rabbit Intestinal M Cells." *Cell Tissue Res* 271:399–405.

Johnson, S. K., J. DeLuca, N. Fiedler, and B. H. Natelson. 1994. "Cognitive Functioning of Patients with Chronic Fatigue Syndrome." *Clin Infect Dis* 18 (Suppl. no. 1): S84–S85.

Khalsa, Dharma Singh, with Cameron Stauth. 1997. *Brain Longevity: The Breakthrough Program That Improves Your Mind and Memory.* New York: Warner Books.

Kidd, P. 2000. "The Gonzalez-Isaacs Program," *Total Health* 22:19–21.

Klaschka, Franz. 1996. *New Perspectives in Tumor Therapy.* Grafelfing, Germany: Forum-Medizin Verlagsgesellschaft mbH.

———. 1996. *Oral Enzymes: New Approach to Cancer Treatment.* Grafelfing, Germany: Forum-Medizin Verlagsgesellschaft mbH.

Klimas, N. G., F. R. Salvato, R. Morgan, and M. A. Fletcher. 1990. "Immunologic Abnormalities in Chronic Fatigue Syndrome." *J Clin Microbiol* 28:1403–10.

Kohen, R., E. Vellaichamy, J. Hrbac, I, Gati, and O. Tirosh. 2000. "Quantification of the Overall Reactive Oxygen Species Scavenging Capacity of Biological Fluids and Tissues." *Free Radic Biol Med* 28 (6): 871–79.

Komaroff, A. L., and D. S. Buchwald. 1998. "Chronic Fatigue Syndrome: An Update." *Annu Rev Med* 49:1–13.

Krupp, L. B., L. Jandorf, P. K. Coyle, and W. B. Mendelson. 1993. "Sleep Disturbance in Chronic Fatigue Syndrome." *J Psychosom Res* 37 (4): 325–31.

Kuby, J. 1997. *Immunology.* 3rd ed. New York: W. H. Freeman and Company.

Leese, G., P. Chattington, W. Fraser, et al. 1996. "Short-Term Night-Shift Work Mimics the Pituitary-Adrenal Dysfunction in Chronic Fatigue Syndrome. *J Clin Endocrinol Metab* 81:1867–70.

Lefrancois, L., and L. Puddington. 1995. "Extrathymic Intestinal T-Cell Development: Virtual Reality?" *Immunol Today* 16 (1):16–21.

Lennard-Jones, J. E. 1983. "Functional Gastrointestinal Disorders." *N Engl J Med* 308:431.

Levine, Barbara. 1996. "Most Frequently Asked Questions about Lactose Intolerance."*Nutrition Today,* March/April: 78–79.

Levine, P. 1998. "What We Know about Chronic Fatigue Syndrome and Its Relevance to the Practicing Physician." *Am J Med* 105:100S–103S.

Liebow, C. 1987. "Specific End-Product Feedback Regulation of Pancreatic Protein Synthesis." *Pancreas* 2 (2):136–40.

Liebow, C., and S. S. Rothman. 1975. "Enteropancreatic Circulation of Digestive Enzymes." *Science* 189:472–74.

Lloyd, A. R., D. Wakefield, C. R. Boughton, and J. K. Dwyer. 1989. "Immunologic Abnormalities in the Chronic Fatigue Syndrome." *Med J Aust* 151:122–24.

Lopez, D. A., R. M. Williams, and M. Miehlke. 1994. *Enzymes: The Fountain of Life.* Charleston, SC: Neville Press.

Lothe, L., T. Lindberg, and I. Jakobsson. 1990. "Macromolecular Absorption in Infants with Infantile Colic." *Acta Paediatr Scand* 79 (4): 417–21.

Macdonald, Ian. 1995. "Carbohydrates." In *Modern Nutrition in Health and Disease,* ed. Maurice E. Shils, et al. Philadelphia: Lea & Febiger.

MacDonald, K. L., M. T. Osterholm, K. H. LeDell, K. E. White, C. H. Schenck, and C. C. Chao. 1996. "A Case-Control Study to Assess Possible Triggers and Cofactors in Chronic Fatigue Syndrome." *Am J Med* 100:549–53.

Maher, K. 2001. "Flow Cytometric Measurements of Perforin and Natural Killer Cell Activity." Poster presented at the American Association for Chronic Fatigue Syndrome Fifth International Conference, Seattle.

Male, D., B. Champion, and A. Cooke. 1987. "Lymphocyte and APC Traffic." In *Advanced Immunology.* Philadelphia: J. P Lippincott and Co.: 14.1.

Malinow, M. R. 1989. "Risk for Arterial Occlusive Disease: Is Hyperhomocysteinemia an Innocent Bystander?" *Can J Cardiol* 17 94(3): 959.

Manyari, D. E., S. Rose, J. V. Tyberg, and R. S. Sheldon. 1996. "Abnormal Reflex Venous Function in Patients with Neruomediated Syncope." *J Am Coll Cardiol* 27:1730–35.

Marcel, B., A. L. Komaroff, L. R. Fagioli, R. J. Kornish, and M. S. Albert. 1996. "Cognitive Deficits in Patients with Chronic Fatigue Syndrome." *Biol Psychiatry* 40:535–41.

Maurer, K. H., and D. Mecke. 1986. "Regulation of Enzymes Involved in the Biosynthesis of the Sesquiterpene Antibiotic Pentalenolactone in Streptomyces arenae." *Antibiot* (Tokyo) 39 (2): 266–71.

McCully, K. S. 1983. "Homocysteine Theory of Arteriosclerosis: Development and Current Status." *Atherosclerosis Reviews* 11:157–246.

McMurdo, M. E. 2000. "A Healthy Old Age: Realistic or Futile Goal?" *Br Med J* 321:1149–51.

Mercola, Joseph, with Alison Rose Levy. 2003. *The No-Grain Diet: Conquer Carbohydrate Addiction and Stay Slim for Life.* New York: Dutton.

Metcalfe, Dean, and Hugh Sampson. 1997. *Food Allergy: Adverse Reactions to Foods and Food Additives.* 2nd ed. Cambridge, MA: Blackwell.

Michiels, V., R. Cluydts, B. Fischler, G. Hoffmann, O. Le Bon, and K. De Meirleir. 1996. "Cognitive Functioning in Patients with Chronic Fatigue Syndrome." *J Clin Exp Neuropsychol* 18:666–77.

Monteny, G. J., and J. A. M. Voermans. 1998. "Ammonia and Odour Control from Animal Production Facilities," 295–301. Review of the International Symposium held at Vinkeloord, The Netherlands, October 6–10, 1997.

Morin, R. J., and S. K. Peng. 1989. "The Role of Cholesterol Oxidation Products in the Pathogenesis of Atherosclerosis." *Ann Clin Lab Sci* 19 (4): 225–37.

Nehler, Mark, et al. 1997. "Homocytseinemia as a Risk Factor for Athero-sclerosis: A Review." *Cardiovasc Pathol* 6:1–9.

Newey, H., and D. H. Smyth. 1959. "Intestinal Absorption of Dipeptides." *J Physiol* 145:48.

Nhat Hanh, Thich. 1998. *Teachings on Love.* Berkeley, CA: Parallax Press.

Nicklin, S., and K. Miller. 1989. "Intestinal Uptake and Immunological Effects of Carrageenan—Current Concepts." *Food Addit Contam* 6 (4): 425–36.

Northrup, Christiane. 2001. *The Wisdom of Menopause: Creating Physical and Emotional During the Change.* New York: Bantam Books.

Nouza, K., and M. Wald. 1995. "Systemic Enzyme Therapy: Problems of Re-sorption of Enzyme Macromolecules." *Cas Lek Cesk* 134 (19): 615–19.

O'Hagan, D. T., K. J. Palin, and S. S. Davis. 1988. "Intestinal Absorption of Proteins and Macromolecules and the Immunological Response." *Crit Rev Ther Drug Carrier Syst* 4 (3): 197–220.

"Oral Enzyme Therapy in Osteoarthritis of the Knee. Proteolytic Enzyme Are Effective with Few Risks." 2001. *MMW Fortschr Med* 143(23): 44–46. German. No abstract available.

Ottaway, C. A., and A. J. Husband. 1992. "Central Nervous System Influences on Lymphocyte Migration." *Brain Behav Immun* 6:97–116.

Ouellette, A. J. 1997. "Paneth Cells and Innate Immunity in the Crypt Microenvironment." *Gastroenterology* 113:1779–84.

Palcic, M. M. 1999. "Biocatalytic Synthesis of Oligosaccharides." *Curr Opin Biotechnol* 10:616–24. A good review with several references about the topic.

Pall, M. L. 2000. "Elevated, Sustained Peroxynitrite Levels as the Cause of Chronic Fatigue Syndrome." *Med Hypotheses* 54:115–25.

Pang, K. Y., W. A. Walker, and K. J. Bloch. 1981. "Intestinal Uptake of Macro-molecules. Differences in Distribution and Degradation of Protein Antigen in Control and Immunised Rats." *Gut* 22 (12): 1018–24.

Passwater, Richard. 1977. *Supernutrition for Healthy Hearts.* New York: Dial Press.

Pastinen, O., K. Visuri, H. Schoemaker, and M. Leisola. 1999. "Novel Reac-tions of Xylose Isomerase from Streptomyces rubiginosus." *Enzyme and Microbial Technol* 25:695–700. Glucose isomerase is a traditional name; xy-lose isomerase would be a more correct name, although it has recently been shown to catalyse many monosaccharide isomerizations.

Perelson, A. S. 1989. "Immune Network Theory." *Immunol Rev* 110:5–33.

Piruat, J. I., and A. Aguilera. 1998. "A Novel Yeast Gene, TH02, Is Involved in RNA pol II Transcription and Provides New Evidence for Transcrip-tional Elongation-Associated Recombination." *EMBO J* 17 (16): 4859–72.

Prochaska, L. J., X. T. Nguyen, N. Donat, and W. V. Piekutowski. 2000. "Ef-fects of Food Processing on the Thermodynamic and Nutritive Value of Foods: Literature and Database Survey." *Med Hypotheses* 54 (2): 254–62.

Prochaska, L. J., and W. V. Piekutowski. 1994. "On the Synergistic Ef-fects of Enzymes in Food with Enzymes in the Human Body. A Lit-erature Survey and Analytical Report." *Med Hypotheses* 42 (6): 355–62.

Ptashne, M. 1992. *A Genetic Switch. Phage Lambda and Higher Organisms.* Cambridge, MA: Blackwell.

Radi, R., M. Rodriguez, L. Castro, and R. Telleri. 1994. "Inhibition of Mitochondrial Electron Transport by Peroxynitrite." *Arch Biochem Biophys* 308:89–95.

Randerath, K., D. Li, and E. Randerath. 1990. "Age-Related DNA Modifications (I-Compounds): Modulation by Physiological and Pathological Processes." *Mutat Res* 238:245–53.

Rath, Matthias. 1993. *Eradicating Heart Disease.* San Francisco: Health Now.

Reader's Digest Association. 1999. *The Healing Power of Vitamins, Minerals, and Herbs: The A–Z Guide to Enhancing Your Health and Treating Illness with Nutritional Supplements.* Pleasantville, NY: Reader's Digest Association.

Rembacken, B. J., A. M. Snelling, P. M. Hawkey, D. M. Chalmers, and A. T. Axon. 1999. "Non-pathogenic Escherichia coli versus Masalazine for the Treatment of Ulcerative Colitis: A Randomized Trial." *Lancet* 354:635–39.

Resch, Karl, et al. 1992. "Fibrinogen and Viscosity as Risk Factors for Subsequent Cardiovascular Events in Stroke Survivors." *Ann Intern Med* 117 (5): 371–75.

Richards, R. S., T. K. Roberts, R. H. Dunstan, N. R. McGregor, and H. L. Butt. 2000. "Free Radicals in Chronic Fatigue Syndrome: Cause or Effect?" *Redox Rep* 5 (2-3): 146–47.

Rimm, E. B., M. J. Stampfer, A. Ascherio, E. Giovanucci, G. A. Golditz, and W. C. Willett. 1993. "Vitamin E Consumption and the Risk of Coronary Disease in Women." *N Engl J Med* 328 (20): 1444–49.

Rimm, E. B., et al. "Vitamin E Consumption and the Risk of Coronary Heart Disease in Men." *N Engl J Med* 328 (20): 1450–56.

Rocco, V., B. De Massy, and A. Nicolas. 1992. "The Saccharomyces cerevisiae ARG4 Initiator of Meiotic Gene Conversion and Its Associated Double-Strand DNA Breaks Can Be Inhibited by Transcriptional Interference." *Proc Natl Acad Sci USA* 89 (December): 12068–72.

Roizen, Michael, F. 2000. *RealAge: Are You As Young As You Can Be?* New York: Cliff Street Books.

Roos, K. F., and M. A. Moser, eds. 1997. *A Manual for Developing Biogas Systems at Commercial Farms in the United States.* AgSTAR Handbook. Washington, DC: U.S. EPA.

Rowe, P. C., and H. Clakins. 1998. "Neurally Mediated Hypotension and Chronic Fatigue Syndrome." *Am J Med* 105 (3A): 15S–21S.

Ruiz, Don Miguel. 1997. *The Four Agreements: A Practical Guide to Personal Freedom.* San Rafael, CA: Amber-Allen.

Ryan, C. M., M. B. Atkins, J. W. Mier, J. A. Gelfand, and R. G. Tompkins. 1995. "Effects of Malignancy and Interleukin-2 Infusion on Gut Macromolecular Permeability." *Crit Care Med* 23 (11): 1801–06.

Sakalova, A., L. Dedik, S. Gazova, J. Hanisch, and W. Schiess. 1998. "Survival Analysis of and Adjuvant Therapy with Oral Enzymes in Multiple Myeloma Patients." *Br J Haematol* 102:353–56.

Salit, I. E. 1997. "Precipitating Factors for the Chronic Fatigue Syndrome." *J Psychiatr Res* 31 (1): 59–65.

Santillo, H. 1993 *Food Enzymes.* Prescott, AZ: Hohm Press.

Saputo, Len, and Nancy Faass. 2002. *Boosting Immunity: Creating Wellness Naturally.* Novato, CA: New World Library.

Schmid A., Dordick, J. S., B. Hauer, A. Kiener, M. Wubbolts, and B. Witholt. 2001. "Industrial Biocatalysis Today and Tomorrow." *Nature* 409:258–68. A good review article on developments of enzymatic and whole cell biocatalytic applications and trends in chemical industry; www.isrs.kagawa-u.ac.jp/ is a page of a recently formed International Society of Rare Sugars.

Schneider, H. J., W. Dedek, R. Grahl, B. Mothes, J. Uhlemann, H. Schwarz, G. Schwachulla, H. Router, and M. Mohring. 1983. "Studies of the Persorption of Large Particles from Radio-Labelled Cation Exchangers." *Urol Int* 38 (2): 116–20.

Schondorf, R., and R. Freeman. 1999. "The Importance of Orthostatic Intolerance in the Chronic Fatigue Syndrome." *Am J Med Sci* 317 (2): 117–23.

Scott, L. V., S. Medbak, and T. G. Dinan. 1998. "Blunted Adrenocorticotropin and Cortisol Responses to Corticotropin-Releasing Hormone Stimulation in Chronic Fatigue Syndrome." *Acta Psychiatr Scand* 97:450–57.

Sebadio, J. L., S. Gnaedig, and J. M. Chardigny. 1999. "Recent Advances in Conjugated Linoleic Acid Research." *Curr Opin Clin Nutr Metab Care* 2 (6): 499–506.

Sellman, Sherrill. 2000. "The Physiology of Hormones." *Healthy and Natural Journal,* October. *Alt HealthWatch.*

Sessler, A. M., and J. M. Ntambi. 1998. "Polyunsaturated Fatty Acid Regulation of Gene Expression." *J Nutr* 128:923–26.

Setala, K. 1986. "The Promise of Enzymes in Therapy of Hyperlipidemia." *Med Hypotheses* 20: 287–315.

Shanahan, F. 2000. "Therapeutic Manipulation of Gut Flora." *Science* 289:1311–12.

Shultz, Arthur R. 1994. *Enzyme Kinetics: From Diastase to Multi-enzyme Systems.* New York: Cambridge.

Sirving O. K., et al. 1996. "Dietary Flavonoids, Antioxidant Vitamins, and Incidence of Stroke" *Arch Intern Med* 154: 637–42.

Smith, P. J., and T. A. Makinson. 1989. "Cellular Consequences of Overproduction of DNA Topoisomerase II in an Ataxia-Telangiectasia Cell Line." *Cancer Res* 49 (5): 1118–24.

Souvannavong, V., C. Lemaire, D. De Nay, S. Brown, and A. Adam. 1995. "Expression of Alkaline Phosphatase by a B-Cell Hybridoma and Its Modulation during Cell Growth and Apoptosis." *Immunol Lett* 47:163–70.

Spanier, J. A., C. W. Howden, and M. P. Jones. 2003. "A Systematic Review of Alternative Therapies in the Irritable Bowel Syndrome." *Arch Intern Med* 163 (3): 265–74.

Spiller, R.C., 1994. "Whether and How Novel Substrates Activate Normal Control Mechanisms Will Be Important Factors Determining Their Effectiveness and Patient Acceptability." *Gut* 35 (Suppl. no. 1): S5–S9.

Steidler, L., W. Hans, L. Schotte, et al. 2000. "Treatment of Murine Colitis by Lactococcus lactis Secreting Interleukin-10." *Science* 289:1352–55.

Strauss, B. S. 1998. "Hypermutability in Carcinogenesis." *Genetics* 148 (4): 1619–26.

Stryer, L., 1995. *Biochemistry.* 4th ed. New York: W. H. Freeman and Company.

Sutton, A. L., K. B. Kephart, M. W. A. Verstegen, T. T. Canh, and P. J. Hobbs. 1999. "Potential for Reduction of Odorous Compounds in Swine Manure through Diet Modification." *J Anim Sci* 77:430–39.

Tagesson, C., L. Franzen, G. Dahl, and B. Westrom. 1985. "Lysophosphatidylcholine Increases Rat Ileal Permeability to Macromolecules." *Gut* 26 (4): 369–77.

Taussig, S. J., and S. Batkin. 1988. "Bromelain: The Enzyme Complex of Pineapple (Ananas cosmosus) and Its Clinical Application. An Update." *J Ethnopharmacol,* 22:191–203.

Thomas, N. W., P. G. Jenkins, K. A. Howard, M. W. Smith, E. C. Lavelle, J. Holland, and S. S. Davis. 1996. "Particle Uptake and Translocation across Epithelial Membranes." *J Anat* 189:487–90.

Truss, C. O. 1983. *The Missing Diagnosis.* Birmingham, AL: The Missing Diagnosis, Inc.

Udall, J. N., K. J. Bloch, A. P. Newman, M. Dixon, and W. A. Walker. 1984. "Intestinal Uptake of Trypsin in Newborn and Weaned Rabbits." *Am J Physiol* 247:G183–G188.

USDA. 2000. "Air Quality Research and Technology Transfer White Paper and Recommendations for Concentrated Animal Feeding Operations." Report by Confined Livestock Air Quality Subcommittee of the USDA Agricultural Air Quality Task Force, Washington, DC, July 19.

Vander, A. J., J. H. Sherman, and D. S. Luciano. 1975. *Human Physiology.* 2nd ed. New York: McGraw-Hill.

Van Osterwijk, M. F., A. Versteeg, R. Filon, A. A. van Zeeland, and L. H. F. Mullenders. 1996. "The Sensitivity of Cockayne's Syndrome Cells to DNA Damaging Agents Is Not Due to Defective Transcription-Coupled Repair of Active Genes." *Mol Cell Biol,* August: 4436–44.

Verma, M., S. Majumdar, N. K. Ganguly, and B. N. Walia. 1994. "Effect of Escherichia coli Enterotoxins on Macromolecular Absorption." *Gut* 35 (11): 1613–16.

Visuri, K. 1995. Preparation of cross-linked glucose isomerase crystals. US Patent 5437993. This patent describes the first preparation of a cross-linked enzyme crystal catalyst.

———. 1987. Stable glucose isomerase concentrate and a process for the preparation thereof. US Patent 4,699,882. This patent describes the first large scale crystallization process of an intracellular industrial enzyme.

Volkheimer, G. 1993. "Persorption of microparticles." *Pathologe* 14 (5): 247–52.

Walker, W. A. 1974. "Uptake and Transport of Macromolecules by the Intestine—Possible Role in Clinical Disorders." *Gastroenterology* 67:531.

Walker, W. A., S. N. Abel, M. Wu, and K. J. Bloch. 1976. "Intestinal Uptake of Macromolecules. V. Comparison of the in Vitro Uptake by Rat Small Intestine of Antigen-Antibody Complexes Prepared in Antibody or Antigen Excess." *J Immunol* 117 (3): 1028–32.

Walker, W. A., and K. J. Bloch. 1983. "Intestinal Uptake of Macromolecules: In Vitro and in Vivo Studies." *Ann NY Acad Sci* 409: 593–602.

Walker, W. A., K. J. Isselbacher, and K. J. Bloch. 1973. "Intestinal Uptake of Macromolecules. II. Effect of Parenteral Immunization." *J Immunol* 111 (1): 221–26.

Walker, W. A., M. Wu, K. J. Isselbacher, K. J. Bloch. 1975. "Intestinal Uptake of Macromolecules. IV. The Effect of Pancreatic Duct Ligation on the Breakdown of Antigen and Antigen-Antibody Complexes on the Intestinal Surface." *Gastroenterology* 69 (6): 1223–29.

Walker, W. A., M. Wu, K. J. Isselbacher, K. J. Bloch. 1975. "Intestinal Uptake of Macromolecules. III. Studies on the Mechanism by Which Immunization Interferes with Antigen Uptake." *J Immunol* 115 (3): 854–61.

Wang, X. D., Q. Wang, R. Andersson, and I. Ihse. 1996. "Alterations in Intestinal Function in Acute Pancreatitis in an Experimental Model." *Br J Surg* 83 (11): 1537–43.

Watson, W. S., G. T. McCreath, A. Chaudhuri, and P. O. Behan. 1997. "Possible Cell Membrane Transport Defect in Chronic Fatigue Syndrome?" *Journal of Chronic Fatigue Syndrome* 3 (3): 1–12.

Weaver, L. T., and R. R. Coombs. 1988. "Does 'Sugar' Permeability Reflect Macromolecular Absorption? A Comparison of the Gastro-intestinal Uptake of Lactulose and Beta-Lactoglobulin in the Neonatal Guinea Pig." *Int Arch Allergy Appl Immunol* 85 (1): 133–35.

Weiner, M. L., M. W. Turner, P. Boulton, J. G. Shields, S. Strobel, S. Gibson, H. R. Miller, and R. J. Levinsky. 1988. "Intestinal Transport of Some Macromolecules in Food." *Food Chem Toxicol* 26 (10): 867–80.

Wessely, S., T. Chalder, S. Hirsch, P. Wallace, and D. Wright. 1997. "The Prevalence and Morbidity of Chronic Fatigue and Chronic Fatigue Syndrome: A Prospective Primary Care Study." *Am J Public Health* 87 (9): 1449–55.

Whiteley, L. O., and D. M. Klurfeld. 2000. "Are Dietary Fiber-Induced Alterations in Colonic Epithelial Cell Proliferation Predictive of Fiber's Effect on Colon Cancer? *Nutr Cancer* 36 (2): 131–49.

Whiteside, T., and D. Friberg. 1998. "Natural Killer Cells and Natural Killer Cell Activity in Chronic Fatigue Syndrome." *Am J Med* 105(3A): 27S–34S.

Williams, Sue Rodwell. 1997. *Essentials of Nutrition and Diet Therapy.* Philadelphia: Mosby.

Wolf, Max, and Karl Ransberger. 1972. *Enzyme Therapy.* New York: Vantage Press.

Wrba, Heinrich, and Otto Pecher. 1997. *Enzymes: A Drug of the Future.* Landsberg/Lech, Germany: EcoMed Verlagsgesellschaft.

———. 1993. *Enzymes: A Drug of the Future.* (Vienna: Verlag Orac Ecomed Verlagsgesellschaft AG & Co.)

Ziboh, V. A., C. C. Miller, and Y. Cho. 2000. "Metabolism of Polyunsaturated Fatty Acids by Skin Epidermal Enzymes: Generation of Anti-Inflammatory and Anti-Proliferative Metabolites." *Am J Clin Nutr* 71 (Suppl): 361S–66S.

Index

Underscored page references indicate boxed text.

Acerola cherry extract, 143, 160, 182, 195, 200,
    221, 234, 245, 265, 292, 326
Acetyl-L-carnitine, 166, 204, 288–89
Acid-forming foods, avoiding, 113
Acid rebound, 40
Acne, 110–15
Acupressure, 74, 100
Acupressure balancing technique, 329–31
ADHD, 147, 161–64
Adrenal enzyme formula, 137, 142, 160, 221
Adrenal exhaustion, 136–37, 159
Adrenal glands, 136–37, 274–75
Adrenaline, 274
Agent Orange, 217
Aging
    alpha linolenic acid for, 288
    antioxidant supplement for, 286–87
    associations with, 269
    caloric restriction and, 277–78
    depression and, 156
    dietary fats and, 273
    digestive enzyme formula for, 287–91
    enzymes and, 4
    enzyme therapy, 268–69, 279–80, 286–91
    exercise and, 279
    food intolerances and, 271–73
    future methods of managing, 279–80
    health problems related to, 281–86
    lifestyle factors and, 268–69, 271–77
    longevity and, 268–69, 277
    nutritional supplements and, 278
    options for, 269–70
    premature, 270
    skin and, 103–4
    stress and, 274–75
    toxins and, 276–77
    vitamin C for, 291
    vitamin E as d-alpha tocopherol succinate for,
        287, 290–91
ALA. See Alpha lipoic acid
Alcohol, 105
Allergies to food, 90. See also Food
        intolerances
Aloe vera juice extract, 64, 183–84
Alpha-galactosidase, 33, 55
Alpha lipoic acid (ALA)
    for diabetes, 221, 223
    for heart disease, 193, 204
    metabolism and, 98
    for weight loss, 98
Alprazolam, 167

Amino acids
    arterial plaques and, 198–99
    collagen and, 102, 276
    enzymes and, 6
    free radicals and, 276
    protease and, 43
    proteins and, 51–52
Amoxicillin, 112
Amphetamine, 81
Ampicillin, 112
Amylase, 11, 32–33, 43, 55, 207
Angina, 188–91
Antacids, 17, 40
Antibiotics, 112
Antigen, 170–71
Anti-inflammatory enzyme solution, 228, 241–42
Antioxidant
    blend, 327–28
    free radicals and, 104, 265, 276–77, 286–87
    supplement
        for aging, 286–87
        for diabetes, 222
        for emotional balance, 160
        for hair, healthy, 119
        for immune system, healthy, 184
        for inflammation, 246
        selecting, 321–23
Apple cider vinegar, 70
Arginine, 198–99
Arousal, sexual, 283
Arterial plaques, 198–99
Arthritis, 8–11
Aspirin, 189
Astragalus root extract, 181, 264
Atherosclerosis, 192
Attention deficit hyperactivity disorder (ADHD),
        147, 161–64
Autoimmune diseases, 12, 172–73, 227

Balding, 120
Banana leaf extract, 97
Bean extract, 89
Beet root extract, 99, 124
Beta-carotene, 182, 265
Beta-glucanase, 33
Bilberry fruit extract, 201
Biotin, 131, 143, 161, 222–23, 325
Bitter melon extract, 220
Black cohosh root extract, 289
Black currant seed oil, 122
Bladderwrack extract, 97, 123, 125

Blood clotting, 199–200
Blood pressure, 196–98
Blood sugar balancing enzyme formula, 219
Blood sugar levels, 150–52, 224
Boron, 327
Boron citrate, 234, 246
Boswellia resin extract, 234
Bowel movements, timing of, 62
Bowel problems, 175–76. *See also specific types*
Bromelain, 31, 196, 263
Bupleurum root extract, 143, 160, 221
Burdock root extract, 123, 182, 265
Butcher's broom, 201
B vitamins, 118. *See also specific types*

Calcium, 327
Calcium citrate, 144, 246
Calendula flower extract, 123
Caloric restriction, 80, 112, 277–78
Cancer
  blood and, 255
  chemotherapy and, 258–59
  circulating immune complexes and, 253
  colon, 261
  conventional treatment, 258–60
  digestive enzyme formula for, 264
  enzymes and
    anticancer benefit of, 262–63
    continued research on, 256–57
    conventional cancer treatment and, 258–60
    history of research on, 253–55
    systemic, 255–57
  enzyme therapy, 251, 261, 263–65
  fear about, 251
  free radicals and, 259–60
  full-spectrum blend digestive enzyme formula
    for, 264
  improvements in care, 260–62
  inflammation and, 260
  lymphedema, 261
  melanoma, 261
  metastasis, 259–61
  process, 251–53, 258
  protease supplement for, 264
  quercetin for, 265
  radiation and, 258–59
  vitamin C for, 265
  zinc for, 265
Candidiasis, 112, 114
Carb blockers, 88–89
Carbohydrate digestive enzyme formula
  best, 55
  blood sugar levels and, 152
  for constipation, 61
  for Crohn's disease, 63
  for diabetes, 222
  for diarrhea, 66
  for diverticular disease, 69
  for hypoglycemia, 138
  for irritable bowel syndrome, 74
  protease supplement in, 55

  for ulcerative colitis, 63
  for weight loss, 95
Carbohydrate intolerance, 50–51
  diabetes and, 205
  identifying, 53–54
  weight gain and, 83–84, 89
Carbohydrate intolerance diet
  for Crohn's disease, 64
  for diarrhea, 67
  dietary fats in, 298
  for diverticular disease, 69
  for emotional balance, 152
  fruits in, 297
  grains in, 298
  guidelines for, 295–96
  for irritable bowel syndrome, 74
  legumes in, 298
  meal plan, 7-day, 302–6
  proteins in, 296
  recipes
    Fruit Slushy, 299
    No-Sugar-Added Tofu Smoothie, 300
    Skillet Eggplant and Tofu Pasta, 300
    Stuffed Zucchini, 301
    Tabbouleh with Buckwheat, 299
  for ulcerative colitis, 64
  vegetables in, 296–97
  for weight loss, 95
Carbohydrates
  amylase and, 11, 43
  cravings, 84
  diabetes and, 207, 224
  diet low in, 273
  energy and, 140
  food intolerances and, 50–51, 53–54
  sugar and, 207–8
Cardiovascular enzyme formula, 193, 199, 202, 287
Cat's claw herb extract, 182, 265
Cellulase, 32–33, 44, 55, 61
Cellulose, 61
Chaste tree berry extract, 290
Chemotherapy, 258–59
Chewing, 14, 41–42
Chewing gum, 96
Children, 83, 207
Chlorella, 246
Cholesterol levels, 191–94, 273, 287
Choline, 325–26
Chondroitin, 235
Chromium, 97, 223, 327
Chromium polynicotinate, 220
Chyme, 42
Chymotrypsin, 255, 263
Circulating immune complexes (CICs)
  acne and, 111
  cancer and, 253
  enzymes and, 275
  foreign substances in body and, 171–72
  immune mediators and, 149
  inflammation and, 195, 226, 228, 243
  mood swings and, 149

purpose of, 149
tissue damage caused by, 172, 195
Circulatory disorders, 199–202
Citrus bioflavonoid blend, 328
Codonopsis root extract, 143–44, 161, 222
Coenzyme Q10, 183, 189, 203, 265, 287–88
Cofactors, 4, 6, 130. *See also* Minerals; Vitamins
Colitis, ulcerative, 62–65, 236–39
Collagen, 102, 122, 276
Collinsonia root, 201
Colon, 105–6
Colon cancer, 261
Constipation, 60–62
Copper, 234
Cornsilk extract, 240
Cortisol, 274
Cortisone, 227
Cosmetic surgery for weight loss, 80
Coumadin, 287
Cow's milk, 216
Cravings
  acupressure for managing, 100
  carbohydrates, 84
  enzyme therapy, 84, 95–100
  overview, 89–92
Crohn's disease, 62–65, 236–39
Curcumin, 99
Cystic acne, 114

Daidzein, 289
Damiana leaf extract, 290–91
Dandelion root extract, 99, 124
Deep breathing, 74
Deglycyrrhizinated licorice root extract, 64, 183, 289
Depression, 154–58, 156
Desire, sexual, 283
Devil's claw bark extract, 234
DHA, 153, 163
Diabetes
  alpha lipoic acid for, 221, 223
  antioxidant supplement for, 222
  carbohydrate digestive formula for, 222
  carbohydrate intolerance and, 205
  carbohydrates and, 207, 224
  children and, 207
  danger of, 206
  diet and, 224
  digestive enzyme formula for, 219, 221
  enzyme therapy, 219–24
  exercise and, 224
  insulin and, 208, 210–12
  magnesium for, 220, 222–23
  metabolic syndrome and, 211, 211
  preventing, 217–19
  quercetin for, 220
  risk factors, 213–17
  sugar and, 207–10, 213–16
  type 1, 206
  type 2, 205–6, 207, 217, 223
  vitamin E as d-alpha tocopherol succinate for,
    219–20

weight maintenance and, 223–24
  zinc for, 220, 223
Diarrhea, 65–68
Diazepam, 167
Diet. *See also* Carbohydrate intolerance diet;
    Protein/fat intolerance diet; *specific foods*
  acid-forming foods in, 113
  acne and, 113–14
  American, 13–14, 51
  blood pressure and, 197
  caloric restriction and, 80, 112, 277–78
  cholesterol levels and, 193
  Crohn's disease and, 64–65
  diabetes and, 224
  diarrhea and, 67
  dieting and, 94–95
  diverticular disease and, 68
  emotional balance and, 164–65
  energy and, 127
  enzyme therapy and, 35–36, 36
  fiber in, 61, 68–69
  grains in, 86–88
  hair and, 118–19
  heartburn and, 71
  heart disease and, 187
  high blood pressure and, 197
  high-fiber, 68
  high-stress, 46–48
  immune system and, 171–73, 180, 185
  inflammation and, 247
  irritable bowel syndrome and, 74
  junk food in, 83, 110
  low-carbohydrate, 273
  low-stress, 46
  organic food in, 14
  overeating and, 114, 277–78
  processed foods in, 62
  raw foods in, 43
  skin and, 103, 109–10, 114
  ulcerative colitis and, 64–65
  weight loss and, 96
Dietary fats
  aging and, 273
  in carbohydrate intolerance diet, 298
  cholesterol levels and, 273
  cooking oil, 110
  food intolerances and, 52–53, 54–55
  free radicals and, 276
  inflammation and, 273
  in protein/fat intolerance diet, 310
  saturated, 273, 276
Dieting, 94–95
Diet pills, 80
Digestion
  acid rebound and, 40
  antacids and, 17, 40
  chewing and, 14, 41–42
  constipation and, 60–62
  Crohn's disease and, 62–65
  diarrhea and, 65–68
  digestive enzymes and, 11–13

Digestion *(cont.)*
  diverticular disease and, 68–69
  emotional balance and, 147
  energy drain and poor, 129–32
  enzyme deficiency and, 15–17
  enzymes in, 11–13, 44–45
  enzyme therapy, 41, 271
  fiber and, 61
  flatulence and, 176
  food enzymes and, 13–14
  heartburn and, 69–71, 188
  hypochlorhydria and, 71–72, 112
  immune system and, 173–75
  incomplete, 12
  inflammatory bowel disease, 62–63, 236–37
  irritable bowel syndrome and, 72–75
  lactose, 51
  leaky gut syndrome and, 93, 141
  metabolic rejectivity syndrome and, 12
  new view of, 75–77
  problems with, 39–40, 43–45
  process of, 41–43
  skin and, 106–7
  stress and, 45–48, 59
  stress management for optimal, 74
  ulcerative colitis and, 62–65
  weight loss and, 82–84
Digestive enzyme formula
  for aging, 287–91
  caloric restriction and, 278
  for cancer, 264
  for circulatory disorders, 200–201
  for Crohn's disease, 64
  for diabetes, 219, 221
  for emotional balance, 160, 165–66
  for energy, 142, 144
  for gastroesophageal reflux disease, 70
  for hair, healthy, 119, 124
  for heartburn, 70
  for heart disease, 203
  for immune system, healthy, 181, 183
  for inflammation, 234, 245
  protease in, 55
  selecting, 22–23
  for skin, healthy, 102–3, 122, 124
  for ulcerative colitis, 64
  for urinary tract infections, 240
  for weight loss, 97, 99
Digestive enzymes, 11–13
Digestive tract, 42–43
Diverticular disease, 68–69
D-mannose, 240
Docosahexaenoic acid (DHA), 153, 163
Drugs. *See* Over-the-counter drugs; Prescription drugs; *specific names*

E chinacea angustifolia root extract, 182, 265
Eczema, 115–17
Edema, 199–200
EFAs, 52, 61, 107–8
Eicosapentaenoic acid (EPA), 153

Emotional balance
  antioxidant supplement for, 160
  attention deficit hyperactivity disorder and, 161–64
  carbohydrate intolerance diet for, 152
  depression and, 154–58, 156
  diet and, 164–65
  digestion and, 147
  digestive enzyme formula for, 160, 165–66
  enzyme therapy, 147–48, 152–53, 160–61, 165–68
  full-spectrum blend digestive enzyme formula for, 152, 160
  hormones and, 151–54
  low blood sugar and, 150–51
  magnesium for, 161
  mood swings and, 148–50
  protein/fat intolerance diet for, 152
  stress and, 158–61
  stress management for, 167–68
  vitamin C for, 160
Endocrine conditions, 120, 120, 138–39
Energy
  carbohydrates and, 140
  diet and, 127
  digestive enzyme formula for, 142, 144
  drains on
    adrenal exhaustion, 136–37
    food intolerances, 132–34
    free radical damage, 134–35
    hypothyroidism, 138–39
    immune dysfunction, 139–40
    poor digestion, 129–32
    sleep disorders, 140–41
  enzyme therapy, 141–45
  exercise and, 145
  magnesium for, 131, 143
  multivitamin/mineral formula for, 145
  supplements for boosting, 131
  vitamin C for, 131, 143
Energy bars, 100, 145
Enzyme program, 21
  digestive formula in, 22–23
  probiotic supplement in, 23–24
  protease supplement in, 23
  Stage 1, 21–24
  Stage 2, 24–28
Enzymes. *See also* Enzyme program; Enzyme therapy; *specific types*
  absorption of, 18
  aging and, 4
  amino acids and, 6
  blood clotting and, 199
  bodily functions and, 4–6
  cancer and
    anticancer benefits of, 262–63
    continued research on, 256–57
    conventional cancer treatment and, 258–60
    history of research on, 253–55
    systemic, 255–57
  catalytic activity of, 3–4
  circulating immune complexes and, 275

deficiency, 14–17, 49, 270
in digestion, 11–13, 44–45
etymology of, 3
in food, 13–14
formulas for healing, 34–35, 55
in health care, 4–6
immune system and, 5
isolation of, early, 3
life and, 3–4
minerals and, 6, 17, 130
molecules and, 4
mushroom, 263
names of, 5
relocation, 12
replenishing, 5–6
in skin, 102
study of, 3–4
tablets, 32
types of
    digestive, 11–13
    food, 13–14
    systemic, 6–11, 255–57
vegetarian, 30–32
vitamins and, 6, 17, 130
Enzyme therapy. *See also specific formulas and*
        supplements
acne, 112–14
adrenal exhaustion, 137
aging, 268–69, 279–80, 286–91
angina, 189–90
attention deficit hyperactivity disorder, 163
basic plan, 32–34
benefits of, 4–6, 13, 18
cancer, 251, 261, 263–65
challenges facing, 17–19
circulatory disorder, 200–201
colon cancer, 261
constipation, 60–62
cravings, 84, 95–100
Crohn's disease, 63–65, 237
depression, 155–57
diabetes, 219–24
diarrhea, 66–67
diet and, 35–36, 36
digestion, 41, 271
early use of, 4–5
eczema, 116
educating people about, 29–30
emotional balance, 147–48, 152–53, 160–61,
        165–68
energy, 141–45
food intolerances, 55–56
formulas for healing, 34–35
gastroesophageal reflux disease, 70–71
hair, 119–26
in health care, 19–20
heartburn, 70–71
heart disease, 202–4
high blood pressure, 197
high cholesterol, 193
hyperhomocysteinemia, 194–95

hypochlorhydria, 72
hypoglycemia, 138
hypothyroidism, 139
immune dysfunction, 140
immune system, 170, 180–85
inflammation, 195–96, 225, 228, 243–47
injury, 243
irritable bowel syndrome, 73–74
lymphedema, 261
melanoma, 261
menopause, 281–82
modern, 5
rheumatoid arthritis, 232–36
safety issues, 36
sexual dysfunction, 284
skin, 112–14, 116, 121–26
sleep disorders, 140
stroke, 199
trauma, 243
ulcerative colitis, 63–65, 237
urinary tract infections, 240
vegetarian enzymes and, 30–32
weight loss, 84, 95–100
EPA, 153
E. purpurea root extract, 265
Erectile dysfunction, 283
Erections, 283
Esophagus, 42
Essential fatty acid blend, 328
Essential fatty acid formula, 163, 184, 222
Essential fatty acids (EFAs), 52, 61, 107–8
Estrogen, 284
Exercise
    aerobic, 279
    aging and, 279
    constipation and, 62
    diabetes and, 224
    energy and, 145
    heart disease and, 204
    irritable bowel syndrome and, 74
Exfoliation, 102, 125–26

Fat. *See* Dietary fats; Overweight
Fenfluramine, 81
Fenugreek seed extract, 220
Fiber, 61, 68–69
Fibrin, 199–200
Ficin, 5
Fight-or-flight response, 274
Figs, 5
5-HTP, 144–45
Flatulence, 176
Flavonoids, 197
Flaxseed oil, 122
Folic acid, 167, 222–23, 288, 326
Food allergies, 90. *See also* Food intolerances
Food Chemical Codex, 32
Food enzymes, 13–14
Food intolerances
    acne and, 113–14
    aging and, 271–73

Food intolerances *(cont.)*
  carbohydrates, 50–51, 53–54
  definition of, 89–90
  dietary fats, 52–53, 54–55
  eczema and, 116
  as energy drain, 132–34
  enzyme deficiency and, 49
  enzyme therapy, 55–56
  mood swings and, 148–49
  pinpointing, 49–50, 53–54, 53–55
  proteins, 51–52, 54–55
  sugar, 213–16
  weight loss and, 100
Foti root extract, 123
Free radicals
  amino acids and, 276
  antioxidant and, 104, 265, 276–77, 286–87
  cancer and, 259–60
  damage of, 134–35
  dietary fats and, 276
  as energy drain, 134–35
  inflammation and, 243
  occurrence of, 104
Fructose, 51, 224
Fruits, 110, 114, 297, 309–10
Full-spectrum blend digestive enzyme formula
  for cancer, 264
  for emotional balance, 152, 160
  for heart disease, 189, 195
  for immune system, healthy, 178
  protease in, 33
  selecting, 33
Fundus, 42

GABA, 166–67
Gamma linoleic acid (GLA), 123
Garlic, 189, 193
Garlic bulb concentrate, 203, 220, 287
Gastric enzyme formula, 63–64, 67, 69–70, 73, 183
Gastroesophageal reflux disease (GERD), 69–71, 188
Generally Regarded As Safe (GRAS) list, 36
Genistein, 289
GERD, 69–71, 188
Ginkgo biloba leaf extract, 165–66, 201, 245, 288, 290–91
GLA, 123
Glucagon, 208–9
Glucoamylase, 33, 55
Glucosamine sulfate, 234
Glucose, 51, 112
Glycation, 118
Glycemic index, 87–88
Glycogen, 85
Goldenseal root extract, 182, 240, 265
Gotu kola herb extract, 165, 201, 288
Grains, 86–88, 111–12, 298, 309
Grapeseed extract, 122, 196, 201, 203, 234, 245, 288
GRAS list, 36
Green tea leaf extract, 97
Guggulipid, 97, 125, 204
Gymnema leaf extract, 98, 219

Hair
  antioxidant supplement for healthy, 119
  diet and, 118–19
  digestive enzyme formula for healthy, 119, 124
  enzyme therapy, 119–26
  hypothyroidism and, 120
  loss, 120
  problems, 118–20
  sugar and, 119
Hashimoto's thyroiditis, 120
Hawthorn berry extract, 189
Hawthorn leaf and flower extract, 203, 287, 291
HCl, 44, 71–72
HDL, 191, 193
Heartbeat, 288
Heartburn, 69–71, 188
Heart disease
  alpha lipoic acid for, 193, 204
  angina and, 188–91
  arterial plaques and, 198–99
  atherosclerosis and, 192
  circulatory disorders and, 199–202
  diet and, 187
  digestive enzyme formula for, 203
  enzyme therapy, 202–4
  exercise and, 204
  full-spectrum blend digestive enzyme formula
    for, 189, 195
  high blood pressure and, 196–98
  high cholesterol and, 191–94
  hyperhomocysteinemia and, 194–95
  incidence of, 187
  inflammation and, 195–96
  lifestyle factors and, 187
  multivitamin/mineral formula for, 204
  stroke and, 198–99
  vitamin E as d-alpha tocopherol succinate for,
    190, 201, 203
  weight maintenance and, 204
Helicobacter pylori, 40
Helper cells, 243
Hemicellulase, 33
High blood pressure, 196–98
High cholesterol, 191–94
High-density lipoprotein (HDL), 191, 193
Holistic approach to health care, 19
Homeopathic remedy, 99
Homocysteine levels, 194
Honey, 70
Hormones. *See also specific types*
  emotional balance and, 151–54
  menopause and, 151–54, 284
  replacement, 151
  sexual desire and, 283
  stress, 274
  zinc and, 98, 125
Horse chestnut, 201
Horsetail extract, 123, 246
Hydration, 62, 110, 114
Hydrochloric acid (HCl), 44, 71–72

Hypercoagulation, 199
Hyperhomocysteinemia, 194–95
Hyperinsulinemia, 217
Hypertension, 196–98
Hyperthyroidism, 139
Hypochlorhydria, 71–72, 112
Hypoglycemia, 137–38, 152–53
Hypothyroidism, 120, 120, 138–39

I BD, 62–63, 236–37
IBS, 72–75
IgA, 174
Immune health enzyme formula, 181, 264
Immune system
  antioxidant supplement for healthy, 184
  bowel problems and, 175–76
  cancer process and, 252, 258
  diet and, 171–73, 180, 185
  digestion and, 173–75
  digestive enzyme formula for healthy, 181, 183
  dysfunction, 139–40
  enzymes and, 5
  enzyme therapy, 170, 180–85
  full-spectrum blend digestive enzyme formula
    for healthy, 178
  function of, 170
  helper cells and, 243
  inflammation and, 226–27
  multivitamin/mineral formula for healthy, 184
  optimal, 180
  other body systems and, 169–70
  protease supplement for healthy, 184
  quercetin for healthy, 183
  stress and, 179–80
  stress management for healthy, 179–80, 185
  sugar and, 177, 185
  toxins and, 177–79
  vitamin C and, 182
  zinc and, 183
Immunoglobulin A (IgA), 174
Impotence, 283
Indigestion, 69–71, 188
Inflammation
  antioxidant supplement for, 246
  cancer and, 260
  circulating immune complexes and, 195, 226,
    228, 243
  Crohn's disease and, 236–39
  diet and, 247
  dietary fats and, 273
  digestive enzyme formula for, 234, 245
  enzyme therapy, 194–96, 225, 228, 243–47
  free radicals and, 243
  heart disease and, 195–96
  immune system and, 226–27
  incidence of, 225
  injury and, 228, 240–43
  magnesium for, 245
  prescription drugs and, 227–30
  protease supplement and, 195–96
  quercetin for, 196, 234

rheumatoid arthritis and, 225, 231–36
role of, 226
trauma and, 240–43
ulcerative colitis and, 236–39
urinary tract infections and, 239–40
vitamin C and, 196, 234, 245
zinc for, 113, 234
Inflammatory bowel disease (IBD), 62–63, 236–37
Injury, 228, 240–43
Inositol, 167, 326
Insulin
  diabetes and, 208, 210–12
  glucose and, 112
  grains and, 111–12
  resistance, 210–11, 217
  sugar and, 111–12
  weight gain and, 88
Invertase, 33, 51, 55
Iodine, 97, 125, 327
Iron, 131, 328
Irritable bowel syndrome (IBS), 72–75

J oint degeneration, 8
Junk food, avoiding, 83, 110

K elp extract, 97, 123, 125

L actase, 32–33, 51
Lactobacillus acidophilus, 34, 107
Lactobacillus casei, 34
Lactobacillus plantarum, 34
Lactobacillus salivarius, 34
Lactose digestion, 51
Lansoprazole, 17
Laughter in stress management, 180
LDL, 191–93, 287
Leaky gut syndrome, 93, 141
Lectins, 12
Legumes, 298, 309
Libido, 283
Lifestyle factors
  aging and, 268–69, 271–77
  depression and, 157
  heart disease and, 187
Lipase, 11, 32–33, 43, 52, 55, 108, 191
Liver, 105–6
Liver detoxification enzyme, 98–99, 125
L-lysine, 123
L-methionine, 99, 123, 125
Longevity, 268–69, 277. *See also* Aging
Low-density lipoprotein (LDL), 191–93, 287
Lymphedema, 261

M acrophages, 149, 192, 226, 228, 243, 253
Magnesium
  for angina, 189
  for diabetes, 220, 222–23
  for emotional balance, 161
  for energy, 131, 143
  for inflammation, 245
  in multivitamin/mineral formula, 327
Magnesium aspartate, 144

Malic acid, 245
Malt diastase, 32–33, 55
Manganese, 193, 220, 327
Manganese citrate, 234, 245
Marshmallow root extract, 64, 183
Massage, 167
Meal plans, 7-day
  carbohydrate intolerance diet, 302–6
  protein/fat intolerance diet, 315–19
Meal-replacement drink, 95–96
Medications. *See* Prescription drugs; *specific types*
Meditation, 74, 167–68, 179, 185, 204
Melanoma, 261
Menopause, 151–54, 281–82, 284
Mental focus enzyme formula, 165, 288
Metabolic balance enzyme formula, 96–97
Metabolic rejectivity syndrome, 12
Metabolic syndrome, 211, <u>211</u>
Metabolism, 98
Methylsulfonylmethane (MSM), 234
Milk thistle seed extract, 99, 124
Mineral enzyme formula, 245
Mineral oil, 126
Minerals, 6, <u>17</u>, 130, 327. *See also specific types*
Molybdenum, 328
Mood/depression formula, 155, 166
Mood swings, 148–50
MSM, 234
Muira puama extract, 291
Multivitamin/mineral formula
  additional nutrients in, 327–28
  for energy, 145
  for heart disease, 204
  for immune system, healthy, 184
  magnesium in, 327
  minerals in, 327
  vitamin E in, 326
  vitamins in, 325–26
  for weight loss, 100
Mushroom enzymes, 263

Natokinese, 287
Natural killer cells, 253
Neuromediated hypotension (NMH), 137
Niacin, <u>131</u>, 143, 161, 221, 326
Niacinamide, 167
Nitric oxide, 198, 283
NMH, 137
Nonsteroidal anti-inflammatory drugs (NSAIDs), 7–8, <u>36</u>, 232
Nutritional supplements and aging, 278. *See also specific types*
Nuts, 114, 197

Oat straw extract, 144, 167, 246
Obesity, 80, <u>83</u>, 92–94
Omeprazole, 17
Oregon grape root extract, 123
Organic catalysts, 3. *See also* Enzymes
Overeating, 114, 277–78
Overweight, 52, 80, <u>83</u>
Oxidative stress, 273

Panax ginseng root extract, 142, 144, 160, 166, 221, 289–90
Pantothenic acid, <u>131</u>, 143, 160, 221, 326
Papain, <u>31</u>, 263
Para-aminobenzoic acid, 326
Passionflower root extract, 144
Pasteurization, 11
Pectin, <u>61</u>
Pectinase, 33
Phen-fen, 80–81
Phentermine, 80
Phlebitis, 200
pH levels, 30, 40, 71, 178
Phosphatidylcholine, 99, 124, 166
Phosphatidylserine, 289
Phytase, 11, 33
Potassium, 197, 204, 288, 327
Premature aging, 270
Prescription drugs, 17, 19, 80–81, 112, 167, 227–30. *See also specific names*
Prevacid, 17
Prilosec, 17
Probiotic supplement, 23–24, 34, 106, 184
Processed foods, avoiding, 62
Products (new molecules), 4
Progesterone, 284
Protease
  amino acids and, 43
  in digestive enzyme formula, 55
  in full-spectrum blend digestive enzyme formula, 33
  function of, 8, 11, 18, 43, 52
  proteins and, 11, 43, 52
  supplement
    for cancer, 264
    in carbohydrate digestive enzyme formula, 55
    cystic acne and, 114
    in enzyme program, 23
    for immune system, healthy, 184
    for inflammation, 195–96
    selecting, 33–34
    units for, 32
Protein/fat digestive enzyme formula, 61, 96
Protein/fat intolerance diet
  dietary fats in, 310
  for emotional balance, 152
  fruits in, 309–10
  grains in, 309
  guidelines for, 307–8
  legumes in, 309
  meal plan, 7-day, 315–19
  proteins in, 308
  recipes
    Asian Salad, 311
    Cauliflower Seldess, 312
    Chilled Pasta Salad, 311
    Perfect Protein Salad, 313
    Wild Rice and Bean Casserole, 314
  vegetables in, 308–9
  for weight loss, 96

Proteins
    amino acids and, 51–52
    in carbohydrate intolerance diet, 296
    food intolerance, 51–52, 54–55
    protease and, 11, 43, 52
    in protein/fat intolerance diet, 308
Pygeum bark extract, 291

Quercetin
    for cancer, 265
    for circulatory disorders, 201
    for Crohn's disease, 64
    for diabetes, 220
    for immune system, healthy, 183
    for inflammation, 196, 234
    for ulcerative colitis, 64

RA, 225, 231–36
Radiation, 258–59
Raw foods in diet, 43
Red clover flower extract, 246
Reishi mushroom extract, 181–82, 264
Rheumatoid arthritis (RA), 225, 231–36
Rhodiola rosea root extract, 97–98
Riboflavin, 109–10, 131, 143, 161, 221, 326
Rice bran, 143, 161, 166, 220–21
Rice protein, 96

Safety issues in enzyme therapy, 36
Safflower oil, 122
St. John's wort extract, 166, 290
Salt, 197
Schizandra fruit extract, 99, 124, 166, 289
Seeds, 114
Selenium, 98, 125, 327
Serotonin, 137–38, 152
Sexual arousal and desire, 283
Sexual dysfunction, 282–86
Shiitake mushroom extract, 182, 264–65
Siberian ginseng root extract, 143, 161, 221
Silica, 328
Skin
    acne and, 110–15
    aging and, 103–4
    basal layer of, 102
    collagen and, 102, 122, 276
    diet and, 103, 109–10, 114
    digestion and, 106–7
    digestive enzyme formula for healthy, 102–3,
        122, 124
    dry, 107–9
    eczema and, 115–17
    elasticity of, 276
    enzymes in, 102
    enzyme therapy, 112–14, 116, 121–26
    epidermis layer of, 102
    exfoliation and, 102, 125–26
    fruits for healthy, 110, 114
    health and, 101–3
    oily, 109–10
    toxins and, 104–6

    vegetables for healthy, 110, 114
    vitamin C and, 126
    zinc for healthy, 109, 113, 123, 125
Skin, hair, and nail enzyme formula, 109–10, 113, 122
Skin-care products, 126
Sleep disorders, 140–41
Sleep-enhancing enzyme formula, 141, 144
Sodium, 197
Soft-tissue enzyme formula, 244
Soy isoflavones and protein, 96, 246, 289
Starches, 55, 207
Steroids, 227–28
Stomach acid, low, 112, 114
Stress
    aging and, 274–75
    digestion and, 45–48, 59
    emotional balance and, 158–61
    emotions and, expressing, 179–80
    fight-or-flight response to, 274
    health problems related to, 274
    hormones, 274
    immune system and, 179–80
    management
        acupressure, 74
        deep breathing, 74
        for digestion, optimal, 74
        for emotional balance, 167–68
        everyday stressors and, 275
        for heart disease, 204
        for immune system, healthy, 179–80, 185
        laughter, 180
        meditation, 74, 167–68, 179, 185, 204
        tai chi, 204
        writing, 180
        yoga, 168, 179, 185, 204
    oxidative, 273
    reaction to, 274
    toxins and, 179–80
    vitamin C and, 159–60
Stroke, 198–99
Substrates (original molecules), 4
Sucrose, 51
Sugar
    addictive properties of, 85–86
    carbohydrates and, 207–8
    diabetes and, 207–10, 213–16
    food intolerance, 213–16
    hair and, 119
    immune system and, 177, 185
    insulin and, 111–12
    weight loss and, 85–86
Supplements. *See* Enzyme therapy; *specific types*
Surtuins, 280
Swedish pollen, 240
Syndrome X, 211, 211
Systemic enzymes, 6–11, 255–57

Tablets, enzyme, 32
Tai chi, 204
Testosterone, 284
Tetracycline, 112

Thiamin, 326
Thrombophlebitis, 200
Thyroid problems, 120, 120, 138–39
Toothpaste, natural, 96
Toxins
  Agent Orange, 217
  aging and, 276–77
  alcohol and, 105
  colon and, 105–6
  immune system and, 177–79
  liver and, 105, 141
  obesity and, 92–94
  skin and, 104–6
  stress and, 179–80
Tranquilizers, 167
Trauma, 240–43
Triterpene glycosides, 289
Trypsin, 263
Turmeric root extract, 99, 124, 234, 245

Ulcerative colitis, 62–65, 236–39
Urinary tract infections (UTIs), 239–40
Uva ursi leaf extract, 240

Valerian root extract, 144, 167
Valium, 167
Vanadium, 223, 328
Vegetables, 110, 114, 296–97, 308
Vegetarian enzymes, 30–32
Vitality. *See* Energy
Vitamin A, 113, 123, 326
Vitamin B$_2$, 109–10, 131, 143, 161, 221, 326
Vitamin B$_3$, 131, 143, 161, 221, 326
Vitamin B$_5$, 131, 143, 160, 221
Vitamin B$_6$, 204, 220, 288, 326
Vitamin B$_{12}$, 166, 288–89, 326
Vitamin C
  for adrenal exhaustion, 159
  for aging, 291
  for cancer, 265
  for circulatory disorders, 201
  for diabetes, 221
  emotional balance and, 160
  for energy, 131, 143
  immune system and, 182
  for inflammation, 196, 234, 245
  in multivitamin/mineral formula, 326
  skin and, 126
  stress and, 159–60
Vitamin D, 326
Vitamin E
  for circulatory disorders, 201
  as d-alpha tocopherol succinate
    for aging, 287, 290–91
    for diabetes, 219–20
    for heart disease, 190, 201, 203
    in multivitamin/mineral formula, 326
Vitamin K, 328
Vitamins, 6, 17, 130, 325–26. *See also specific types*
Warfarin, 287
Water hyssop herb extract, 166, 289

Water intake, 62, 110, 114
Weight gain
  carbohydrate intolerance and, 83–84, 89
  in children, 83
  grains and, 86–88
  obesity and, 80, 83, 92–94
  overweight and, 52, 80, 83
  as public health issue, 80
  sugar and, 88
Weight loss
  alpha lipoic acid for, 98
  amphetamine for, 81
  carb blockers and, 88–89
  carbohydrate digestive enzyme formula for, 95
  carbohydrate intolerance diet for, 95
  children and, 83
  commercial products for, 80–81
  cosmetic surgery for, 80
  diet and, 96
  dieting and, 94–95
  diet pills for, 80
  digestion and, 82–84
  digestive enzyme formula for, 97, 99
  enzyme therapy, 84, 95–100
  fenfluramine for, 81
  food intolerances and, 100
  grains and, 86–88
  leaky gut syndrome and, 93
  multivitamin/mineral formula for, 100
  phen-fen for, 80–81
  phentermine for, 81
  prescription drugs for, 80–81
  protein/fat intolerance diet for, 96
  struggle, 79–82
  sugar and, 85–86
  zinc and, 98
Weight maintenance, 204, 223–24
Wheat germ extract, 89
White willow bark extract, 234, 240
Wild lettuce leaf extract, 144
Writing in stress management, 180

Xanax, 167
Xylanase, 33, 55

Yeast, 112, 114
Yoga, 168, 179, 185, 204
Yogurt, 107
Yohimbe bark extract, 291

Zinc
  for cancer, 265
  for diabetes, 220, 223
  hormones and, 98, 125
  immune system and, 183
  for inflammation, 113, 234
  in multivitamin/mineral formula, 327
  for skin, healthy, 109, 113, 123, 125
  weight loss and, 98
Zinc citrate, 290